Maneuvering the Maze of Managed Care

Skills for Mental Health Practitioners

KEVIN CORCORAN
VIKKI VANDIVER

THE FREE PRESS

New York   London   Toronto   Sydney   Tokyo   Singapore

The Free Press
A Division of Simon & Schuster Inc.
1230 Avenue of the Americas
New York, N.Y. 10020

Printed in the United States of America

printing number

1 2 3 4 5 6 7 8 9 10

Text design by Carla Bolte

Library of Congress Cataloging-in-Publication Data

Corcoran, Kevin (Kevin J.)
    Maneuvering the maze of managed care : skills for mental health practitioners/
Kevin Corcoran, Vikki Vandiver.
        p.   cm.
    Includes bibliographical references and index.
    ISBN 0–684–82310–1 (cloth)
    ISBN 0–684–82309–8 (pbk)
    1. Managed mental health care—United States.   I. Vandiver, Vikki.
II. Title.
    [DNLM: 1. Managed Care Programs—organization & administration—
United States.   2. Mental Health Services—United States.
3. Quality Assurance, Health Care—United States.   4. Physician's Practice Patterns—
United States.   W 130 AA1 C7m 1996]
RC465.6.C67   1996
362.2'0973—dc20
DNLM/DLC
for Library of Congress   95–47008
                                                                                            CIP

One more time:
To my beloved G. Olivetti and 14,000 sunsets from Stonefield Manor.
—K.C.

And to J. S. Siegerson, whose recipe for "Champagne Picnic du Jour"
is one of life's more effervescent joys.
—V.V.

Contents

Appendixes

Preface

If you have ever scratched your head in bewilderment to an inquiry from a managed care organization, or furrowed your eyebrows in disbelief over a managed care decision, or sighed in frustration over the demands of another managed care review, this book is for you.

The purpose of this book is to help practitioners and students from a variety of mental health disciplines—psychologists, social workers, psychiatrists, and counselors of all other types—to work effectively, efficiently, and successfully with their clients within the purview of managed mental health care. Managed mental health care is relatively new in the field of mental health, and it was not a program that was coordinated or even consistent in its policies and procedures.

The goals of managed mental health care, like managed physical health care, are to control the cost of services while ensuring the quality of care. As such, managed mental health care essentially strives to determine whether a person needs clinical services, what services are most appropriate for the client's problem, how long treatment should last, and what is expected as an outcome of treatment. These issues may be addressed two ways: on a program level, as in the case of capitation programs, such as health maintenance organizations (HMOs) and community mental health associations, or on a case-by-case approach to the management of fee for service by independent practitioners.

Because of the rapid development of managed mental health care and the numerous differences among programs, this area is truly a maze. There are demands, restrictions, regulations, and procedures used to determine if treatment will be authorized—and more demands, restrictions, regulations, and procedures used to evaluate the services and authorize financial reimbursement. Many clinicians are uncertain how to make their way through this maze. Moreover, many believe managed care interferes with their ability to work effectively with clients. And most find the demands intrusive, frustrating, and cumbersome at the least.

The goal of this book is to help mental health professionals meet the needs of both managed mental health care and their clients. It contains a variety of tools used by managed care organizations to demonstrate the need for clinical services and the structure of systematic interventions, and to evaluate the quality of care.

Practitioners of every discipline are learning how to cope with the managed care system. For the most part, the difficulty many clinicians have is that there is no single system or set of procedures. What is expected, of course, is fairly consistent: to ensure quality while containing costs. The problem is that different managed care programs approach this goal in different ways, and the procedures they use are constantly and rapidly changing. Some managed care procedures consist of a simple telephone call to discuss the need for services or reimbursement. Others ask for a brief written description of the type of treatment and the client's progress. Others use standardized forms to determine the necessity for and quality of clinical services. And still others use an in-depth review of the client's records. Some programs may restrict services or require providers to use a limited range of interventions or services. Such programs might well include a utilization review of services provided, and most likely include some survey of each client's satisfaction with the services he or she received.

Thus, managed care programs are not a single system of mental health care but a variety of systems, although they share common factors. One is the transfer of control of clinical services from the hands of clinicians and clients to the financial ledger of business corporations. At the same time, managed care organizations often tend to be rather independent of the actual treatment process. And yet the managed care organization may well determine if clinical services are necessary, who may provide what specific intervention and for how long, what the outcome should be, and how much it should cost—or at least how much will be paid. Much of what was once negotiated between practitioner and client is now influenced, and sometimes determined, by a fourth party. (Technically, managed care companies are fourth parties to the treatment of a client's problem, with the insurance company or payor serving the role of the third party.) It is not surprising that many clinicians find themselves quite frustrated trying to help their clients within the restrictions and regulations of managed care.

Without oversimplifying this task, we suggest that learning the skills necessary to wind your way through the managed care maze is relatively easy. Consequently, in providing some useful skills in working efficiently and successfully within managed care we do not mean to suggest that you will not find that managed care continues to be confusing, challenging, and downright frustrating. We cannot tell you exactly when to turn left or right or go forward to reach the reward at the end of the maze. We do not believe anyone can. The mazes are just too different from program to program, locale to locale, and changing rapidly all the time. We do believe, however, that the skills and knowledge acquired from the materials in this book will make managed care work more straightforward and easier.

This book is directed as well to students of counseling and psychotherapy, regardless of whether the discipline is psychology, clinical social work, psychiatry, psychiatric nursing, or counseling. Just like practitioners who have enjoyed the challenge of clinical practice, managed mental health care has caught many professors off-guard and unprepared for the new reality of practice in an era of cost containment. If professors are unfamiliar with managed care and how to work within its confines (and many are), then their students' education for this new business of clinical practice will also be limited. It is important for students to be prepared to work in a variety of settings, including managed care settings. Indeed, there are few settings left that are unaffected by the fourth-party management of care. Consequently, this book will prove useful to students who must demonstrate treatment necessity, goal-oriented interventions that are implemented systematically, and evidence outcomes.

This text will have a special appeal to students, practitioners, and professors who are trying to integrate research and practice. Many of the demands of managed mental health care, in fact, may be epitomized in a single word: *accountability*—accountability for the quality of a client's care and accountability for the costs of that care. Many of the skills necessary to show accountability are taught in various research courses. In particular, the knowledge and skills are part of idiographic research, which is often called single-subject research. Managed care, then, has accomplished what many professors have not: getting practitioners to use single-case evaluation tools in order to evaluate practice.

Regardless of whether we call this method single-subject research (as is frequently the case in clinical and counseling psychology) or single-system designs (as the term is used in social work), only a limited number of students and practitioners find these classes enjoyable and relevant. Managed care has changed all of that. Because of managed care, topics that once were research are now practice. Suddenly skills of research (e.g., measurement and cutting scores) are also practice skills (i.e., assessment and triage). As applied to managed mental health care, easy-to-use and rudimentary single-system designs, observational tools, and methods of interpretation will help practitioners maneuver the maze and find the reward at the end.

Our goal is not simply to provide yet another book on single-system evaluation. Others can, and have, done a good job in this area. Moreover, we do not believe many students or practitioners will rush out to buy a book on research. In contrast, our goal is to provide a variety of tools from the practice evaluation model to enable clinicians to work efficiently and successfully with managed mental health care. We believe that many of the tools and skills learned in this way will also help in working with clients' problems. Consequently, this book is designed to reflect one of the possible integrations of research and practice in public and private mental health service delivery.

In fact, we hope this book will demonstrate to student readers that certain single-system research design skills are actually practice skills. This book may prove useful to students and professors in research courses who are searching for a way to demonstrate the relevance of research to practice. We think it will be useful for research courses and a helpful supplement to such outstanding works as Barlow, Hayes, and Nelson (1984), Bloom, Fischer, and Orme (1995), Hersen and Barlow (1986), Jayaratne and Levy (1979), Kratochwill (1978), and Tripodi (1995).

Finally, this book seeks to help clients of mental health services, the audience we believe will benefit most from practitioners' improved competency to work with managed mental health care. Indeed, professionals who are not able to work within managed mental health care will find that their ability to serve clients will be limited. If a managed care program refuses to authorize services or denies authorization of reimbursement for services, clients will suffer, either immediately or eventually. Perhaps they will not receive necessary treatment and will continue to experience distress that interferes with their functioning and quality of life. Or the professional may not be paid for services already provided or that continue to be necessary. In the long run, the client and his or her family, friends, employer, and society will experience the adverse affects.

Clients can take an active role in managed mental health care through health promotion and disease prevention practices and by participating in meeting the utilization review demands of managed care. In this book, we illustrate how to engage clients in the managed mental health care process. It may be beneficial for them to read a couple of chapters, particularly chapter 1, to familiarize themselves with the managed care elements of their treatment, and chapter 9, designed to facilitate their involvement in determining quality assurance. The more that clients are familiar with and involved in this aspect of treatment, the more fully their consent is truly *informed*. A client's participation in the managed mental health care process helps make the treatment process and mental health promotion one of mutual participation between the client, the treatment provider, and the managed care fourth party.

This book reflects our belief that managed mental health care is more of a friend than a foe of clinical treatment. We inform readers of particular content and then describe the various skills necessary for evidencing the two purposes of managed mental health care: cost containment and quality assurance. These managed care goals are accomplished primarily by some form of utilization review, before, during, or after treatment. We discuss many of the utilization review procedures and show how to use them in practice. The appendixes contain forms useful for documenting clinical work in various public and private managed care settings.

Chapter 1 defines managed care and the roles of the private and public third-party payor in clinical practice.

Chapter 2 reviews the controversy about managed care as it contrasts with fee-for-service arrangements, which have dominated the mental health field until recently. We believe the relationship between these two forces is bound to improve, with changes guided by cost-effectiveness, responsiveness, cooperation, and the best interests of the client.

The next four chapters outline managed care procedures. Chapter 3 discusses capitation programs, health promotion, disease prevention, treatment of the chronically mentally ill, and client satisfaction surveys. Services and their coordination are offered within self-contained programs to manage care, such as HMOs, employee assistance programs, behavioral health networks, and community mental health organizations.

Chapter 4 then reviews the role of the prospective utilization review in determining treatment necessity and presents a number of methods of evidencing this to a managed care reviewer. Chapter 5 addresses treatment demands of managed care, which tend to be goal-directed, structured, and systematic interventions that include client participation in the process of change. Chapter 6 considers managed care when some or all of the treatment has occurred (either a concurrent utilization review or a retrospective utilization review). Both concurrent and retrospective utilization reviews are concerned primarily with demonstrating quality of care in terms of adequacy, treatment implementation, and outcomes. Common outcomes include a reduction in the presenting problem, goal attainment, and client satisfaction.

In chapter 7 the demands of managed care are considered in the context of client diversity and culturally competent practice. We focus on culturally competent practice with Asian Americans, Hispanic Americans, African Americans, and American Indians.

Chapter 8 outlines many of the ethical and legal challenges facing practitioners in the managed care setting: conflict of interest, confidentiality, informed consent, malpractice, contractual and fiduciary obligations, and emerging duties under managed care practice.

Chapter 9 considers various ways to involve clients in the managed care process in order to promote client autonomy, empowerment, and treatment effectiveness. This participation includes the client as a player in determining mental health service needs and in the process of change.

Finally, in chapter 10, we conclude by offering a few thoughts about the future of managed mental health care and ways of keeping abreast of developments.

Often managed mental health care organizations will expect the practitioner to document various aspects of the treatment process—for example, by providing evidence of the medical necessity of treatment, what the practitioner has done during the course of treatment, and the outcomes of that treatment. Sometimes a managed mental health care reviewer may even specify the type of treatment that is authorized and how long it may be used. Interventions that are systematic and even include step-by-step protocols are often not only helpful in working effectively with clients but required by a managed mental health care organization. We have provided some general guidelines and forms for these purposes.

Managed care is about cost containment—maybe more so than it is about quality assurance. In this respect we stress the importance of not overpricing this managed care business. Managed care and its procedures should be seen as aids, suggestions, or guidelines that supplement a practice, and not as a substitute for sound clinical judgment.

We are going to argue the value of a variety of methods of evidencing client change, including easy-to-use goal attainment scales, self-anchored rating scales, rapid assessment instruments, and the General Assessment of Functioning. These observational systems are designed to assess a client's behavior, regardless of whether that behavior is the way a client is feeling, thinking, or acting. These observational systems are estimates, and the scores are referents to these phenomena. They are extremely useful in assessing client change before, during, and after treatment. For example, if a measurement tool of depression indicates a client is functioning well and yet your clinical judgment is contradictory, we recommend you discuss this with your client and supervisor, and not necessarily assume the veracity of the measurement tool. This is true even if a managed care reviewer says enough change has occurred to warrant termination and the discontinuation of reimbursement. As you well know, and probably believe (or you would not be in the helping professions), your commitment and obligation is first and foremost to your client. No score on an assessment tool or the opinion of a managed care reviewer can replace your training, years of experience, and supervision in terms of what is necessary to help your client or determine your client's continued need for clinical services.

We hope that this book, with its forms and guidelines, are helpful supplements to professional training and clinical judgment. But there is no substitute for sincere and well-trained clinical judgment, professional supervision and—of course—paid malpractice premiums.

We thank those who made this book possible: our clients, students, and colleagues who served as the laboratory for developing many of the ideas of this book. Among those we single out are Dr. Joseph Madonnia of Plan 21, one of the early employee assistance programs offering utilization reviews; John Parker, president of an innovative community mental health organization; Ginny Gay, who typed our tables and figures at warp speed; and Dr. James Ward, dean of the Graduate School of Social Work at Portland State University, who promoted scholarship in the marketplace of ideas. We especially acknowledge our editor and her assistants at The Free Press, Susan Arellano, Jennifer Schulman, and Elizabeth Wright, respectively. Without all these individuals, this book would not have been possible.

And, finally, the order of authorship is alphabetical (So there!).

Chapter 1

Managed Care and the Emergence of Cost Containment and Quality Assurance

An Overview

M anaged care is the administration or oversight of health and mental health services by someone other than the clinician and the client. This management of client care is designed to meet two major goals: controlling costs while ensuring the quality of care.

Managed mental health care, a relatively recent phenomenon, stems from managed care in physical health, which became prominent in various forms in the early 1980s (MacLeod 1993). As a relatively new aspect of mental health service delivery, *managed mental health care* is a term used for a wide variety of programs and procedures. Kongstvedt (1993) prefaces his fine glossary of terms, jargon, and acronyms by acknowledging that even within the managed care industry, there are differing opinions on the definition of terms. He defines managed care, in part, as "a regrettably nebulous term." He is not alone in this opinion. Previously, Dorwart (1990, p. 1087) had stated, "It is difficult to know exactly what is meant by the term." In general, managed care refers to "any method to regulate the price, utilization, or site of services" (Austad and Hoyt 1992), restricting those who are authorized to provide services, ascertaining that those who receive services truly warrant treatment, determining that the treatment itself is systematic and has a likelihood of success, and evaluating the outcome of treatment to assess its quality and value.

1

In spite of the lack of a clear definition of managed care, one aspect is consistent: the management of clinical practice is done by an entity independent of the clinician-client treatment relationship that characterizes much clinical work. The independent entity, often called a managed care organization or program, may be performed by a community mental health organization, an employee assistance program (EAP), or another distinct party who intervenes between the clinician and the client's third-party payor. The managed care organization is often an agent of the payor of services, such as an insurance company, the government, or someone in a self-insured corporation's department of human resources. Since the payor of services is considered the third party (as in the phase *third-party payor*), managed care must be considered the fourth party. In its efforts to control costs and ensure quality, managed care organizations intervene between the first two parties (clinician and client) and on behalf of the third party.

TYPES OF MANAGED CARE

Throughout this book, we consider two general approaches to managed care. One is managed care by means of an entire treatment program, such as a health maintenance organization (HMO) or an EAP. These self-contained organizations provide in-house services as much as possible and coordinate other services. Their source of financing is in terms of a lump sum for whatever services will be needed, not a fee for services that were provided. That is, the organization offers most of the needed services and contracts out for others. This financing is typically called a *capitation model* and is found in both the public and private sectors. This is typically called *capitated managed care*.

The other general approach to managed care is independent case-by-case reviews of services that are paid for by a fee-for-service policy. Additionally, the clinician is usually an independent practitioner in an individual or group setting (independent practice associations and preferred provider panels) who provides services for a reduced fee and the agreement to participate in the management of client care. In contrast, capitated managed care has practitioners who are employees of the organization.

In capitated and independent managed care organizations, the quality of care and its costs are assessed primarily by reducing the costs

Figure 1.1   Overview of Managed Mental Health Care

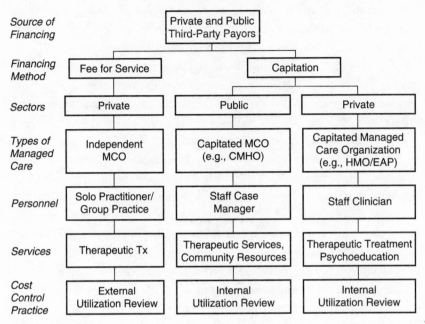

charged by clinicians, restricting services to those in need of treatment, participating in the development of the treatment plan, and evaluating the outcome of treatment. The evaluation of outcome usually includes changes in the presenting problem, the attainment of goals, and client satisfaction. With capitated managed care, these practices would occur for a group of enrolled members and would be contained within the service delivery organization. They would be self-contained. With independent managed care, these practices would be independent of the service delivery and may be conducted by a managed care organization in a different location—perhaps even on different coasts of the country. This model of managed care is summarized in Figure 1.1.

Capitated Managed Care

In this general approach to the management of mental health care, all, or most, of the clinical services needed by a group of potential clients are provided by a program or network of programs. An example is a company's EAP, which offers a limited number of clinical visits per employee, such as four or fewer sessions. This type of managed care organization delivers many of the services it manages. In the public sector, capitated managed care may include community mental health organizations that provide services and service coordination.

Probably the most familiar managed care programs are those found in an HMO. In fact, one author asserts that the term *managed care* has replaced the term *HMO* (Mizrahi 1993). Managed care is much more than an HMO, although it too uses many principles and procedures of cost containment and quality assurance.

HMOs, like other forms of capitated managed care, are based on a capitation financing model. Capitation programs essentially place a cap on how much a third party will pay for specific services or a cap on the costs of services needed for a specific person. These programs operate on a cost per unit of consumer basis instead of a cost per specific services provided (fee for service). Capitation programs contract with a third-party payor to provide a fixed set of services used by an entire group at a fixed amount per individual, such as all employees of a school district or all the mentally ill in a catchment area (Paulson 1996). Capitation programs attempt to control costs by guaranteeing that all the required services will be provided, but they are quite careful in predetermining when a procedure is actually required (that is, clinically necessary). In other words, capitated managed care controls costs by reducing the amount paid to providers and carefully ascertaining whether treatment is necessary. Capitated managed care organizations ensure quality by authorizing the use of only certain treatment interventions (ones believed to be effective) and monitoring the satisfaction of those enrolled in the program who receive services.

Managed mental health care has numerous programs and procedures for controlling costs—for example, changing the focus in treatment from inpatient to outpatient and from long-term, insight-oriented psychotherapy to goal-oriented and planned short-term treatment (Wells 1994). These interventions and clinical services often include specific treatment protocols, established clinical guidelines, recommendations for structured intervention (Barlow 1993; Corcoran 1992), and coordinated clinical case management (Vandiver and Kirk 1992).

Cost controls could include changing the extent to which one may rely on a private third-party payor—for example, decreasing the total amount paid per year or per lifetime, restricting the number of sessions or the particular mental health provider (such as by a panel of preferred providers), or reducing the level of care, such as what type of treatment will be covered, and the magnitude of the coverage (e.g., major mental disorders might be reimbursed at 100 percent, while V codes are reimbursed at 50 percent of the costs).

Independent Managed Care

The other general approach to managed mental health care is the review on a case-by-case basis of those services requested or used. These services and providers are often independent of the managed care organization. Here the clinician could be a member of an individual provider association (IPA) or a preferred provider organization (PPO), with treatment offered to members of a group at reduced fees (Mizrahi 1993). These reduced fees are one of the reasons the practitioners are preferred over others. They are also preferred because they agree to use certain interventions and to comply with the managed care requirements (e.g., assessments of treatment outcomes and client satisfaction).

Sometimes this type of managed care is called a *utilization review organization* (Hamilton 1992) because a primary method of quality assurance is reviewing the use of services. Utilization reviews are also often part of capitated managed care procedures, as with the management of services provided by contract therapists employed at an HMO. Moreover, utilization reviews are frequently used in the management of services provided by a private practitioner or members of a panel of preferred providers.

The utilization review approach to managed care might include determining if services are medically necessary, directing the potential client to the most appropriate provider of the most effective intervention (a referral process called *channeling*), or evaluating the outcome and costs of such services. This approach to managed care includes the following kinds of reviews (Tischler 1990a, 1990b):

Prospective utilization reviews: Those that evaluate the need for services in advance of treatment and may authorize a particular practitioner to provide a preferred intervention (Giles 1991, 1993).
Concurrent utilization reviews: Those that occur during the course of treatment (APA 1992) to determine if additional care is required.

Retrospective utilization reviews: Those that evaluate the course and outcome of treatment in order to assess the quality of care and determine whether reimbursement is warranted.

Record reviews: In-depth inspections of the entire record to evaluate all aspects of care; usually reserved for high-cost clients, such as those requiring hospitalization.

Both capitated and independent managed care organizations incorporate a variety of different review procedures to assess the quality of care and to control its costs, but there is no standard. There is an incredible variability in the expectations of different managed care programs, differences in the level of scrutiny of managed care reviewers, and the ever-changing landscape of what problems and services will be authorized at what level of payment. The procedures themselves can range from telephone interviews, to open-ended surveys requesting a brief statement of a client's progress, to standardized forms, to an occasional in-depth review of a client's records.

Although managed mental health care procedures are similar to those developed for physical health care, there are differences, in part due to the stigma associated with being a "mental patient" and the fact that there is less agreement among mental health professionals about acceptable theories and methods of intervention. But even if there was much agreement, there would still be a lack of standardization of how practitioners implement a theory or an intervention. Techniques and interventions vary depending on the client, the severity of the problem, and the talents and professional proclivities of the clinician. As Anderson and Berlant (1993) note, mental health needs often accompany an erosion in available social supports, such as family and friends, and include a correspondence between societal stress and individual distress. Thus, one mental health discipline may see a client's problem as needing intrapersonal change, while another may see the need for changing the environment.

These approaches to cost containment and quality assurance are not without serious limitations. One limitation is the uncertainty of whether managed care organizations are effective in reducing costs or simply deny coverage. Some invite felonious fraud, such as overestimating the severity of the client problem or intentionally misdiagnosing a client. Because of these potential abuses, it is anticipated that managed mental health care will respond with even more assertive over-sight of cases. The mechanisms are already in place in the form of high cost case management, which is not to be confused with clinical case management (Vandiver and Kirk 1992). Managed mental health care case management directly monitors a client's treatment (it may even make the diagnosis), may conduct periodic evaluation of the client's progress through interviews with the client and the clinician, may even direct the type of treatment that will be reimbursed (e.g., locating appropriate supportive groups instead of group therapy), and may attempt to eliminate substandard care (Anderson and Berlant 1993).

THE ORIGINS OF MANAGED CARE

In many respects, managed mental health care emerged as a consequence of—and a contributor to—America's current health care crisis. We say "current crisis" because, like others (Harris 1994; Starr 1982), we believe the crisis in health care has been going on for nearly a hundred years. The current crisis is primarily a matter of costs and access to health care.

In order to understand why managed mental health care exists, it is necessary to understand who pays for services, regardless of whether those services are for physical health or mental health. More often than not, the entire cost is not paid by those who use the services, whether we call them patients, clients, consumers, or just persons.

Not long ago, maybe only seventy-five years or so, there was no concern over quality assurance and cost containment. Before the 1930s the majority of health care costs were paid for by those who benefited from the use of the services. Estimates are that approximately 90 percent of the cost of health care was paid by those persons receiving the services (Harris, 1994). As a consequence of a client-sponsored system of paying for care, many medical needs went untreated. It was a fairly simple and straightforward two-party system of an individual provider and purchaser—usually a physician and a patient. The provider was free to charge whatever the market would bear, and the system was chiefly one of caveat emptor, or let the buyer beware (Patterson and Sharfstein 1992). A third party, particularly in the unique role of payor, was relatively uncommon. This system changed when the primary pay-ors became private insurance companies and eventually the public sec-tor—the government.

The Private Third-Party Payor

Employer-provided health insurance has become commonplace for much of America's full-time workforce. Indeed, most workers in America have come to expect it, or at least to hope for it. To illustrate, approximately 80 percent of Americans believe employers should be required to offer insurance, in spite of the overwhelming rejection of President Clinton's proposed health security act (Harris 1994).

All insurance policies work about the same way: most of those who have it do not use it. In other words, insurance is the ability to spread the cost of care for a few people over a large number of individuals. A small payment (the premium) is made by a large number of persons to offset the costs of paying the benefits used by only a few. In exchange for this cost, everyone who subscribes can trust that if there eventually is a need for the benefits, those costs will be covered, or at least the costs will not represent the same financial loss to the person needing the services.

The current need to control the costs of health and mental health care is in sharp contrast to the circumstances prior to the advent of health insurance coverage as part of employment. The early insurance policies were typically available for purchase through employers, unions, and fraternal organizations, such as was found in major industries—railroad, lumber, mining, and textile. When insurance was available from an employer, the cost was paid primarily by the worker through payroll deductions, and much of the coverage was limited to work-related injuries.

The Great Depression changed that system. After this economic debacle, when huge numbers of people had no work, could not afford to buy insurance, and could not afford to pay the medical bills they incurred, the system of purchaser and seller collapsed. The outcome of this widespread unemployment was that physicians, and hospitals, in turn, were not getting paid and risked insolvency. As a consequence, individual hospitals began to offer insurance in order to ensure payment. Later, consortiums of hospitals began to offer insurance. This became the model for Blue Cross.

The first Blue Cross plans were offered through a group of teachers in Dallas, Texas, in 1929 (MacLeod 1993) and another group of teachers from Sacramento, California, in 1932 (Furrow, Johnson, Jost and

Schwartz 1991). These plans offered a premium rate based on a single community-wide risk pool (that large group of insured who do not use the benefits but offset the costs of those who do). These fees guaranteed payment for selected health care procedures to participating hospitals.

Backed by the American Medical Association, Blue Cross was exempt from state insurance regulations, which often require large cash reserves to ensure the ability to cover the eventual costs of claims. Several states offered this exemption upon the condition that Blue Cross would serve the entire community, including low- and moderate-income citizens who could not afford the premiums. In turn, the plans were eligible for federal tax exemptions as a charitable organization.

By 1945 the Blue Cross plans provided basic coverage of hospitalization costs of over 19 million subscribers; that is, Blue Cross paid all costs of hospitalization. But the Blue Cross benefits typically did not cover the fee of the physician, a lacuna filled by Blue Shield. A forerunner of insurance for physician fees were state medical bureaus, with the first established in Washington in 1933 (MacLeod 1993) The first Blue Shield plan was California Physician Services, which began in 1939. Like Blue Cross, Blue Shield emerged as a means of ensuring that physicians would be paid for the services they provided. Blue Shield was also a basic coverage, where the entire fee for the service was paid.

Throughout the country the "Blues" dominated the health insurance market until World War II. The costs of premiums were still primarily at the expense of the insured. During World War II, however, when the wartime economy instituted wage and price controls in an effort to ensure stability, union-management negotiations often provided noncash remuneration. Employees could be recruited and retained by offering generous advantages in lieu of higher salaries; moreover, these benefits were exempt from federal income taxes. As the new demand for insurance policies grew, Blue Cross and Blue Shield faced competition. Instead of determining premium rates based on a community risk pool, commercial insurance companies could offer lower premiums based on the experience rate of a particular group of employees—that is, how likely a particular member of the group would be to use the benefits. Thus, unlike Blue Cross and Blue Shield, which offered rates from an entire community, commercial insurance carriers were only insuring those particular workers and their dependents. Obviously it was less expensive to insure a thousand young, healthy workers in a school district than an entire community in a coal mining community of western Pennsylvania.

This marketplace competition resulted in the eventual blurring of the original distinctions between the "Blues" and commercial insurers. In order to be competitive, Blue Cross and Blue Shield began to change their rate structure to include experience rates of particular groups of insured.

Paralleling the development of employer-purchased insurance as an employee benefit, some businesses began offering benefits at their own expense—that is, self-insurance. Instead of paying for insurance premiums through an independent insurance company, these businesses paid the costs of the care itself. Currently, the federal Employee Retirement Income Security Act (ERISA) provides employers a considerable incentive to be self-insured. Still, many companies have recognized the great risk in being self-insured: if the use of benefits or costs of care escalate, so do the costs of doing business. Additionally, self-insurance requires a company to be in two businesses: its actual business and the insurance business.

Because of the potential for loss, many self-insured employers purchase "stop-loss" insurance: secondary insurance that applies to an entire self-insured plan. For example, if a company's total costs exceed $1.5 million or if any single component of the plan rises above a certain level (e.g., an employee's care exceeds $300,000), the remaining costs are covered by the stop-loss policy. Stop-loss insurance takes effect only when a certain level of cost has been incurred (Kongstvedt 1993).

Another approach to offering employee benefits is through HMOs, such as Group Health Association of Washington, D.C., Health Insurance Plan of Greater New York, and Kaiser Permanente. The forerunner of HMOs was introduced in 1929 in a small farming community in Oklahoma that did not have a hospital. In order to raise money for the facility, a physician sold shares in a health organization and in consideration offered services at a discount rate (MacLeod 1993). In many respects, an HMO can be a form of self-insurance that offers medical coverage by directly contracting with the providers of the care at a predetermined fee. Similarly, some companies offer health care benefits through their own providers. The ship's doctor and the company nurse are probably the oldest and simplest examples.

Insurance and Costs. The costs of providing insurance coverage have gone up because more of those who are insured use the benefits and the cost of what is covered has increased. There are six basic ways to control the increased costs:

1. Have the employer pay the increased costs of labor.
2. Pass the extra cost on in the stream of commerce in the form of more expensive goods and services.
3. Offset the higher cost of coverage by charging more to use the benefits, as in the form of higher insurer-paid premiums or copayments.
4. Have fewer people use the benefits.
5. Offer less coverage for the same price of the premium.
6. Reduce the actual costs of the care itself.

These are the rudimentary means to control the financial loss by the private third-party payor; they become complicated when implemented, as the entire field of managed care illustrates. Few employers claim to be able to absorb more costs of production. Inflation seems once again under control, and most people want things to stay that way; thus, most would object to higher premiums, lower coverage, or more expensive goods and services. Few people favor the alternatives of more costs or less coverage, especially if they are combined, so those who are insured pay more for less. Reducing the cost of services may be the most appealing, since it is clearly the least painful alternative. It is also the most difficult alternative.

In an era of managed care of a third-party payor's cost, all six mechanisms are used to control cost, and none is as dreadful as it may seem. The reduction of use, for example, does not mean denying coverage for needed services but, rather, educating clients about health promotion and disease prevention (as discussed in chapter 3), or wiser decisions about when and which services are necessary (as discussed in chapters 4 and 5). Similarly, reducing the costs of services does not necessarily translate to lower quality of care but may mean using less expensive providers (such as a master's-level practitioner instead of a licensed psychiatrist or other expensive specialists), decreasing excessive overhead, and eliminating waste and fraud.

Cost of Coverage. This third-party system of paying for someone else's health care is costly, in part because those who are in poorer health and are more likely to use the benefits of an insurance policy are the very people who are the most likely to seek out insurance coverage, a concept known as *adverse selection*. Those who have good health (e.g., young graduate students) are less likely to have insurance.

Employer-provided insurance pays the majority of nonpublic costs of physical and mental health care in America. Some 211 million Americans are fortunate enough to have coverage (Health Insurance Association of America 1992). This is approximately 31 percent of the costs, or about $179 billion. Estimates are that medical benefits cost about $4,000 per employee and that, by the year 2030, benefits will exceed the average salary (Harris 1994). Consequently, instead of offering health care to all citizens (as is found in every industrialized country of the world except South Africa and the United States), the American system puts much of the financial burden on willing—although quite possibly reluctant—employers. Business, in turn, passes these costs on in the form of higher prices for the goods and services found in the stream of commerce (the second cost-control practice noted). Thus, one way or another, directly or indirectly, the costs of health and mental health care are borne by all of us.

The Other Working Americans. Amid all this discussion of employer-paid insurance coverage, it is important to remember the uninsured and the underinsured—disproportionately women, persons of color, and people with low incomes (Wolf 1994). Often these people are full-time or part-time workers, usually in jobs that pay around the minimum wage, but their employer does not provide adequate benefits.

For these working people the alternatives to employer-provided insurance are to purchase insurance in the marketplace or go without insurance and—most likely—without care. The first alternative is of limited feasibility for a person earning minimum wage. Further, individual purchasers of insurance must buy their coverage in the same marketplace where small to large firms shop for insurance. An individual, however, does not necessarily have the large risk pool of that same 1,000 young, healthy employees in the school district to offset the cost of the few who use the benefits. Over 14 million people purchase these "nongroup" policies. The costs are higher, the ability to limit or deny coverage greater, and the ease of cancelling coverage more probable than is found with group policies.

There are also numerous people who are not within the ranks of the adequately insured, including those who are not full-time paid workers or cannot afford individual policies. This included over 36 million persons in 1991, of whom 79 percent were workers and their dependents (Harris 1994). Since Medicare provides coverage to 97 percent of people over the age of sixty-five, the uninsured include a great number of people who are employed in companies that are small or not incorporated. For example, nearly half of all uninsured workers are employed in companies with fewer than twenty-five employees (Furrow et al. 1991). The lack of coverage is, in part, a result of higher premium rates due to a small risk pool. The federal tax structure also contributes to this problem because it allows incorporated firms to deduct 100 percent of the cost of benefits as a legitimate business expense, while unincorporated firms can deduct only 25 percent. In this respect, the federal government is clearly willing to subsidize larger, incorporated employers with a lower tax liability. That is, this tax reduction decreases the costs of doing business for one type of company but not another. Because of such silent subsidies, the federal government makes it easier for incorporated businesses to offer employer-provided benefits. In essence, government fiscal policy directly affects the probability that an employer will offer insurance and how much insurance will be considered a benefit of employment. This brings us to the other largest payor for health care in America: the public third-party payor.

The Public Third-Party Payor

The complexity of who pays for physical and mental health coverage greatly increases when we consider public third-party payors. The topic itself warrants much more attention and detail than we could possibly provide here. We will attempt, however, to give you a flavor of the incredible extent and diversity of the system of public third party payors.

The private and public third-party payor systems are highly interdependent, as is illustrated with the tax subsidy for some types of businesses and not for others. The interdependence is recognized by Katz and Trainor (1988) as the "waterbed effect," where compression at one end makes the other end bulge. In the case of physical and mental health care insurance, if fewer companies were to provide coverage, a greater burden would shift to the public sector. Similarly, corporate incentives to provide adequate coverage lessen the demands on the public third-party payor.

A variety of people are provided some form of insurance through public third-party payors. Those who are not insured through private employer-paid or subsidized insurance coverage include persons who work for federal, state, and local government; persons with low revenues (pejoratively referred to as "the poor"); children; older adults; those with disabilities; and a number of retired workers (most notably railroad retirees and government retirees). These people receive coverage by public third-party payors.

Historically, public provision of care for selected groups of individuals is nothing new. Government-sponsored health care was established shortly after America's independence from England. In 1798 federally provided health care was offered to seamen, an offer facilitated by the fear that diseases could be spread by a group whose employment took them up and down the coast and elsewhere in a relatively short period of time. Shortly after, America witnessed the creation of public hospitals, including local hospitals and state-sponsored hospitals for persons with mental illness. The highwater mark during this period of public-sponsored care was undoubtedly Dorothy Dix's hope for a federal land-grant program for hospitals for the mentally ill—a dream and a need recognized by Congress, only to be vetoed by President Franklin Pierce in 1854 (Starr 1982).

Medicare and Medicaid. The most widely recognized federal programs today are Medicare and Medicaid, although they are by no means the only public health and mental health care programs. Medicare expenditures totaled $159.5 billion in 1994, and the federal-state Medicaid program spent $158 billion in 1994 ($90 billion of it from federal funds and $68 billion from state budgets). Medicare is available to social security recipients over the age of sixty-five, railroad retirees, and persons with end-stage renal disease. It is similar to Blue Cross and Blue Shield in that it offers coverage for hospital costs. Supplementary medical insurance (SMI) operates much like Blue Shield and covers the costs of physician services and related services.

This coverage is becoming increasingly expensive. For example, the annual budget per person for hospital insurance was around $1,500 in 1970; it reached approximately $2,800 in 1994. SMI was approximately

$800 in 1970; it was about $1,600 in 1994. Expenditures are increasing at a rate of 10 percent per year, with the system expected to go bankrupt by 2002 and run a $126 billion deficit by 2004 (Toner and Pear, 1995).

Because Medicare is the largest federal program for health care, it is the target of numerous efforts to reduce its costs by various managed care approaches, such as contracting with HMOs to provide services instead of paying the traditional fee for services (Zarabozo and LeMasurier 1993). Cost containment is particularly critical in advance of the onslaught of the baby boomers' reaching the age of eligibility around 2010.

Medicare is like other health insurance policies in that it is available for purchase by qualified buyers. Any citizen (or legal resident who has lived in the United States for at least five years) and who is over sixty-five years of age may enroll in Medicare, provided he or she can pay the costs of the premium. Thus, Medicare is an entitlement program for senior citizens, an eligibility program for certain health services (e.g., end-stage renal disease), and an insurance policy for those of a particular age who can afford it.

Medicare and Cost Containment. Because Medicare pays for over 25 percent of all hospital care, it puts the federal government in the enviable position to offer cost-containment alternatives on a take-it-or-leave-it basis (Furrow et al. 1991). Probably the most dramatic and well-publicized method is through the prospective payment system based on diagnosis-related groups (DRGs).

DRGs classify inpatient procedures into one of more than 460 groups for the purposes of payment. The classification is based on primary and secondary diagnoses, the necessary treatment procedures, and comorbidity conditions. Reimbursement rates for the procedures are based on the hospital as an entirety and not all the other possible services that were part of the patient care (Goodman, Brown, and Deitz 1992).

Originally DRGs excluded psychiatric hospitals and psychiatric units in general hospitals, for several reasons. Out of the numerous DRGs, only fifteen related to psychiatric conditions, and nine of these are different classifications of substance abuse. The major psychiatric DRG is the general category of psychosis, which consists of several specific diagnoses with substantial differences in severity and the necessary length of hospital stays (Namerow and Gibson 1988). Psychiatric DRGs do not adequately predict utilization of services, contributing to random underpayment and overpayment for services covered under a psychiatric DRG (English, Sharfstein, Scherl, Astrachan, and Muszynski 1986; Namerow and Gibson 1988).

Although psychiatric facilities were exempt from DRGs, they were not exempt from government efforts to control costs. In particular, mental health services were subjected to prospective payment systems. Prospective payments of Medicare beneficiaries are reimbursed and regulated through the Tax Equity and Fiscal Responsibility Act. As Bachofer (1988) notes, this system may be even less desirable than DRGs. There are difficulties in individual cases that require collateral providers, and prospective payment systems tend to lack provisions for atypical cases, which usually require the largest amount of care and the most expensive care.

Although mental health services have exemptions and limitations from Medicare cost-containment practices, eventually restrictions will be imposed for most, if not all, Medicare-reimbursed services. We believe this will happen in the very near future and will regulate the type, duration, and reimbursement rate of mental health services through capitated managed care and utilization review procedures. This may be from encouraging enrollment in a capitated managed care organization such as an HMO or mandatory reviews.

Medicaid and Cost Containment. Medicaid is much more complex than Medicare because it is a joint federal-state program; thus, it consists of fifty-six programs for the different states and territories. There are tremendous differences in programs found in these different jurisdictions. Compare, for example, Oregon's health care rationing plan with any other state's distribution of health care (Wiener 1992).

Medicaid benefits are available to those who meet various eligibility standards and are considered the "deserving poor." Currently over 36 million Americans receive Medicaid in the fifty states and the District of Columbia. Two-thirds of all long-term nursing home residents are covered under Medicaid.

Some politicians would lead us to believe that Medicaid is primarily for women and children with low income, that is, those receiving Aid to Families with Dependent Children. Although they may be the largest proportion of persons covered by Medicaid (approximately 70 percent of those people in the program are beneficiaries of Aid to Families with Dependent Children), only 10 percent are on general public assistance (Herrick 1993), and they do not receive an equal proportion of the expenditures. Two-thirds of all expenditures are for long-term care for the elderly and disabled citizens, a group comprising about a third of those covered by the program. Medicaid generally excludes single people without children who have no money. Presumably these individuals are the "undeserving poor."

When it began in 1966, Medicaid was a fee-for-service third-party payor, much like Medicare. It has seen significant increases in costs over the past thirty years. In 1984, it was only 8 percent of a state's budget; in 1994, it was 20 percent. In spite of this, Medicaid has not embraced cost containment with the same enthusiasm Medicare has. For example, there are only 200 HMOs nationwide that have contracts with state Medicaid agencies, and twenty-two states have no Medicaid HMO program (Herrick 1993). Only a few states have instituted DRGs for inpatient physical health care or require utilization reviews. And yet these cost-containment procedures can reduce high-cost fee for services; emergency room visits, for example, can be reduced by 70 percent (Herrick 1993).

There are numerous reasons for the less aggressive pursuit of cost containment by Medicaid. For example, because of inadequate reporting, the extent of Medicaid funding is difficult to determine, although it is known that it is the largest federal funding source of mental health services. Another reason is that a reduction in the federal-state shared costs might easily become cost shifting. In particular, cost containment in Medicaid may simply shift the costs to hospitals funded only by the state (Katz and Trainor 1988), once again illustrating the waterbed effect.

We believe this disregard of cost containment will not last much longer. In the very near future, almost every state Medicaid program will develop alternatives to the fee-for-service approach, much like what is found in Medicare and by private third-party payors. For most states, this will include physical and mental health services. Some states will make even bolder efforts to contain costs, ensure quality, and increase access. Probably the boldest of these efforts so far is the Oregon Health Care Plan, which works on the principle that, depending on state funds, complete coverage is provided to all eligible recipients but only those with certain health and mental health conditions. For other conditions, no coverage is provided at all. For example borderline personality disorder is paid for from state funds, but anti-social personality disorder is not. Managed care procedures to contain the cost while ensuring quality are also integral to the Oregon plan (Thorne 1992). Currently, this state's approach is restricted to physical health care. Mental health services will be folded into the plan in the near future, provided there is adequate state funding. We believe that soon every state Medicaid program will include many of the principles and procedures of managed care.

Other Public Third-Party Payors. There are a number of other public health and mental health services. Government payments for health care coverage also include the cost for veterans of the armed services and civil servants. Veterans' services for active and retired military personnel and their dependents are provided in over 172 hospitals and in hundreds of community clinics, as well as 168 military hospitals and hundreds of medical and dental clinics.

The armed services are also augmented through benefits paid to nonmilitary facilities through the Civilian Health and Medical Program of Uniformed Services (CHAMPUS). Approximately 6 million persons are covered by CHAMPUS, which has an annual budget of $3.9 billion (Boyer and Sobel 1993).

Government-sponsored health coverage is also provided in over 600 hospitals, centers, and clinics for nearly 1 million Native Americans who are enrolled members of federally recognized Indian tribes.

And let us not forget the over 1.3 million persons in federal and state prisons in 1992 (Forer 1994), with the number of incarcerated people predicted to exceed 4 million by the year 2000 (Dilulio 1991). Government pays the cost of health care for those who are incarcerated in federal and state prisons, local jails, boot camps, and juvenile detention centers. It is worth noting that these health and mental health costs are for a group of people not known for being healthy, nor is the environment known for its health promotion.

The system of government as the third-party payor does not stop here. When we consider the state and local levels, government programs also provide funding for state university hospitals, student health clinics, aid to the medically indigent, and local health clinics.

The government is also the third-party payor through workers' compensation programs, which provide payment for health and mental health injuries arising out of—or in the course of—employment or are from occupational diseases. This coverage is provided to all workers except domestics and those in agriculture (Larson 1992).

There are also indirect ways in which government becomes the third-party payor for health and mental health services. One of the major ways is through tax subsidies. Recall the discussion about subsidies for incorporated versus nonincorporated businesses. Tax-exempt status is essentially a subsidy created by reducing tax liability, which is nothing less than revenue enhancement and a decrease in the cost of doing business. There are a variety of local, state, and federal tax benefits to charitable health and mental health care facilities. Some tax benefits include little or no federal and state income tax, sales tax, and property tax. One estimate is that over $4 billion of potential government revenue is not available because of tax-exempt status granted to the not-for-profit health care industry (Furrow et al. 1991).

Clearly government is a major player in physical and mental health care coverage. In 1990, for example, it spent $269 billion on health and mental health care—representing 42 percent of the country's entire expenditure for health care (Furrow et al. 1991).

PRIVATE AND PUBLIC PAYORS OF MENTAL HEALTH CARE

During the early years of private health insurance and the beginning of federally funded health care, mental health services generally were not covered, in part because care for persons with mental illness was provided chiefly through state-run hospitals and in part because there were few psychiatric treatment options available besides supportive care in restrictive environments (Patterson and Sharfstein 1992). Those with psychiatric diagnoses also tended to have more chronic than acute conditions, and thus they were less likely to be found in the workforce where insurance was available. From the perspective of the insurance industry, mental illnesses were excluded from coverage because of a reluctance to accept the high cost of care that did not seem to ameliorate the problem and was already financially supported on a state tax level.

This outlook began to change in the 1950s as psychiatric epidemiological studies suggested that mental health problems were much more pervasive than originally believed (for discussion see Regier and Burke 1989) and as general hospitals began to include psychiatric units (Starr 1982). Moreover, psychotropic medication made advances. Not only had medication long been recognized as an acceptable fee-for-service component, but phenothiazine seemed to make a difference. Medication ameliorated much of the symptomatology of mental disorders.

Consequently, insurance carriers began to offer coverage for various psychiatric conditions. The most common coverage was for psychiatric conditions considered severe enough to warrant hospitalization. Thus, some of the financial burden of care for persons with mental illness was shifted to the insurance industry and private third-party payors.

Insurance coverage of mental health needs expanded throughout the 1960s into the 1980s in terms of the types of services covered (inpatient and outpatient), number of persons with insurance coverage, and which disciplines were recognized as qualified to provide mental health services. And as coverage became increasingly available, more and more services were provided. This trend was most noticeable in the areas of substance-abuse treatment and adolescent psychiatric hospitalization.

There was a massive buildup of for-profit facilities during the late 1970s and 1980s. Similarly, state statutes began to recognize a variety of qualified providers besides physicians, such as psychologists, social workers, and licensed professional counselors, resulting in a more rapid growth in such disciplines as psychology and social work in comparison to psychiatry. Currently the vast majority of treatment is provided by psychologists and social workers, not psychiatrists (American Psychiatric Association 1987b).

Similarly, the government's role as a major payor in mental health care began in the 1960s, developing from President Kennedy's concern for mental health and mental retardation. Probably the most significant change resulted from the publication of *Action for Mental Health* (Appel and Bartemeier 1961), which established the design for a nationwide system of community mental health centers.

Originally, community mental health centers provided five essential services: inpatient care, outpatient care, partial hospitalization, psychiatric emergency care, and consultation/education. Subsequent devel-

opments from 1968 through 1970 included additional mandated services for children and the elderly, substance abuse, screening prior to
admission to state psychiatric hospitals, posthospitalization follow-up,
and transitional housing (Shore 1989). An emphasis on persons with
low incomes became a priority.

Community mental health centers were designed with a gradual decrease in federal funding and increased funding at the state and local
levels. By the early 1980s, the so-called new federalism of the Reagan
administration shifted much of the financial burden from the federal to
the state level through block grants, which provided funds that states
could use as they saw fit (Cutler 1992). By the end of the 1980s, this
shift in funding had resulted in a greater burden on states, which now
provide the largest mental health system in the world: 29,000 programs
(Katz and Trainor 1988).

Community mental health centers were also amended in 1977 to include a requirement of quality assurance or utilization reviews. These review programs were quite different from those today. Sometimes they
were rigorous assessments of the actual quality of care and effects on a
client's functioning. More often than not, the initial quality assurance
and utilization review were primarily "compliance policing" to determine
if a client's treatment plan and records were up to date and complete.

More rigorous quality assurance reviews were initiated with CHAM-
PUS in 1977 when the Department of Defense contracted with the
American Psychiatric Association to provide case reviews. The eventual outcome included a set of standards of care based on major psychiatric diagnostic categories. Much of this quality assurance was a determination of whether there was a medical necessity for treatment and if
the intervention was implemented efficiently (Hamilton, 1992). These
procedures were later adopted by the Aetna insurance company, which
concluded that peer reviews improved the quality of care and contained the costs. These reviews were primarily retrospective utilization
reviews based on written reports submitted by practitioners. They were
time-consuming to complete, occasionally taking up to a month to get
a response.

Not surprisingly, the two issues of treatment necessity and appropriately implemented treatment interventions continue to be the chief
concerns of prospective managed care programs. Because denying reimbursement is difficult once services have been provided, prospective

and concurrent utilization review procedures were developed. In fact, the retrospective utilization review to assess the need for services has largely been replaced by prospective reviews. It is, after all, rather difficult to tell a clinician and a client that payment for services that have already been provided were not necessary. It is infinitely more acceptable to deny payment prior to their delivery.

These forms of utilization reviews were frequently based on a telephone interview with the practitioner or a structured questionnaire. These efforts at utilization reviews became much of the basis for the current methods of prospective, concurrent, and retrospective utilization procedures addressed throughout this book.

THE HEALTH CARE COST CRISIS AND MANAGED CARE

The outcome of this involvement by third-party payors is a health care crisis focused primarily on costs and, possibly, availability of services. (Actually, the crisis of availability is a result of the costs; if services were not so expensive, access would be easier to accomplish.)

To a great extent this crisis has resulted not simply because of the third-party payor but because the first two parties (the provider and the patient) are relatively insulated from the financial burdens of purchasing and selling health care services. The noticeable exceptions are higher copayments and deductibles, and possibly higher premiums (Harris 1994).

As DuVal (1998) comments, the entire system of private and public third-party payors is a "sure-fire formula for pushing expenditures through the roof" (p. 2). For example, the determination of who needs treatment and for how long is frequently defined by the availability of a private or public third-party payor and the limits of the insurance policy's coverage. Most purchasers of mental health care believe that whatever care is desired or recommended is the best and preferred intervention. In mental health, one illustration of this is seen with practitioners' preferred treatment, which continues to be expensive, long-term, insight-oriented psychotherapy. There seems to be little delivery of short-term treatment (Rabinowitz and Lukoff 1995). The preference for profitable long-term treatment continues in spite of the repeated evidence indicating that time-limited and brief treatment may be as effective—

and maybe more effective (Bloom 1992; Reid and Shein 1969; Smith, Glass, and Miller 1980; Videka-Sherman 1985; Wells 1994).

Moreover, much of the development in the health care fields has been additive growth, not growth that replaces older technology. That is, many new and effective procedures and specialists do not replace older ones; rather, they may supplement them at greater financial costs (Eisenberg et al. 1989). Additional and lengthy procedures, whether for physical health or mental health, add to the costs of care but not necessarily to effectiveness.

As Starr (1982) noted in a remarkable book, health care has begun to undergo a major revolution driven by the high costs of care. Due to political and media attention to the need for health care reform, most Americans are now aware of just how troubled the system is. For example, over 12 percent of the total 1990 gross national product went to health care, representing approximately $660 billion. About 12 percent of that $660 billion was allocated to mental health care (Dorwart 1990). And the costs keep going up. By 1993 the total gross national product dedicated to health care was 14 percent, or $838.5 billion (Harris 1994). At current rates, by the year 2000 health care costs are expected to exceed $1.6 trillion (Harris 1994).

Moreover, health care costs have been increasing at a rate unparalleled by other components of the economy and have outpaced inflation by three or four times. Mental health care costs were the fastest rising costs throughout the 1980s (Patterson and Sharfstein 1992).

CONCLUSION

Managed care is necessary, for complex reasons. Escalating benefits compete with real wages and lower the standard of living. This means there is less money available for other sectors of the economy, which in turn means fewer jobs and, then, even less money in the economy. Such a scenario will be accompanied by the exacerbation of additional social problems, from violence to substance abuse, to stress and distress.

Let us consider the effect of the current economic pace of growth in the physical and mental health industry. At the current pace, the entire gross national product will be devoted to health care by the year 2030. If this comes to pass, there will be no goods or services produced besides those of health care. No food. No clothing. No automobiles. No tickets or Geritol for the Rolling Stones' Octogenarian Tour.

Clearly this will not happen because unlimited growth cannot occur. It will not happen, in part, because of private and public efforts to control cost. Managed mental health care is one of those efforts, and almost every psychologist, social worker, counselor, and mental health worker needs to develop skills to work efficiently and effectively within the new four-party system of client, clinician, payor, and managed care program.

Chapter 2

Every Stick Has Two Ends

The Managed Care Controversy

Managed care is a new and pervasive force in mental health services. Under the guise of being able to contain costs while ensuring the quality of care, managed care may determine who receives what services for how long, by whom, and with what expected outcomes. Understandably, managed care has not been greeted warmly by many practitioners. On the other hand, proponents of managed care are convinced that this loosely woven system of fourth-party programs and procedures is effective and necessary to ensure a future of affordable health and mental health services. It is as if the two sides of the debate were addressing different issues, like night and day. In this chapter we will consider some of the positions for and against managed care, drawn from the furious and voluminous debate.

The context in which the debate takes place seems to center on three themes: (1) control of the treatment process, (2) money (who gets how much), and (3) the cost-effectiveness of managed care itself. A related theme is whether managed care impedes treatment by being detrimental to clients' needs. Much of this concern falls squarely in the area of control. Nearly every practitioner would argue that if he or she controlled treatment, it would be to the benefit of the client. Managed care organizations make the same argument. For example, referral to less expensive master's-level practitioners reduces the unnecessarily high cost of using psychiatrists. Similarly, managed care channeling prevents a client from wasting time and money on a provider who may define the limits of treatment as the end of the insurance coverage. In other words, both sides think their approach is better for the client. Consequently, we think that much of this aspect of the quarrel is best addressed as an issue of control.

We will organize some of the controversy under the three headings of clinical control and professional autonomy, money and who gets it, and the cost-effectiveness of managed care. By conceptualizing the debate within this context, it is more likely to move toward a resolution of the conflicts between managed care and clinicians. At a minimum, the solution to the conflicts must include a managed care system that itself is cost-efficient, reasonable, and responsive to clinicians who are cooperative and committed to cost containment and, and above all, operate from the position of what is in the best interests of clients.

Not only do we believe that these three standards should facilitate the development of managed care, but they should be used as a north star that guides practitioners' involvement in managed mental health care. In advance of the discussion, we suggest that practitioners refuse to work with any managed care program or procedure that costs society more money, not less; is unreasonable in the expectations placed on clinicians; and whose practices are not in the best interests of clients.

"YOU'RE EITHER WITH US OR AGAINST US"

The views on managed care are quite divided, extreme at times, and difficult to resolve on common ground. Managed care has been considered an unreasonable burden that adversely affects clinical judgment (Zuckerman 1989). Others charge that it intrudes into the confidential client-clinician relationship and threatens the public policy of encouraging individuals to seek the services they need (Corcoran and Winslade 1994; Paris, Winslade, and Corcoran 1995). Others call managed care an ineffective marketplace mechanism for rationing care (Bornstein 1990). Independent practitioners, especially those specializing in treatment of interpersonal problems (Wylie 1994), consider managed care a threat to the future of private practice and a threat to entire schools of thought, e.g. humanistic psychology (Kuhl 1994). Managed care contracts that provide services at a reduced rate, restrict client coverage, and require systematic treatment pose serious threats to solo practitioners whose primary skills are with insight-oriented psychotherapy. Still others have argued that since managed care will need many aggressive procedures to control costs, the inevitable outcome will be an adverse effect on the quality of care, accompanied by limited client access (Dorwart 1990).

On the other side of the debate are those who believe that managed care is a realistic way to contain costs while ensuring quality (Paulson 1996; Winegar 1992). Moreover, by directing clients to less expensive providers, more clients are serviced. From this view, managed care may redistribute services and maximize access to those most in need (Patterson 1990). The denial of services is seen as restricting only services that are not warranted or not covered by the third-party payor. In this sense, the restriction of services may prevent fraud and waste (Patterson 1990). Still, once services are restricted or guidelines and protocols are established, the fourth party to some extent is usurping the clinical judgment and professionalism of the practitioner. Clinical decision making is now outside the treatment relationship and in the hands of someone who may never interact with the client. In effect, this seriously weakens the autonomy of the client and the clinician and restricts choice in the type of intervention considered preferable (Office of Technological Assessment, 1993).

Clearly, the opinions on managed care are quite divided and the distance between their perspectives quite large.

THE CONTEXT OF THE CONTROVERSY

Clinician Autonomy and Clinical Control

Chief among the many reasons that the managed care controversy runs so deep is that managed care has removed the control of treatment from the hands of the clinician to the profit margin and bottom line of entrepreneurs (Hall 1994a, 1994b). As Stern (1993) notes, traditionally a professional has been defined by the ability to make judgments as to what is an appropriate intervention. Yet the mandate for short-term treatment for managed care removes this professional element and renders the clinician more of a technician who simply applies the prescribed procedures.

For example, in many cases, especially those requiring costly services such as hospitalization, prospective utilization reviews may require a second opinion. This not only questions the practitioner's clinical judgment and integrity but also directly contributes to the velocity of the second opinion business. Additionally, a second opinion mandate is a risky cost-containment practice because the eventual cost savings must take into account the cost of the second opinion. When the two opinions concur, the managed care practice simply contributed to the cost for that particular client. It is wasteful. Savings, then, must come from another case where the opinions disagree *and* the treatment clinician's opinion is the incorrect one. If the opinion disagrees and the treating clinician is not in error, it continues to be wasteful.

Another example of control and autonomy is seen from those managed care organizations that make the determination of whether a potential client's problem is severe enough to warrant treatment. If treatment is necessary, the managed care organization may even recommend or require that certain preferred providers be used for particular problems and specify the treatment intervention considered appropriate for that reimbursable problem. These prospective utilization review decisions will also determine how long that treatment may last and with what specified outcome. This fourth party involved will determine the dollar value that will be paid—on the condition that the treatment was adequately implemented and effective. With the exception of some limits on insurance coverage, such as lifetime limits and preexisting illness, most treatment in the past was determined privately by the client and whichever clinician the client trusted enough to seek out (Smith and Meyer 1987). Much of the relationship was part of the treatment process and was considered nobody else's business.

This transfer of control of many clinical decisions has resulted in outright indignation among clinicians (Sabin 1994). It is understandable that many resent the introduction of a fourth party in the treatment process. Imagine if a similar approach was imposed when people sought absolution for religious transgressions. A parallel to prospective managed care review would be that whether a sin had occurred and penance was necessary would be determined by an ecclesiastic fourth party, who would review the thought, word, or deed to see if it was truly sinful and, if so, whether it was severe enough to warrant absolution as a minor or mortal sin. Provided the thought, word, or deed was determined to be a transgression severe enough to warrant absolution, the managed care fourth party would then determine if the potential penance needs dictated the assistance of a less experienced or specialized clergy. This fourth-party-managed religious care might even determine the appropriate penance.

When so much of clinical treatment is governed by others, it not only results in resentment but a considerable number of misguided decisions. In essence, then, much of the controversy begins with the fact that someone besides the clinician and client is determining much of the clinical relationship. Moreover, this determination may adversely affect treatment and at the same time is seen as burdensome to the clinician (Bernstein 1994).

Conflicts over control also materialize when some managed care programs require their preferred providers to participate in mandatory supervision, clinical rounds, or inservice training (Anderson and Berlant 1993). This supervision is quite different from what might be useful for one's professional development, such as advanced certification or licensure. The managed care supervisor might be a psychologist or psychiatrist whose goals and commitment are primarily to the managed care employer. Such practices are designed to ensure quality by having informed and up-to-date clinicians. The need, however, may be more of the managed care organization than of the clinician.

There may be complaints of poor administration of services, slow claims processing with inadequate reimbursement, and unrealistic requested reduction in fees (Poynter 1994; Sargent 1992). Thus, not only is managed care controversial because it reduces a clinician's professional autonomy, but the new control may very well be done inefficiently. A case in point occurred when one of our colleagues was authorized to provide three sessions of treatment at $18 per session after spending three hours negotiating with the managed care organization, which was three time zones away. The time zone difference reduced the window of opportunity to communicate during business hours. Let's admit it, the business hour on the East Coast is quite different than it is in Yachats, Oregon or Honolulu, Hawaii.

The problem of clinical control and professional autonomy is exacerbated by the fact that many of the procedures for control by the managed care company are confusing and include elusive expectations for evidencing quality. The argument is furthered by the fact that this confusing control may easily be accompanied by excessive paperwork. Thus, not only has the clinician lost some professional autonomy, but the fourth party in control is working in a baffling manner. Bornstein (1990) contends that managed care organizations employ reviewers who may not be qualified to evaluate all types of cases and treatment and that the requirements for appealing a reviewer's recommendations are onerous and expensive. Grumet (1989) contends these burdens are intentionally inconvenient in order to discourage utilization.

These problems have not gone unnoticed by the private managed care industry. As Winegar (1992) points out, the managed care organizations that will be successful will be those that provide quality services with cost containment and quality assurance to three constituencies: the individual client, the clinician or provider, and the third party who contracts with the managed care organization. Although Winegar's opinion seems to be based on Adam Smith's "unseen hand of the economy," successful private managed care organizations will probably be those that are responsive to the frustrations and burdens imposed on clinicians.

Currently the balance of control clearly favors managed care over the independent clinician. To some, it is arguable that the balance is so uneven that managed care organizations have an unfair advantage and a take-it-or-leave-it attitude. Woolsey (1993) questions the unregulated and unavailable criteria for evaluation services. Many managed care organizations refuse to release the information, claiming it is a proprietary interest. Woolsey cites a case of a managed care organization that issued a gag policy restricting providers' speech if it undermines or could undermine confidence in the managed care plan. As remote and attenuated as it may sound, indeed the managed care organization was insisting on clinicians' waiving their rights of free speech if they believed that what they said could cause the client to think something unkind about the organization. This same company was found guilty of price fixing, racketeering, and security law violations. The fact that very few providers refused to renew their status with the managed care organization supports Woolsey's observation that clinicians are passively accepting and silently complying with a questionable system.

Woolsey also observes that managed care disproportionately affects women's care, since the majority of clients are women. Moreover, the treatment of women has resulted in trouble for some men, such as treatment that leads to discovering sexual abuse, escaping an abusive relationship, overcoming a poor marriage, or learning to be assertive. Woolsey concludes that managed care is silencing the voice of those women who are not affluent and do not have control over their own money, leading Woolsey to question who is being contained.

Money and Who Gets It

Not everyone agrees with Winegar's (1992) opinion of a self-correcting industry. After all, in the opinion of managed care, clinicians and clients were not self-correcting and required fourth-party intervention. Managed care organizations are in business for basically the same reason clinicians are: to make money. As such, the argument against managed care contends that its primary concern is to satisfy the third-party payor with lower costs. Bernstein (1994), for example, believes this is primarily done by evidencing cost containment as a result of providing shorter treatment to fewer clients. Such a consequence must not be taken lightly. The result of denying services may leave without treatment a growing number of people who are in need of services. Indeed, some research indicates that the majority of people with mental health needs do not in fact receive services even if they can afford them (Klerman, Olfson, Leon, and Weissman 1992). The suggested conclusion is that instead of cost containment by restricting coverage, targeted groups need better access to services.

This brings us to the second element in the context of the managed care industry: money. At one end of the argument, managed care proponents argue that clients and clinicians have contributed to the escalated expense of care by not considering the cost of providing services. Opponents assert that managed care does not simply shift the financial risk of treatment but transfers the same profits from the clinician to the fourth-party organization.

Criticism of managed care goes beyond cost containment practices to quality assurance procedures as well. Sharfstein, Dunn, and Kent (1988), for example, assert that managed care primarily assesses the length of treatment, inpatient versus outpatient, and costs in determining quality. The criticism is furthered in that those who receive authorization are often channeled to short-term treatment with standardized protocols. There is little value in the integrity of the therapeutic relationship under this disguise of quality assurance (Stern 1993).

The context of money includes how much one will be paid for mental health services and how much another will have to pay for them. Managed mental health care is quite unpopular with many—if not most—clinicians because cost containment translates into less income or, at its worse, doing more for less—that is, seeing more clients at a lower fee for service, a charge that was well demonstrated in two recent surveys of mental health providers conducted by the Ridgewood Financial Institute (1992, 1995). The 1992 survey excluded psychiatrists but included 1,905 psychologists, social workers, professional counselors, marriage and family therapists, and other types of clinicians. The second survey included 1,659 providers, including psychiatrists. The pervasiveness of managed care seems to differ for the solo practitioner from the clinician in an independent professional organization. Solo practitioners report that 46 percent of their income is derived from managed care clients, while independent professional organizations report approximately 35 percent of theirs is derived from managed care.

Sixty-six percent of the practitioners in the early 1990s indicated they had signed contracts with managed mental health care fourth parties to provide clinical services at a reduced fee. The previous year, only 51 percent indicated they had reduced-fee contracts. In the mid-1990s this figure was 79 percent. About 25 percent of the clinicians' client contact in the early 1990s was administered under a managed mental health care contract. It was approximately 30 percent in the mid-1990s. In other words, clients who were seen at a reduced fee for service generated a sizable proportion of clinicians' client contact. This work, however, was done at a reduced fee. For example, psychologists are paid $75 per session for a managed care client while the median usual and customary fee paid directly by a client is $90 per session. Similar reductions are reported for social workers, professional counselors, marriage and family therapists, and psychiatrists.

Psychologists, social workers, family and marital therapists, and counselors of all other sorts saw about 25 percent of their clients for less money than they normally charged, and 50 percent of those surveyed in the early 1990s indicated that managed care programs actually decreased their income. This figure was 60 percent in the mid-1990s. The decrease in income seems more severe for marriage and family therapists, who reported a 2.4 percent decrease from the early to the mid-1990s. Other professions reported higher incomes and generally higher fees for service than earlier in the decade. Psychologists reported a 6.1 percent increase, from about $75,000 to slightly more than $80,000. Social workers reported the largest increase in income (over 12 percent), from around $51,000 to about $59,000. The counseling fee increased during this same period by only $5 (from $75 to $80) for professional counselors and social workers and to $90 per session for psychologists. Only marriage and family therapists did not report an increase in fees during this period.

Finally, 40 percent of the clinicians surveyed in the early 1990s indicated that managed care reduced their case load. In the mid-1990s this figure was 47%. Based on these surveys it would seem that cost controls are not only a result of lower fees, but there is some evidence that it is denying services to more people who would have received services.

The surveys provide informative data on the issue of how managed care might have an adverse impact on clients. Forty-four percent of the respondents in the early 1990s indicated that more potential clients were disallowed for treatment because of managed care, a figure that grew to 47 percent in the mid-1990s. Presumably these potential clients were persons the clinicians believed would benefit from treatment and may well have been seen in therapy. Thus, the number of persons with unmet mental health needs may be continuing to grow as a consequence of denying services as Klerman's (1992) study would suggest.

The results also indicate that what clinicians do and with whom is different because of managed care. Thirty-seven percent of the mental health providers in 1991 indicated that their approach to treatment had changed because of managed mental health care, a 10 percent increase from 1990. In the mid-1990s nearly 53 percent of clinicians reported they changed their treatment approach because of managed care. Finally, 52 percent indicated that the length of treatment was shorter because of managed care, a figure that rose to 63 percent in the mid-1990s. These figures further the argument that managed care contains costs by reducing utilization and limiting the length of treatment (Sharfstein, Dunn, and Kent, 1988). In the light of these efforts to contain cost, it is not surprising that over 55 percent of these clinicians reported problems in collecting their fees from insurance companies.

Criticism over the restriction of money is also noted by Woolsey (1993). Her contempt for managed care is primarily directed toward capitation programs, programs that she compares to futures traders who buy low, by providing limited service to as few people as medically necessary, and sell high, by contracting for a sufficient fee that is greater than the cost of care.

Many of these impediments and inconveniences posed by managed care are a welcome relief to the financial burden of the third-party payor. From their point of view, the decrease in the length of treatment does not spell truncated needed services but an increased reliance on interventions that have persuasive evidence of effectiveness. Treatment may not necessarily offer fewer services but rather eliminates the financial waste and inefficiency of a "one-size-fits-all," long-term, insight orientation. Similarly, to benefits manager in charge of the third-party payments, the disallowing of requests for clinical services is not seen as a denial of legitimate benefits but the prevention of needless services for a condition that does not appear to warrant treatment or is not covered by the payor.

A helpful analogy is auto insurance. Not everything is covered under the terms and conditions of the insurance policy, and the insured can select most of the level of coverage and what it covers. Perhaps a car has a legitimate need for a new carburetor, but such an expense should not be paid by the insurer if coverage is for collisions. Similarly, a newly purchased used car that has a smashed bumper would be a preexisting condition, not covered by auto insurance. The insurance company is not denying a need for a new carburetor or repair of the unsightly dent; rather, it is saying the responsibility to pay for these services is not theirs. And when a needed repair is an insurable interest, most insurance companies want two or three estimates so *they* can choose the lowest bid in an effort to control costs. If one mechanic can repair the car in less time and for less money than another equally qualified one, then it is reasonable and financially sound to use the first mechanic. A frequent rebuttal is that the two providers of services, mechanics or clinicians, may not be equally qualified. Perhaps not. And yet a specialist in repairing classic 1983 XJ6 Jaguars may not be necessary to fix a dented finder. By comparison, managed mental health care may select a less expensive but equally effective master's-level practitioner over a more expensive psychiatrist. This could occur, and we believe should, even though the client wants a "real doctor." Patterson (1990) contends that managed care makes services more available by directing potential clients toward less expensive providers, mandating clinical accountability and fiscal responsibility.

In sum, those opposed to managed mental health care suggest that clinicians of most disciplines find that it is influencing where one works, how much one works, what type of work is done and for how long, with whom one works, how much one gets paid, and how easily one collects those fees. Often this is all determined by methods that are needlessly burdensome and intrude into the confidential client-clinician relationship.

Does Managed Care Work?

The third major context of the controversy centers around whether managed care is cost-effective. Does it contain costs and ensure quality?

Research on the effectiveness of managed care in the mental health field is relatively recent, rather limited, and fairly inconsistent. It seems ironic that the external parties demanding accountability have little evidence of their own effectiveness. Be that as it may, what research is available does not speak favorably for managed care or is mixed at best (Bickman et al. (1995).

One study considered the effectiveness of managed care by surveying thirty-one benefits managers from managed care vendors or companies using four different approaches to utilization reviews (Garnick, Hendricks, Dulski, Thorpe, and Hogen 1994). Two-thirds of the programs used prospective utilization reviews, concurrent reviews, and case management for inpatient treatment. Forty percent of the companies used utilization reviews for outpatient treatment, practices that are similar to those outlined in this book.

As for the common criticism that managed care personnel are not qualified, Garnick et al. (1994) found that most managed care organizations use a variety of professionals: psychiatric nurses, clinical social workers, psychologists, and physicians. Three programs used only nurses. Similarly, the criticism that decisions are often arbitrary is also questioned because the managed care organizations indicated they have explicit criteria for authorizing hospitalization and extension of the length of stay. Admittedly, some of these criteria were reported to be "proprietary information" (p. 1202)—trade secrets, if you will, that are not available to those who must comply with the criteria. This tends to support the criticism that practitioners believe they must guess at what is expected from the managed care program. Garnick et al.

(1994) did report, however, that several of the managed care companies *sell* their criteria to authorized providers. In other words, managed care will tell practitioners what is expected of them, for a price.

An evaluation of managed care's own effectiveness must bear in mind that these programs are run by a number of educated and experienced professionals, who are an expensive labor force, and the managed care organization has offices and overhead. It is not an inexpensive service. To survive by containing costs, managed care must exceed the added costs of operating the managed care program. For example, if a managed care program trimmed $100,000 from the mental health expenditures of a public or private payor but itself cost $75,000, the $25,000 saving may not be worth the aggravation to consumers of mental health services, the burden it places on practitioners, or the loss of goodwill in the program, not to mention possible increases in other service areas (such as use of the emergency room). If the treatment is as effective and accessible as it was before the savings, then it may be worth it. Cost-effectiveness, though, must factor in the added costs of the managed care program.

Cost-effectiveness must also take into consideration how managed care may further reduce increases in expenditures. As Winegar (1992) reports, managed mental health care is cost-effective by reducing the yearly increase of cost. Winegar reports three examples: CIGNA decreased its percentage increase for mental health coverage from 25 to 30 percent to between 6 and 8 percent; the mental health costs of Metropolitan Life fell by 50 percent; and Aetna saved over $30 million on mental health costs by implementing a utilization review program.

Not all accounts claim such dramatic effects. A case study of a family service center indicated that the number of people served increased from around 20,000 to over 50,000 with the signing of a single HMO contract to provide mental health services (Robinson 1989). The author points out many of the struggles that accompany such rapid growth. Most noticeable was the need to use a sliding scale for client fees subsequent to running out of HMO benefits. Interestingly, this attempt to offset financial losses to an agency or individual provider by some form of cost sharing with the client may no longer be permissible. As Woolsey (1994) points out, there is a catch-22 in the managed care contract such that the need for additional sessions (even at a sliding scale rate) indicates the need for long-term treatment, and the plan covers only brief treatment.

The research on managed care effectiveness is led by a study by Dickey and Azeni (1992) of inpatient mental health services before and after implementing two managed care cost-containment programs. The results were based on the "covered lives" of workers and their dependents at two large corporations between 1985 and 1987. The goal of these programs was to reduce the costs of hospitalizing patients whose condition did not warrant such expensive services. One of the programs was a prospective utilization review that authorized hospital admissions and the length of stay. The other was a concurrent utilization review program that evaluated treatment and discharge plans. Both programs required mandatory participation by members who used employee mental health benefits.

The results were based on a sample of 6,534 persons who submitted insurance claims for mental health or substance abuse treatment. The concurrent review produced a decrease in hospital admission rates from 9.4 per 1,000 before the program was implemented to 9.0 per 1,000 after implementation The prospective utilization review resulted in an *increase* in admission rates, from 4.2 per 1,000 to 5.6 per 1,000. Both programs resulted in an increase in the number of bed-days used, from 217 to 291 for the concurrent review program and from approximately 80 to 175 for the prospective utilization review program. As these increases in utilization would suggest, the costs of mental health care expenditures rose from approximately $4.25 million to $4.8 million for the concurrent review program and from approximately $2.8 million to approximately $3.9 million for the prospective utilization review.

These results initially suggest that managed mental health care results in higher costs and more use of services—hardly the scenario of denying coverage to save money. This interpretation is not necessarily so, especially when we take into consideration Winegar's (1992) argument that controlling the rate of cost increase is an indicator of success. During the time of Dickey and Azeni's study, the rates of costs and utilization were rising nationwide. Thus, the question of effectiveness turns on whether the programs resulted in a lower increase than would have occurred otherwise. When the data were statistically adjusted for such client characteristics as age, gender, and diagnosis, and for hospital characteristics (such as tax status and teaching hospital status), the results suggested that the concurrent review program contained the average annual increase in the cost of a claim. Concurrent reviews also tended to decrease the likelihood of being hospitalized. Such encouraging results were not found for the prospective utilization review program.

These findings are not encouraging for the managed care industry. The effects found seem rather minimal, especially since the savings did not appear to factor in the cost of the managed care programs, which further undermines the probative value of the results. Moreover, because of the decrease in the rate of hospitalization, those who were admitted were more seriously mentally ill and frequently included comorbidity of substance abuse as a secondary diagnosis. All of these characteristics contributed to longer lengths of stay. Dickey and Azeni cautiously note, however, that these results may be a consequence of the increase in documented severity that is necessary for obtaining authorization to hospitalize the patient. It may not reflect an actual increase in the severity of symptomatology. Nevertheless, in general, the results indicate only a minimum effectiveness of the concurrent utilization review program. There was no impact resulting from the prospective utilization review program.

Other studies produce similarly sobering results. For example, although Staines (1993) reports that estimates from the Congressional Budget Office show "strong evidence" of the cost-effectiveness, the results suggest that prospective and concurrent utilization review reduced cost by only 1 percent or less.

The research shows as well that managed care's quality assurance has not fared well, especially when compared to fee for service, one of the original cost problems managed care was going to correct. A study on effectiveness examining a sample of 617 clients in psychotherapy seeking services for depression question's managed care's assertion that costs are containable at no expense to quality (Rogers et al. 1993). The results suggested that those whose treatment was administered under a prepaid system had less functional outcomes compared to those whose care was provided by fee for services. In other words, quality assurance by managed care may be of lower quality than that by independent fee-for-service providers. A similar study examined clients' ratings of outpatient care and found that fee-for-service treatment received the highest client evaluation. HMO care, an example of capitated managed care, was seen as the worst (Rubin et al. 1993).

Empirical research on managed mental health care continues to be fairly limited in terms of determining whether it improves the quality of care. Based on interviews with clinicians, Luft, Sampson, and Newman (1976) found that most clinicians reported appreciating the professional feedback, while patients raised concerns about the review committee's interference in their treatment. A randomized study of treatment that was reviewed as compared to a control whose care was not reviewed suggests that quality assurance monitoring is not very effective either. That is, the groups were no different on service utilization or treatment outcome. However, a study by Price and Greenwood (1988) showed that reviews of existing treatment plans as the source of information for monitoring care resulted in staff's taking the treatment plans more seriously, although they provide no data that the reviews actually related to outcome. Similarly, a review by Siverman, Comerford, and Stoker (1988) indicated a high compliance rate of implementing the recommendations from a quality assurance reviewer but did not determine if the recommendations were actually related to effective outcomes of treatment. In general, then, the research does not seem to point to a conclusion that utilization reviews produce results that are more likely to provide effective outcomes than might occur when the practitioner and client develop the treatment interventions.

Finally, the research supports the criticism that managed care is cost-effective only if it decreases hospitalization. As Thompson et al. (1992) summarize, the savings attributed to managed care are largely due to decreases in inpatient treatment; this determination was the result of differences in ratings of patient functioning by the clinician and the managed care reviewer. Managed care reviewers tended to rate functioning higher than clinicians did, thus questioning the need for the particular service.

COMING TO TERMS WITH THE
MANAGED CARE CONTROVERSY

Which side is correct in these arguments for and against managed care? Probably both. Both sides have a rational basis, cogent arguments, and some supporting empirical evidence. A clinician whose income is dropping, whose patience is exhausted, and whose clinical judgment is challenged will surely be opposed to managed mental health care. Yet, if this clinician's insurance rates are escalating, he or she may find the efforts to control costs while ensuring quality to be persuasive. Even the clinician who wants to provide services and receive reimbursement does not want to face unaffordable insurance premiums.

This balanced understanding of the benefits and detriments of managed care is well illustrated by Paulson (1996), who considers the predictable polarity for the future of managed care. He sees growth in managed care with decreased government involvement. The current political climate is clearly one of less government involvement, and yet even a Republican Congress is calling for hearings on managed care.

Changes are demanded and will be forthcoming on behalf of all who participate in mental health services, including the thoughtful practitioner who is learning new methods of working with managed care and potential clients who will need to take a more active role in managing the mental health care benefits and participating in reaching demonstrative treatment outcomes. Change will also be necessary on behalf of the managed care industry. The majority of the published voices of practitioners and much of the empirical evidence support the need for improvements. One common complaint is that the process of determining need has become needlessly adversarial. Instead it should be reasonably collaborative, an outcome that will require change by the managed care industry as a whole, individual managed care programs, and each managed care reviewer as a contributing member of a treatment team (Gabbard 1994).

Managed care must distribute criteria of expectation (the criteria used in a review) so that clinicians can successfully reply to managed care and clients will be informed when they consent to managed care treatment. Managed care needs to accommodate clinicians with more expedient processing and appeals, and develop thorough mechanisms for protecting clients' rights to privacy and confidentiality.

Some of these changes may come from inside the managed care industry, although more serious and active regulation may be necessary at the state and federal levels, especially in the area of client privacy and confidentiality (Alpert 1993; Gostin et al. 1993). Such outcomes are inevitable in the future. What is needed is maximum participation by clients, clinicians, advocacy groups, and the managed care industry.

STANDARDS FOR CHANGE

Any changes made must be professionally sound and ethically based. The same principles we suggest be used in evaluating the managed care controversy should be used to guide the needed changes: managed care must be cost-effective, it must be reasonably responsive to cooperative clinicians, and its decisions must first and foremost be in the best interest of the client.

In essence, managed care must be cost-effective. It means taking into consideration the amount it costs to save money by complying with managed care demands. If managed care is not cost-effective, it should not intervene between clinician and client and the third-party payor.

Managed care should also be evaluated against a standard of reasonable responsiveness to providers of mental health services. A small proportion of time spent to complete prospective utilization reviews or concurrent and retrospective utilization reviews is reasonable. Spending two or three hours to get authorization for only three or four sessions of treatment is not. If practitioners are going to be expected to participate in a fourth-party intervening system, that system must include the clinician in the formula of cost containment and quality assurance, especially since the clinician is providing services at a reduced fee in the first place (Graham 1995).

Most of all, the changes in managed care must be guided by a standard of the best interest of the client. This standard is not new to clinicians and is often recognized as a legal expectation in the mental health field. As we will discuss in chapter 8, it is also emerging as a legal duty for the managed care fourth party (Appelbaum 1992). In all likelihood, however, when the client's best interest is considered, it is balanced against the commitment to a specific profit.

Together these three standards form a series of thresholds. First and foremost, managed care must conduct its business in the best interest of the client. Having done so, it must proceed in a fashion that is reasonably responsive to mental health providers. It then must be cost-effective. Failure at any of these levels should result in deliberate improvement or the dismantling of managed care.

CONCLUSION

The issue of cost-effectiveness brings us back to where managed care began, as a response to the demands of a marketplace economy. Both sides of the argument have to concede the unquestionable conclusion that the controversy has arisen to a large extent because such an essential service as mental health is bought and sold in the marketplace. When services as important as physical and mental health are bought and sold in a marketplace where someone besides the seller and buyer pays the majority of the costs, it is understandable how some things have spun out of control. In a sense, the marketplace has been relatively unchecked in terms of what is purchased, how much of it is used, with what expected outcome, and at what costs.

The alternative is to establish health and mental health services as an entitlement for all citizens, but it is unlikely that this will occur in the near future. And even when, or if, universal coverage is made available, it will in all likelihood include a fourth party that will intervene on behalf of the payor to ensure that the quality of services is the highest the money can provide.

Managed care is here to stay, although it will continue to change considerably, as it has since its inception. Any changes should be guided by sound decisions derived from a rational basis. We believe the three legs of managed care are cost-effectiveness, reasonable responsiveness to clinicians, and conformity to the client's best interest. To accomplish these three principles may well include a variety of state and federal regulations and management of those who manage. Inevitably, state and federal regulations will emerge to help guide these new guardians of mental health services. What must accompany the change is not the bifurcated argument of what is right or wrong with managed care but how to improve managed care and how to work cost-efficiently, reasonably responsively, and in the best interest of the client. Indeed, these are the goals of managed mental health care and professional clinicians.

Chapter 3

Capitated Managed Care in the Public and Private Sectors

Mental Health Services for the Persistently Mentally Ill

M anaged care may be an entire program that offers all or some of the services its clientele may need, or it may proceed on a case-by-case approach. In this chapter we look at the model of capitated managed care and its role with the merger of public and private sector mental health services.

Figure 3.1 provides an overview of the similarities and distinctions of two types of mental health programs that are influenced by capitated managed care: public sector and private sector. Although both are considered in this chapter, more discussion will be given to public sector services because they represent the more dramatic changes in the mental health care system, particularly for persons with severe and persistent mental illness.

CAPITATION

Durham (1994) defines managed care as "providers offering a comprehensive package of health care services to a defined population for a fixed, predetermined ('capitated') fee for each enrolled individual or family without regard to the number or nature of services provided to each person" (p. 336). Under a capitation model, the managed care organization has a single administrative structure that assumes fiscal and

Figure 3.1   Capitated Managed Care in the Public and Private Sector

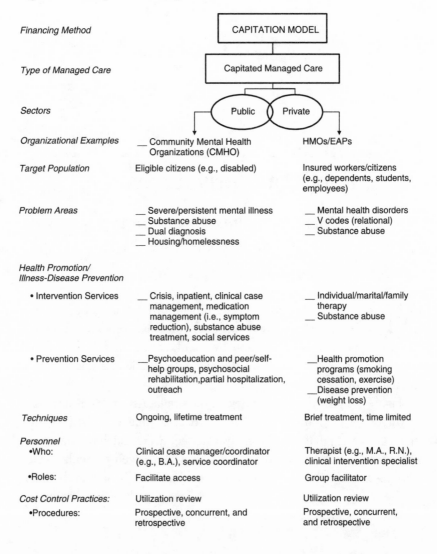

	Public	Private
Financing Method	**CAPITATION MODEL**	
Type of Managed Care	Capitated Managed Care	
Organizational Examples	__ Community Mental Health Organizations (CMHO)	HMOs/EAPs
Target Population	Eligible citizens (e.g., disabled)	Insured workers/citizens (e.g., dependents, students, employees)
Problem Areas	__ Severe/persistent mental illness __ Substance abuse __ Dual diagnosis __ Housing/homelessness	__ Mental health disorders __ V codes (relational) __ Substance abuse
Health Promotion/ Illness-Disease Prevention		
• Intervention Services	__ Crisis, inpatient, clinical case management, medication management (i.e., symptom reduction), substance abuse treatment, social services	__ Individual/marital/family therapy __ Substance abuse
• Prevention Services	__Psychoeducation and peer/self-help groups, psychosocial rehabilitation,partial hospitalization, outreach	__Health promotion programs (smoking cessation, exercise) __Disease prevention (weight loss)
Techniques	Ongoing, lifetime treatment	Brief treatment, time limited
Personnel •Who:	Clinical case manager/coordinator (e.g., B.A.), service coordinator	Therapist (e.g., M.A., R.N.), clinical intervention specialist
•Roles:	Facilitate access	Group facilitator
Cost Control Practices: •Procedures:	Utilization review Prospective, concurrent, and retrospective	Utilization review Prospective, concurrent, and retrospective

clinical responsibility for the client in his or her community. Capitated managed care operates with a cap to the entire costs. In other words, funding for all of a person's care is internal to the managed care organization, and that funding for all the enrolled members is capped. (This is why it is called a capitation model.) The most familiar examples of capitation models are HMOs and some EAPs.

Some will say that the goal of a capitated financing system is to provide fewer services in order to increase profits. In truth, the overall goals are to contain costs by providing the best care at the lowest price, to engage and sustain the client in the community, and to develop lower-cost alternatives to expensive inpatient care. Structurally, managed care does this by providing the services or coordinating services external to the program, or both. A capitated managed care program uses external agencies to provide services that are unavailable in-house. This is a likely occurrence since the program is responsible for all the mental health needs of the "covered lives." The funding structure of a capitated model is often called a *prospective system*, in reference to a financing and reimbursement system whereby a service or set of services is predetermined. This prospective financing structure establishes an upper limit on costs to the payor (Durham 1994). Costs are controlled by terminating services as soon as they are no longer necessary or cost-effective (Durham 1994; Lazarus and Sharfstein, 1994). The mechanism for funding is provided on a per capita payment in advance, so some of the fiscal responsibility for comprehensive care is in the hands of the provider (McGovern, Lyons, and Pomp 1990). If the costs of care exceed the established upper limit, the programmatic managed care organization must pay for those services. In this sense, capitation programs are called *risk sharing*.

Once the targeted population has been identified (e.g., all potential eligible citizens/members within a catchment area) and a provider identified (e.g., a mental health center or network of providers), federal and state funding mechanisms (Medicare, Social Security, Department of Public Assistance, etc.) make prospective capitated payments to the provider for a given period of time (such as quarterly or annually). Capitation rates may be varied and based on risk-adjusted factors such as diagnosis, symptom severity, prior resource utilization, and possibly social and familial support (McGovern, Lyons, and Pomp 1990). The capitated program either provides all services or contracts out for certain services (e.g., psychosocial rehabilitation services or residential).

The amount of funding provided for each case would have to be comparable to the expense of providing the necessary services. Understandably, some clients will cost more than this amount, and some will cost less. Because of the high cost of care for many of the persistent and severely mentally ill, when certain cases exceed the limits, risk-sharing strategies allow a renegotiation of capitation rates. In essence, capitation programs provide all the services a group needs at, say, $1,500 per person/annually. The financial goal is for the average to be less than $1,500, which becomes the profit for the managed care program.

From a clinical standpoint, a capitated system tries to promote a conservative use of resources by encouraging clinicians to be mindful of economic resources and sound practice techniques while planning for optimum clinical outcomes. The clinician and agency make the decision about what services are to be utilized. However, it is the capitated managed care organization that manages the care so that the available pool of money is not exhausted (Schreter 1993).

Even services once held unchallengable, like psychotherapy, have a new relationship to practice in capitated managed care programs. The use of long-term psychotherapy to produce intrapsychic change is now seen as beyond the scope of capitated services (Schreter 1993). Instead, short-term interventions aimed at stabilization and resolution of the presenting problem are considered preferred practices.

Capitated managed care is increasingly making its presence evident in two service sectors, one public and the other private. The most familiar example of public sector capitated managed care programs are community mental health organizations (CMHOs). Examples of private sector capitated managed care programs are HMOs and some EAPs. However, there is considerable overlap between public and private sectors, particularly as public sector payors (i.e., CMHOs) look to managed care programs as a means to contain costs. Similarly, private sector payors (HMOs) are looking to the public sector as their next area of expansion by proposing to establish behavioral health programs for Medicaid and other eligible beneficiaries (Ray and Oss 1993).

THE PRIVATE SECTOR

Private sector mental health services are assessed on a prospective basis, and a spending cap (or limit) is assigned. In an HMO, for example, treatment may be offered to any enrolled member when it is determined to be necessary. These members may be insured workers who have employer-sponsored health benefits, their dependents, and students. Illustrating the overlap of the public and private sectors, in some states, Medicaid may elect to become an enrolled member in a private HMO.

In the private sector, clinicians typically work with clients with mental health disorders (e.g., depression, anxiety disorders, phobias), substance abuse disorders, and relational problems. As Durham (1994) notes, untreated depression is associated with much higher than average levels of health care utilization and costs; thus, rapid intervention is critical here, and it is cost-effective for an organization that is responsible for the person's total care. Access or entry into the system could be through intake, assessment, and triage to the appropriate type of service provider.

In private sector organizations (as well as public ones), the notions of health promotion and disease and illness prevention are driving forces in the design of health care programs. It has been well established that the major causes of death and disability are preventable through changes in collective and individual lifestyles (Public Health Service 1991). Thus, increasing emphasis has been placed on health promotion and enhancement and illness and disease prevention through behavioral change rather than relying solely on medical (e.g., pharmacological) treatment. Consequently, many HMOs provide members with two kinds of services: intervention services, such as individual, marital, or family therapy or for substance abuse, and prevention services, such as health promotion classes on smoking cessation or stress reduction and disease prevention classes on weight loss and how to live with chronic illness.

The techniques for these services, derived from behavioral approaches, include brief treatment approaches that are time limited (perhaps eight to twelve sessions). Short-term interventions aimed at stabilization and resolution of the presenting problem are considered preferred practices, in keeping with empirical findings that support the efficacy of brief treatment techniques. The personnel who provide these services—licensed therapist, nurse, or health worker—act as clinical intervention specialists or group facilitators.

Cost-containment practices are built into the system in the form of selective hiring, training, program development, and utilization reviews (Schreter 1993). The private sector use of utilization reviews is similar to that found in public sector organizations and consists of three types: prospective, concurrent, and retrospective. *Prospective* refers to a system in which the rate of service is established prior to service delivery.

Concurrent refers to assessment of the medical necessity or appropriateness of services that occurs while services are being delivered. *Retrospective* review refers to the determination of the appropriateness of services after they have been delivered.

THE PUBLIC SECTOR

Like the private sector, public sector services are moving to a capitation model of financing. Community mental health organizations (CMHOs), for example, target a client population consisting of all eligible citizens who qualify as disabled (which includes those who are unemployed or underemployed as a consequence of chronic mental illness). The National Institute of Mental Health defines severe mental illness as a nonorganic psychosis or a personality disorder accompanied by major limitations in life activities, which persists over a prolonged period of time (Durham 1994). Epidemiologic research suggests that in any given six-month period, 19 percent of the American population carries a DSM-IV diagnosis that warrants treatment (Schreter 1993). The prevalence of schizophrenia and bipolar affective disorders, two of the most pervasive chronic mental disorders, is 0.5 to 1 percent and 0.4 to 1.6 percent, respectively (American Psychiatric Association 1994a). With regard to problem areas, people with serious mental illness are an extremely heterogeneous population, at high risk for health and social problems, and are disproportionately represented by the lowest socioeconomic strata (McGovern, Lyons, and Pomp 1990). Often they are the poorest of the poor. As a group, they are the greatest consumers of the most expensive mental health care resources, use of the emergency room and inpatient hospitalization, yet studies indicate that only 18 percent of the severely mentally ill who need mental health or substance abuse services are receiving care (Schreter 1993).

Health promotion and illness and disease prevention are gaining recognition in public sector service delivery systems. Because of the proclivity of people with severe mental illness to health problems, many community mental health organizations are beginning to offer prevention services along with their regular intervention services. These notions embrace the belief that much of illness and disability is preventable through changes in the individual's lifestyle and behaviors. Although this notion has established merit in the behavioral health care field, it should be used with sensitivity with people who suffer from severe and persistent mental illness. Mental health problems tend to be less visible, fluctuate over time more than physical disability does, and are not always responsive to early intervention or prevention programs (Durham 1994). Further, as most research shows, the natural history of most mental conditions is unknown or poorly understood, so even close adherence to a prevention plan may not bring about symptom improvement.

For many who already feel stigmatized and troubled by an illness whose origins are unknown, programs that stress individual responsibility for illness may be unwittingly blaming the victim. On the other hand, many excellent health promotion efforts can be focused on health (including all levels of physical and mental health) to encourage people to think about the aspects of themselves that are healthy and strong. Some general examples include wellness programs such as exercise, nutrition, and symptom management (e.g., medication education). Additionally, this has the benefit of opening the door to using both formal support systems, such as traditional services, and informal ones, such as family and community resources.

In setting up health promotion and prevention programs, the clinician must take responsibility for considering the client's financial and health care resources as well as the cost-effectiveness and clinical efficacy of the services. In particular, clinical decisions must be based on the best available data about the effectiveness of interventions in both the short and long term (Schreter 1993). What is consistent is that chronicity and recidivism in psychiatric illness are inevitable for this population.

Although a central goal of intervention services in a capitated model is to engage and sustain the client in the community with the appropriate resources, avoiding hospitalization does not always lead to cost reduction. Durham (1994) reports that length of stay in psychiatric hospitals and the total cost of care may be reduced in some programs but not in others. More important, she argues, the critical issue is to determine whether reductions in psychiatric hospital admissions and length of stay have an adverse impact on clients' mental health and general functioning. Further, primary care physicians report that between 15 and 60 percent of their patients exhibit some form of emotional disorder (e.g., anxiety and depression), that could be more appropriately treated by outpatient mental health services (Simon et al.,

1995). This suggests that primary care is likely to remain an entry point for many mental disorders, though physicians in prepaid practice are even less effective than fee-for-service doctors in detecting some mental disorders, such as depression (Wells et al. 1992).

Types of Service

There are numerous types of preferred treatments in a capitated managed care program for people with severe and persistent mental illness. Many are internal to the managed care program, such as intervention services (clinical case management, medication compliance) and prevention services (psychoeducation, peer and self-help groups). Others are external and contracted as providers for persons who are enrolled members or clients in the capitated community mental health organization.

Intervention services include clinical case management, which attempts to link clients to necessary services outside the managed care setting and to monitor their progress. Additional intervention services include crisis intervention, medication management, substance abuse treatment, referral, and social services. The mechanism to implement and overview these services has typically been a case management system in which a worker or team of workers is responsible for the treatment plan of the individual client.

In a general sense, case management refers to coordinated clinical practices that seek to relieve symptoms of an acute episode (secondary prevention) and reduce the likelihood of deterioration (tertiary prevention) (Durham 1994). Durham describes clinical case management as "creating a care plan for an individual patient which is expected to maximize functioning and independence as well as reduce unnecessary utilization of services at present and in the future. This may include encouraging service use to manage extant problems and prevent subsequent use" (p. 341).

Case management allows for better coordination of care, accomplished, in part, by assessing client needs, linking those needs with the best available service, and monitoring the chronically mentally ill client's adjustment to community living (Vandiver and Kirk 1992). The case management treatment plan typically focuses on coordinating a wide variety of services, for example, day treatment, medication check, group therapy, rehabilitation, and money management, with emphasis on identification and follow-through, while encouraging high utilization of needed services. It might encompass managing contracted psychosocial services, medical services, and other clinical needs (Hood and Sharfstein 1992).

The benefits of case management have been consistently demonstrated. A recent study (Quinlivan et al. 1995) found that clients who received intensive case management had fewer inpatient days and lower overall costs for mental health services. Yet despite its demonstrated efficacy, traditional case management is not always welcome in a managed care or capitated system. As Durham points out, coordination of clinical care is a costly investment given the broad range of medical and psychosocial needs that people with severe mental illness require. Scheduling costly and time-consuming follow-up visits and the use of expensive medications or referrals may not be encouraged (Durham 1994).

The typical prevention services in a capitated managed mental health program are psychoeducation and family education, peer and self-help support groups, and psychosocial rehabilitation or partial hospitalization. In the broadest sense, these services are referred to as *step-down services* and have become somewhat of a trend in the mental health industry (Schreter 1993). Step-down services are secondary levels of services that are less driven by the medical model, and services that are influenced more by the client. These kinds of services exist on a continuum and range from family and peer self-help groups, to partial hospital programs, to residential care in group homes (Schreter et al. 1993). Each of these activities may have an emphasis on social skills training and brief behavioral interventions provided by paraprofessionals (McGovern, Lyons, and Pomp 1990).

An example of a step-down program is family psychoeducation, which is used to provide client support in the community and to empower family members to cope with a family member with mental illness (Sands 1991). Empirical studies support its use with families of chronic patients who participate in a problem-solving and educational format (Hood and Sharfstein 1992).

Quinlivan and colleagues (1995) found that mental health peer consumers employed as case aides can play a vital role in the delivery of mental health services, particularly with frequent users of mental health services. Increasingly, peer consumers (e.g., people who have a psychiatric diagnosis and history of psychiatric treatment or hospitalization) are being employed in mental health programs in the role of support staff or case aids. Their roles may include assisting clients with transportation, maintaining phone contact, or acting as liaison with community resources and the clinicians (Bachrach, 1989). Quinlivan et al. report that assertive outreach programs that used consumer case aids contributed to fewer bed-days and reduced costs.

In a related service, a study by Dobson et al. (1995) found that social skills training appears to be more effective in reducing negative symptoms for people with schizophrenia than milieu therapy; however, there was a gradual decline in improvement of negative symptoms at a six-month follow-up, which supports the argument for extended care over many years of the client's life. Treatment, then, should include relapse prevention and ongoing monitoring of the client's functioning.

In our opinion, work in capitated managed care will include a proliferation of step-down services, which will increase in both number and complexity because they facilitate the managed care goals of being cost-efficient while providing quality of care.

Intervention and Prevention Service Techniques

The techniques employed in the delivery of intervention and prevention services in public sector CMHOs are seldom time limited as they are in the private sector. Since the very nature of chronicity sets the persistent mental illness apart from other health conditions, the coordination of care over time becomes vitally important (Durham 1994). Like many chronic physical conditions, a severe mental illness presents a pattern of increasing disablement that may persist for life (Durham 1994). Consequently, the emerging patient profile is of individuals who present with long-standing, refractory, behavioral-based problems (Durham 1994) whose need for long-term services outstrips the system's capacity to manage them (Schreter 1993).

Clients are often seen as "treatment noncompliant" when symptoms or behaviors do not subside, though providers cannot predict with accuracy the cause of the problem or the length of treatment (Durham 1994). Studies have consistently shown that people with a chronic course of mental illness benefit from long-term, integrated care systems. These long-term services are often lifelong and may include most aspects of community living, from housing and social and occupational functioning to legal services.

Ecomaps are one technique that case managers use to understand and organize the comprehensive networks and needs in clients' lives. Ecomaps are graphic tools for portraying client-family-environment transactions at a point in time (Mattaini 1993) and were developed to assist the clinician in assessment and intervention techniques and the client in reflecting on his or her emotional and cognitive connections to the support systems.

In the ecomap in figure 3.2, arrows connecting the circles signify the

Figure 3.2   An Ecomap

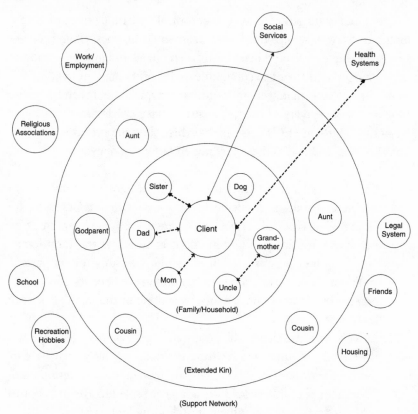

Arrows are used to indicate the direction of the flow of energy or resources between systems.

———— Positive (reflects strong relationship)

------ Negatives (reflects a stressful or conflicted relationship)

Family/Household consists of all people/pets residing in household.
Extended Kin consists of all relatives (extended/adopted) who may be involved in the client's life.
Support Network consists of all support systems that the client is connected with.

flow of interactions and resources (perceived as either positive or negative). This technique is quite valuable when working with many clients, regardless of whether they are chronically mentally ill or more functional. The purpose is to identify as many resources as possible available to the client. Many of the resources identified in an ecomap become the client's indigenous treatment, and they are integrated into the treatment plan. (Appendix A contains an ecomap form.) In Figure 3.2, the client identifies numerous family contacts and support yet indicates that relations are negative between immediate family members (as indicated by hyphened lines) and positive between self and the social service system.

Capitated managed care for the chronically mentally ill must take a long-term view of service needs and treatment outcomes. Change comes slowly for the severely and persistently mentally ill and may be as modest as striving for adjustment to community living and symptom stability.

A clinical case manager or coordinator typically is involved in the assessment or delivery of mental health services and carries out many functions. Durham (1994) asserts that this role is important in the capitated system and makes these recommendations to managers:

1. Be involved early in the process of treatment planning, before benefits are exhausted. Because costs are legitimate factors in deciding what types of services to arrange, case managers must be involved early in the planning process to assess the total family and insurance resources. For example, planning for outpatient treatment will be restricted unless inpatient benefits can be exchanged for outpatient benefits, as is done in the management of high-cost cases.

2. Discuss with the clients the potential impact of managed care and the course of approved treatment, including alternative treatment or payment methods if inpatient benefits are terminated. Treatment planning should include aggressive linkage and coordination efforts between inpatient and outpatient care.

3. Work to coordinate a full range of medical, psychiatric, and social services even when the benefit package does not include a specific, nonmedical service (e.g., personal attendant). In other words, the case manager must serve as a liaison between the client and the uncovered service (Durham p. 345). Clearly practi-

tioners working in capitated managed care organizations need a wealth of knowledge about available social services, support networks, and community resources.

4. Help to establish a plan of care that minimizes reliance on hospitalization or other unnecessary financial costs. Although prevention of mental illness is not as causal as in other medical conditions, good case management is nevertheless important.

Evaluation

Cost control practices are built into the system through selective hiring, training, program development, and utilization reviews (Schreter 1993). Community mental health organizations' use of utilization reviews is similar to that found with independent managed care of private sector fee for services.

Managed care attempts to control costs and ensure quality by evaluating the outcomes of treatment. The purpose of evaluation is to identify which practices are associated with better outcomes and how cost-effective the services have been (Kane, Bartlett, and Potthoff 1995).

Managed care organizations are known more for their utilization review teams than for implementing case management teams. In fact, many public sector mental health case management teams are converting to utilization review teams. Despite persuasive arguments for the ability of clinical case management to work collaboratively within capitated models of care, many public sector organizations are choosing not to use traditional case management programs. The argument provided is that the nature of the system is to encourage service use for a subset of individuals who typically have far-reaching psychosocial problems outside the traditional scope of medical and psychiatric care (Durham 1994).

All managed care organizations use some form of concurrent utilization review procedure to assess a client's continued need for treatment. In other words, if the treatment plan has as its goal maintaining health and avoiding future health care costs through prevention, the techniques used to increase health functioning will need to be measured for effectiveness. One way that community mental health organizations evaluate quality and treatment outcomes is by assessing the satisfaction of its members. Since we will focus on treatment outcomes in chapter 6, we will forgo much discussion here.

We will point out, though, how difficult it is to measure outcomes with persons who are chronically mentally ill, in part because change is slow and the primary goal may be to facilitate community adjustment. There is difficulty as well in trying to measure outcomes on disorders that do not have a predictable course. As Durham (1994) suggests, even close adherence to a treatment plan may not bring about symptom improvement. The result is that providers may be unable to predict the likely length or course of treatment that will be required.

As a consequence, an outcome evaluation is more likely to be based on how satisfied the enrolled members or clients are. Indeed, satisfaction surveys are fairly routine in both public and private capitated managed care settings, and the results are frequently used for marketing purposes.

Among the standardized measurement tools for assessing satisfaction, one of the most widely used is the Client Satisfaction Survey (Larson et al. 1979) which is found in *Measures for Clinical Practice* (Fischer and Corcoran, 1994a). Most managed care organizations, however, develop their own satisfaction survey, tailored to the program's needs. An example of a typical satisfaction survey is displayed in figure 3.3.

Satisfaction surveys are beneficial to programmatic managed care and also helpful in work with clients. For example, you might discover a consistently different level of satisfaction for clients with a certain disorder in comparison with those with other disorders. Satisfaction survey results may also prove validating for clinical efforts. For example, in our experience, some clients who seem very challenging to work with, such as the severe and persistent mentally ill, are often very satisfied with their care. Moreover, if a satisfaction survey is conducted prior to the end of treatment (or phase of treatment for the chronically mentally ill), the result may be helpful in termination. If the client appears less than satisfied, you can explore which aspects of services were satisfying and which were not. Of course, a lack of satisfaction may not necessarily reflect poor services. Sometimes clients do not want a good thing to end and are dissatisfied not with the actual services but with facing the end of treatment.

Satisfaction surveys provide meaningful feedback to the clinician and the managed care organization. The results may be valuable in supervision and professional development. For example, since a satisfaction survey can be very brief—Larson's scale has a short form of only

Figure 3.3   Client Satisfaction Survey

Below are questions designed to assess your opinion of the clinical services you received. Your honest opinion is very important in determining the quality of your treatment. Please take a few moments and answer each item honestly by recording your answer in the space to the left of each item.

Please use the following scale to answer each item:
1 = Definitely no
2 = Somewhat no
3 = Neither no nor yes
4 = Somewhat yes
5 = Definitely yes

_____ 1.   Did you receive a prompt response to your request for services?

_____ 2.   Were you satisfied with the clinician's professionalism and competency?

_____ 3.   Were your services directed toward a specific goal?

_____ 4.   Were you and your clinician able to reach your goal?

_____ 5.   Would you select us again in the future if you have a need for services?

_____ 6.   Would you refer a family member or close friend to us for services?

_____ 7.   Do you believe that you needed additional services that were not provided?

_____ 8.   Do you believe there has been improvement in your social life?

_____ 9.   Do you believe there has been improvement in your mental and emotional health/ adjustment to the community?

_____ 10.   In an overall sense, are you satisfied with the quality of your care?

Thank you for completing this survey.

---

three items—it might be used to ascertain client satisfaction after each component of treatment or at the end of collateral services.

Satisfaction surveys are not the only or even the best assessment of treatment outcome, but they are a valuable means of assessing an entire program of managed care, as well as the client's perception of the quality of the care.

LIMITATIONS AND BENEFITS OF CAPITATED CARE

Like other aspects of the containment and quality assurance movement, capitated managed care has grown with unprecedented and unchecked growth. There are both limitations to and benefits of this approach.

Chief among the limitations is that the capitation model creates an adverse incentive to limit treatment. More treatment runs the risk of exceeding the funding cap—at times to the detriment of clients who need services and are denied them or whose treatment is prematurely terminated.

Capitated mental health care programs are also more likely to limit a patient's choice of providers than fee-for-service insurance coverage, although fee-for-service coverage under an independent managed care organization may also restrict a client's choice of clinicians and types of service. Capitated managed care poses a risk for persons with severe and persistent mental illness who may have difficulty making well-informed choices among competing mental health coverage plans (Durham 1994). Additionally, providers may be forced to choose between financial loss and inadequate patient care if medical or psychiatric need exceeds the cap (Durham 1994).

Families, too, experience a greater cost due to the service needs of the chronic mentally ill family member. Because of lack of adequate public funding (as well as the relative absence of private third-party-payor involvement), families experience some of the cost-shifting strategies of capitation models. Many become lifelong caregivers. These families may be the least able to bear this added financial burdens. Chronic mentally ill clients often come from families who have severe financial losses complicated by the mental illness of a family member (Hood and Sharfstein 1992). As treatment needs escalate and funds decrease, families are less able to pick up the financial costs of inpatient care. Often the only alternative is Social Security Insurance disability and no active treatment. As Hood and Sharfstein (1992) note, the costs are shifted away from the health care budget and toward the family budget, social service budget, and disability payments. Often patients and families find themselves caught between clinicians who want more time to work with a treatment-resistant depression and reviewers charged with containing costs (Hood and Sharfstein 1992). What this means to family members and practitioners in capitated managed care is addressed in the family empowerment literature (Friesen and Poert-ner 1995). This literature evidences that family empowerment for the benefit of the chronic mentally ill family member mobilizes resources and badly needed services.

Capitation programs also run the clinical risk of restricting needed services. Many capitated payment systems prevent the use of innova-tive treatment approaches despite data showing that a certain percent-age of patients can be helped with assertive and continuous care strate-gies (Hood and Sharfstein 1992; Soloman and Draine 1995).

On the side of benefits, in many ways a prepayment program elimi-nates uncertainty about future health costs and manages activities that promote health while minimizing illness (Durham 1994). Three benefits stand out for the treatment of persons with severe mental illness: (1) an emphasis on creating less expensive, community-based alternatives; (2) efforts to minimize hospital care in favor of community care; and (3) pro-motion of interdisciplinary referral, use of natural support systems, and coordination of psychosocial services through case management. More-over, each of these benefits recognizes the potential of the long-term value of such interventions for reducing future costs (Durham 1994).

In terms of administration, a capitation model encourages care across a spectrum of internal and external services consistent with this population's needs (McGovern, Lyons, and Pomp 1990). There are also administrative cost savings, including the need for utilization reviews by an external organizations.

For these reasons and others, clinicians may prefer the capitated model. A capitation model can contain costs while allowing for better coordination of care through case management. Consequently, capita-tion models are a logical funding basis for mental health services for people with serious mental illness. It reduces the fragmentation of ser-vices and resources and encourages greater accountability and respon-sibility across clinical, administrative, and fiscal dimensions. Clinically, patients may receive more integrated services that represent known ef-ficacious treatment approaches (Solomon and Draine 1995).

Chapter 4

Prospective Utilization Reviews

Demonstrating Treatment Necessity

The initial step in the process of using prospective utilization reviews for cost containment and quality assurance is to make certain that only conditions covered by the third party or capitated program are provided to a potential client who truly needs treatment. Costs are contained by denying payment for a personal problem that is not covered by the program or policy. This most likely includes many V codes from the DSM-IV, i.e., clinical treatment not due to a mental disorder, e.g., parent-child relational problems, and many of the services provided by marriage and family therapists (Ridgewood 1995).

Both capitated programmatic managed care and independent case-by-case managed care organizations use prospective utilization reviews to determine treatment necessity. These reviews are a major tool in case-by-case managed care, but capitated managed care organizations use them too. If, for example, a potential client presents with a bona fide need for treatment due to distress or disability from an adjustment disorder but the third-party coverage is restricted to certain major mental disorders, treatment would not be authorized. This does not mean there is no need for treatment; rather, the capitation program or insurance policy will not pay for it.

The evaluation and determination of treatment necessity are handled differently in programmatic and independent managed care organizations. In the former, this is often done at an interdisciplinary clinical team meeting of clinical case managers and allied clinical staff. In the latter it might be between the clinician and an independent managed care reviewer. Since both types of managed care program rely on utilization reviews of some form, the content and skills covered in this chapter are useful regardless of work setting.

DEMONSTRATING TREATMENT NECESSITY

One of the major functions of a prospective utilization review is to evaluate if treatment is necessary *at the time* the client is requesting services. We emphasize the time that services are requested because one cost-containment practice is to be certain that the condition that might be authorized for treatment is not a preexisting one because such a condition most likely would not be covered by the program or plan.

The first and foremost step in demonstrating treatment necessity is to evidence the need for treatment with sufficient persuasiveness to result in the necessary authorization of a particular treatment. Consequently, the challenge is not simply whether a client should receive treatment but whether the clinician can persuade a managed care program that the problem is severe enough to warrant reimbursement of treatment. As clinicians, we believe that few clients who seek treatment do not actually need it. This does not mean, however, that a managed care program sees the circumstance the same way.

The consideration of the necessity of treatment may include whether the presenting problem is covered by the third-party payor. Many of the decisions of what clinical problems are covered and will be authorized are based on the DSM-IV (APA 1994a; Anderson and Berlant 1993). Programmatic managed care relies on this system to ensure that those needing services are identified and given access. Independent managed care organizations rely on accurate diagnosis to authorize and deny coverage.

Consequently, regardless of the system of managed mental health care, the clinician will need to provide an accurate diagnosis and delineate the presenting problems. We cannot stress enough the importance of the accuracy of diagnosis. It is essential for clinicians not to fall into the trap of overstating the diagnosis of a potential client's problem "for insurance purposes." Not only is this an intentional fraud of the third party, but it introduces more distrust into the fragile alliance between managed care and clinical care. Deception and the resulting distrust will eventually adversely affect the client's services. All parties must take steps to avoid it.

Consequently, one of the first determinations of treatment necessity is not whether the diagnosis and presenting problem warrant intervention but whether they warrant reimbursement by the private or public third party. Once this obstacle is surmounted, the question becomes whether the presence of symptomatology has a severe enough impact on the client's functioning to require the particular intervention considered. The degree of scrutiny in making this decision varies with the projected cost of the care. For example, a client whose presenting problem is clinical depression (dysthymia in DSM-IV terms) and requesting planned short-term treatment is evaluated with less demand and detail than when the client's problem is major depression or a bipolar affective disorder–depressive type, when expensive hospitalization is recommended. In general, longer-term, higher-cost cases will demand more time to obtain authorization for services.

Less severe mental health conditions with short-term treatments available and amenable to the client's circumstances are usually more routine in the prospective utilization review. This does not necessarily translate into a saving of time. Managed care programs may deny treatment for easier cases because the diagnosis and presenting problem are not covered by the third-party program or policy or because they do not warrant the level of care being offered. Since there seems to be emerging a clear duty to make every reasonable effort to obtain services for a potential client (see chapter 8), denying services may result in even more demands on time in order to appeal the managed care decision.

With an independent managed care organization, the determination of treatment is facilitated by a standardized form used to conduct a telephone interview or to be completed in writing. The answers to the prospective inquiry are used to determine if treatment will be authorized. Appendix B contains an example of a typical pencil-and-paper prospective utilization review form. The portion used to determine treatment necessity is shown as figure 4.1.

The same content for pen-and-paper forms is ascertained in a telephone interview schedule, although the format is different. Since the two forms have similar purposes, we will present only the pen-and-

Figure 4.1   Determinant of Treatment Necessity

Date of intake assessment: _____/_____/19 _____
Client's presenting problem:

(a) 1 _____

(b) 2 _____

(c) 3 _____

What was the date of onset of each presenting problem?
(a) Problem 1: _____ (b) Problem 2: _____ (c) Problem 3: _____

Please identify current symptoms observed for each problem for which you are requesting authorization of services:

(a) Problem 1: _____

_____.

(b) Problem 2: _____

_____.

(c) Problem 3: _____

_____.

What is the client's current functioning in each of the following areas?

(a) Psychological: _____

_____.

(b) Social: _____

_____.

(c) Occupational/educational: _____

_____.

How have you assessed the client's problems, symptoms, and functioning?

_____

_____

_____.

Please provide the following DSM diagnoses:

(a) Axis I: _____

(b) Axis II: _____

(c) Axis III: _____

(d) Axis IV: _____

   Stressors: _____

(e) Axis V: (GAF) _____

B. History of Treatment

  1. Was the client ever treated before for this or a similar problem?

      ____No ____Yes

  2. If yes, what type of clinical services were provided?

      _____

  3. Please summarize the outcome of previous treatment or clinical services.

  4. Please indicate if medication was provided before, and include the type,

      dosage, and duration of the medication. _____

      _____.

      _____

paper form. Not only is it becoming commonplace in managed care, but it greatly helps in preparing for a telephone review.

MEASURING THE NEED FOR TREATMENT

In our opinion the primary issue in demonstrating the need for treatment is not much different from a typical intake assessment. Here, though, the clinician must convince the managed care reviewer of the accuracy of his or her assessment, diagnosis, and clinical judgment. This is facilitated by using standardized procedures in conjunction with typical assessment techniques—for example, mental status examinations, diagnostic and screening tools, problem checklists, rapid assessment instruments, and the Global Assessment of Functioning. This information is of great value throughout the managed mental health treatment process, including concurrent and retrospective utilization reviews of the treatment process and outcome.

Operationalization

In many respects the demand to demonstrate the need for treatment, and even those of evidencing the process and outcome of treatment, is one of *operationalization*: the process of developing an observable and quantified definition of the problem. In managed mental health care's use of prospective utilization review, this definition is used to show a need for treatment.

The ability to observe a client's problem must also be seen from the view of the managed care reviewer. The task in managed mental health, then, is not simply to observe the need for treatment but also to provide evidence to a fourth party that the need warrants treatment. Managed care programs are intentionally designed to evaluate all aspects of treatment, from treatment necessity, to the adequacy of the implementation of the intervention, to the outcomes of the treatment. The concern is how the clinician operationalizes or observes clinical practice.

Operationalizing the necessity of treatment is as easy as the client's presenting problem is severe. It is more difficult when the problem is less severe and much easier when the client presents with a more distressful and debilitating problem.

Once the potential client's presenting problem is determined to be covered by the program or policy, the issue becomes one of whether the severity of the problem warrants the level of care. Inevitably the determination is in response to the question, "How bad is it?" implying a comparison to some referent group—that is, "How bad is it compared to whom?" From this perspective, it is compared to how the potential client was functioning or is functioning in comparison to others. For the practitioner and the managed care program, the comparison may be to others in similar or different circumstances. Is the condition worse than those in similar circumstances who do not receive treatment? If so, how much so? If not, what benefit would treatment provide to a problem with which many seem to do all right without professional services?

In our opinion, and that of many of our colleagues, the typical client we see at intake has sufficiently severe symptomatology to warrant treatment. Rarely do potential clients present with a problem so inconsequential as not to warrant treatment, although this does happen occasionally. To many practitioners the very fact that a client is seeking treatment, even at the insistence of some relevant other such as a spouse or parent, is sufficient to warrant treatment.

Referent Groups

The greater challenge in persuading a managed care program of the necessity for treatment may be met by having convincing comparison or referent groups. This is a method of answering the question, "How bad is it compared to whom?"

The clinician can use referent groups from two different views: (1) to demonstrate that the client's problem is more troublesome than that of those who are not affected by the condition or (2) to show that the client is similar to those with the same problem who are receiving treatment. In this respect, we will consider two approaches to answering the question. One is a comparison to norms available from others who are from the general population (nonclinical samples) and from mental health clients (clinical samples). The other referent comparison is when the potential client's problem is compared to how the person once was and how he or she wished to be after treatment. The comparison is to oneself. The first approach is called *norm-referenced comparison*. The other is called *self-referenced comparison*. Both approaches compare scores on standardized clinical measurement tools with some other score or scores.

CLINICAL INSTRUMENTS FOR NORM-REFERENCED COMPARISON

Norm-referenced comparison is the process of interpreting an assessment score with a large sample of scores. Most of us are familiar with this from our experiences in the school system. You may have taken any number of standardized tests, such as a college admission exam. Your score may have been interpreted as above or below a population mean and in a certain percentile. The same approach is useful in managed mental health in order to determine if a client needs treatment.

The client's score will be interpreted in comparison to a sample that has completed the same instrument.

Diagnostic Screening Instruments

Probably the more common method of norm-referenced comparison is to compare a client's functioning with others from either a general population or a clinical sample. The assessment instrument may be a standardized diagnostic screening test or a variety of other instruments that are more readily available and less expensive. Some well-established and common screening instruments that consider a wide variety of possible disorders are the Minnesota Multiphasic Personality Inventory, the Clinical and Personality Scales of the Multiaxial Diagnostic Inventory (Doverspite 1990), and the Millon Clinical Multiaxial Inventory (Millon 1985a, 1985b). There are also a number of screening tools for specific disorders, such as dysthymia and major depression (Hakstian and McLean 1989; Zimmerman et al. 1986); bulimia (Thelan et al. 1991); and substance abuse (Selzer 1971).

Diagnostic screening instruments tend to assess the client on a wide range of potential diagnoses. The results of these assessment tools produce scores that are compared to the average scores for the general population and clinical samples of clients in treatment. Generally if the client's score is similar to that of the general population, a managed care reviewer will probably determine that there is no clinically significant problem, and treatment most likely will not be authorized. If the client's score is similar to the clinical sample or even more severe, the managed care reviewer will probably decide the problem does warrant clinical intervention.

Such an approach to determining the need for treatment is an effective method of persuading the managed care program the client warrants treatment. Moreover, the instrument may even cause the clinician to take a different view of the client's needs.

The use of diagnostic instruments is not without impediments. These screening instruments are not inexpensive, and if the managed care program does not authorize reimbursement for treatment, the practitioner is left with the cost of the assessment. (As we will discuss in chapters 6 and 8, the client should not be held liable for this bill if payment for treatment is not authorized.) Diagnostic instruments are also limited in their usefulness with diverse populations, although recent advances have occurred in the assessment of ethnic and racial groups (Dana 1993). Further, such broad-band assessment tools ascertain general problems or a number of problems, often in the form of a clinical diagnosis that may not necessarily reflect the nuances of that problem for a particular client. And they generally are too long to allow monitoring of a client by repeated assessment.

Ideally, the assessment tool used for determining the necessity of treatment should also be used as a monitoring device to assess the client's progress during the course of treatment. But because of their length, costs, and difficulty in scoring, diagnostic assessment tools are not good for subsequent monitoring of the problem over the course of treatment. The exception is a mental status exam, which can be short, inexpensive, or even free. Mental status exams are usually conducted as part of the intake process, are standardized structured or semistructured interview schedules. Some are available with quantified scoring procedures (Doverspite 1990). With all mental status exams that are in interview form, the actual assessment is made by the clinician, who bases a comparison on clinical judgment and familiarity with functional and dysfunctional behavior. An example of a standardized mental status exam is displayed in appendix C. A brief assessment consisting of twenty-five items, it may be used as a semistructured interview or a rating form to record clinical impressions.

A standardized mental status exam is designed to direct attention to critical symptomatologies, which will facilitate diagnosis. Those that are quantified have the added benefit of providing a score of the client's general mental status. The example in appendix C allows this for a general score of mental status (the summation of scores for all twenty-five items) or for any of the four areas: self, action, behavior, or cognition. When used at intake and as an exit interview, scores can be reported and differences used to reflect stability, improvement, or deterioration.

Problem Screening Inventories

Recently some screening instruments have become available that are amenable to monitoring a client's progress over the course of treatment. These are alternatives to diagnostic instruments, which screen for clinically meaningful problems, have the benefit of not only provid-

Table 4.1   Problems Assessed with the Multi-Problem Screening Inventory and Representative Items

Problem	Representative Item
Depression	I feel downhearted.
Self-esteem	I feel that people do not enjoy my company.
Partner problems	I feel that I would not choose the same partner if I had it to do over again.
Sexual disorder	Sex with my partner has become a chore for me.
Child problems	My child is too demanding.
Mother problems	My mother is very irritating.
Father problems	My father's behavior embarrasses me.
Personal stress	I feel that I cannot keep up with all the demands on me.
Friend problems	I really feel left out by my friends.
Neighbor problems	I wish I were not part of this neighborhood.
School problems	I really do pretty shoddy work at school.
Aggression	I am quick to let people know they cannot walk all over me.
Problems with work associates	My work associates are a bunch of snobs.
Family problems	There seems to be a lot of friction in my family.
Suicidal	My life is so grim that I have considered ending it.
Nonphysical abuse	My partner demands obedience to his or her whims.
Physical abuse	My partner throws dangerous objects at me.
Fearfulness	I am terrified that something awful is going to happen.
Ideas of reference	People around me really resent my ability and talent.
Phobias	I am terrified of driving in even moderate traffic.
Feelings of guilt	When things go wrong, I feel I should apologize even if it is not my fault.
Work problems	My boss is a fool.
Confused thinking	There are times when my thinking does not seem to work right.
Disturbing thoughts	Disturbing ideas come to me, and I cannot get rid of them.
Memory loss	I forget where I put my keys, glasses, or other objects that I use regularly.
Alcohol abuse	My drinking interferes with obligations to my family or friends.
Drug use	I take drugs several times a week.

ing information about the need for treatment, but are direct measures of what you are going to be working on with your client.

Notable among useful problem inventories are the Multi-Problem Screening Inventory and the recently published South Shore Problem Inventory (O'Hara 1995).

The Multi-Problem Screening Inventory (MPSI; Hudson 1992) is a lengthy instrument that identifies twenty-seven potential clinical problems. It can be made shorter by excluding subscales that are not appropriate for a particular client (e.g., children's problems subscale for a couple with no children). As the name implies it is an inventory to screen multiple problems (table 4.1). Like the other screening inventories, the MPSI is useful at intake in order to isolate the presenting problems warranting treatment. It can even be mailed to a potential client in advance, for completion prior to the intake interview.

Unlike the MMPI, the MPSI is designed not to arrive at a diagnosis but to assess a client's problems. The inventory has several added benefits, including a score range from 0 to 100 for all twenty-seven subscales so that a profile of a client's problem can be conveniently created (figure 4.2). The individual subscales are short enough to be used for monitoring the client's problem throughout treatment, once the problem is isolated, to determine whether there is progress, stability, or deterioration over the course of treatment. The MPSI is quite inexpensive (about $2) and easy to interpret, and it takes less than an hour to complete.

For the purpose of evidencing the necessity of treatment, many of the MPSI subscales have cutting scores. A *cutting score* is one that indicates with a high degree of certainty whether the client has a clinically significant problem. It is a criterion that can be used to judge the severity of the client's problem. Many of the diagnostic screening instruments also have cutting scores, where a score above a particular range indicates the likelihood of the diagnosis (Hakstian and McLean 1989). A cutting score, then, is an easy and convenient way of asserting that the client's problem is as severe as others that have required treatment.

The South Shore Problem Inventory is a self-report instrument that assesses psychophysiological problems, community and health problems, family problems, and marital-familial stress. These four subscales can be considered miniglobal measures. The psychophysiological subscale ascertains problems that are primarily intraindividual. The community health subscale ascertains problems with the community (e.g.,

Figure 4.2   MPSI Score Profile Graph

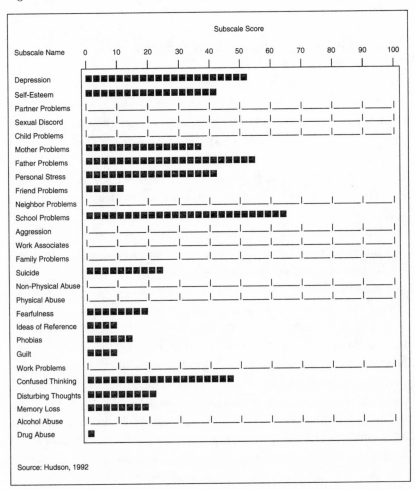

the legal system) and problems with one's health (e.g., medical care). Family problems include sexual victimization, interfamily conflicts, and problems due to the abuse of drugs or alcohol. The fourth subscale taps into problems of stress in the familial or marital relationships (e.g., financial and children). This instrument takes very little time to administer and score, and it has respectable normative data to use for interpreting a client's scores.

Both of these problem inventories are recommended because they include a focus on the client's social environment of the community and family. This readily available and useful information may also help managed care administrators to see treatment necessity in a broader context of the social environment.

Rapid Assessment Instruments

Another method of documenting the necessity of treatment is to compare scores to some norm with rapid assessment instruments. Rapid assessment instruments are narrow-band measures that assess a specific and narrowly defined construct, such as a client's presenting problem. Like the subscales on the problem inventories, these assessment tools ascertain the duration of a problem, its frequency of occurrence, or its severity.

The difference between using a rapid assessment tool for determining the necessity of treatment and a screening tool is that the screening inventory enables the clinician to isolate a client's problem or arrive at a diagnosis; a rapid assessment instrument requires that the clinician and potential client know what the presenting problem is prior to selecting an instrument. We believe that this is a fairly common situation in clinical practice since most potential clients present with an understanding of what is troubling them.

Rapid assessment instruments and screening inventories can be used to determine the need for treatment by comparing the client's scores with those from a norm of the general population or a clinical sample. Rapid assessment instruments are also extremely useful for monitoring the client's progress throughout treatment.

There are many examples of rapid assessment instruments scattered throughout the social science, behavioral, and psychiatric literature; many are discussed in resource books and professional journals (Fischer and Corcoran 1994a). A useful source of rapid assessment instruments is the two-volume *Measures for Clinical Practice*, which reprints over 325 rapid assessment instruments for children, couples, family problems, and problems found in adults (Fischer and Corcoran 1994a, 1994b). The instruments are listed in appendix D. A number of these tools are appropriate for determining the necessity of treatment, especially those with cutting scores. When a cutting score is available with a rapid assessment instrument, it usually demarks a clinically significant problem. Many managed care organizations recognize a cutting score on a rapid assessment instrument as sufficient evidence of the need for treatment.

Establishing Treatment Necessity

There are two relatively straightforward approaches to using problem inventories and rapid assessment instruments for evidencing the necessity of treatment. One is to compare the potential client's score with those from appropriate normative groups, much as is done with a diagnostic instrument. The client's score is interpreted in comparison to the sample from the general population or from clinical settings. The other way is to compare the client's score with how he or she was before the onset of the condition and as how he or she hopes to be at the end of treatment.

Consider, the client who states at intake, "I just feel lousy. I can't sleep at night, and I don't have much of an appetite. I just seem to be moping around all the time." This would suggest that the client is depressed, though a managed care program might want to dismiss the complaint as "just a bad mood" and thus insufficient to warrant treatment. Here the task is to convince the managed care program that the client's magnitude of depression is sufficient to warrant treatment and third-party reimbursement. You can compare the client's depression with the level of depression for those in the general population or compared against a sample of clients who are already receiving treatment for depression.

Clearly, in order to advance the argument that your client warrants treatment, you should illustrate that he or she is different from the general population or similar to the clinically depressed sample. Our experience is that it is difficult for a managed care program reviewer to deny authorization of treatment if the client is noticeably more distressed than the general population or similar to a sample of patients who are already determined to require treatment. Let's consider each approach separately.

Comparison with General Norms. In order to compare a client's functioning with that of the general population, select an instrument that best reflects the client's problem and also has appropriate norms. This instrument must be one with normative data of at least a mean and a standard deviation. Moreover, the client should be as similar as possible to the population with which he or she is being compared. The norm should be from a sample of the same age, gender, race, ethnicity, and educational level, for example.

Once the instrument is selected, administer and score it. Then compare the score to the mean score reported for the nonclinical population.

To illustrate, let us assume you have a client whose presenting problem is depression. After examining the relevant instruments in appendix D, you decide that the depression subscale of the Symptom Checklist (Kellner 1987) is appropriate for your client. You administer the subscale, and your client scores 4 on a score range of 0 to 17. The score of 4 is then compared to the scores for the general population. The average score for a sample from the general population is approximately 1.8, with a standard deviation of 2.2. This is a positively skewed distribution because many from the general sample report no or very few symptoms of depression. Your client's score is nearly one standard deviations above the average scores for the general population. This means that your client's depression score is greater than was reported for almost 83 percent of those in this normal sample.

This figure was derived from the characteristics of the central tendency and variability found with a normal distribution. A normal distribution is displayed in figure 4.3. For the sake of future discussion, the scores on this normal distribution display the mean and standard deviation for Z scores. The figure also reflects the percentage of scores within the standard deviations of the distribution. The scores of a normal distribution are distributed with an equal mean (the sum of all scores divided by the number of scores), mode (the score that occurs

Figure 4.3   A Normal Distribution

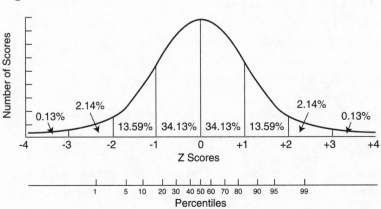

most often), and median (the score halfway between the highest and lowest scores).

Along with the standard deviation, which reflects deviation from the mean, we can determine the percentage of scores below your client's. In other words, with this information you are able to say that your client's score reflects more severity, for example, than a certain percentage of the general population. With a normal distribution, half of the scores are below the mean. One standard deviation above the mean includes an additional 34 percent, and so on up to 100 percent. Thus, the figures for the client who scored 4 on the Symptom Checklist and is about 83 percent more depressed than the general population is derived from 50 percent below the mean plus 33 percent for one standard deviation above the mean. Consequently, in comparison to this example, you would be able to state to the managed care program that your client is more depressed than approximately 83 percent of a sample from the general population.

Comparison with a Clinical Sample. Similar steps are involved when comparing a client's score with the norm from a relevant sample of persons receiving treatment. Using the Symptom Checklist again, the average score for a sample of nonpsychotic patients is 10.6, with a standard deviation of 5.9. It is negatively skewed because many psychiatric patients report numerous symptoms of depression. This time let us assume that your client's score is 5 and will be compared to those from the clinical sample. You would be able to state that your client's level of depression is greater than about 16 percent of those persons who are nonpsychotic psychiatric patients.

Does a score reflecting no more severity of depression than only 16 percent of the norm warrant treatment? Probably. Remember that you are comparing your client who appears to need treatment with those who have already been deemed to need treatment and are receiving it.

A Combination Approach. The procedures of comparing a client to a normal sample and a clinical sample can be combined for an even more persuasive argument for the need for treatment. It is quite a compelling argument to be able to say a client warrants treatment because he or she seems more depressed than nearly 83 percent of a general nonclinical sample *and* more depressed than approximately 16 percent of pa-tients receiving treatment for depression.

Calculating with Precision

This approach to determining treatment necessity with comparison to either a normal sample or a clinical sample is actually more compli-cated than our discussion suggests because we have simply estimated the percentage of scores below the client's. We also used scores that made these estimates easy and more accurate. Our simplified examples were constructed in such a fashion that the scores were close to a stan-dard deviation. But it is not very often that a client will score approxi-mately one standard deviation above or below the mean as in the ex-ample. A client's score, however, may be anywhere within the range of scores and most likely will not be at a standard deviation. Additionally, the actual percentage, not an estimate, must be reported.

In order to determine the percentage above or below your client's score, it is necessary to convert the scale score to a standardized score, called a Z score. A Z score is determined by subtracting the normative mean from the client's raw score and dividing by the standard deviation of the norm. This is illustrated in the following formula: $Z = X - \bar{X}/S.D.$ This procedure puts the raw score into a distribution ranging from -3 to $+3$ with a mean of 0. Figure 4.3 uses Z scores. Once you have calculated your client's Z score, you can then consult a table of Z scores (table 4.2) to determine the percentage of scores above your Z score and below it.

To illustrate how to use Z scores, we will use the same depression sub-scale of the Symptom Questionnaire. This time, let us say the client's score is 7. The Z score for the distribution of the nonclinical sample is 7 $- 1.8/2.2 = +2.4$. From table 4.2, a Z score of 2.4 is higher than 99.18 percent of the distribution. In other words, this client's score on depres-sion is higher than 99 percent of the sample from the general popula-tion. Similarly, the Z score for the distribution of scores for nonpsychotic psychiatric patients is $7 - 10.6/5.9 = -0.6$. As displayed in table 4.2, a Z score of $-.6$ is greater than 27.42 percent of the scores for the clinical sample. These findings warrant the statement that the particular client is more depressed than about 27 percent of psychiatric patients who are receiving treatment. Since this client is more depressed than the vast

Table 4.2   Table of Standard Scores and Proportions

| | Proportion of Score | | | Proportion of Score | |
| | Lower | Higher | | Lower | Higher |
Z Score	Than	Than	Z Score	Than	Than
−3.0	.13	99.87	.1	53.98	46.02
−2.9	.19	99.81	.2	57.93	42.07
−2.8	.26	99.74	.3	61.79	38.21
−2.7	.35	99.65	.4	65.54	34.46
−2.6	.47	99.53	.5	69.15	30.85
−2.5	.62	99.38	.6	72.58	27.42
−2.4	.82	99.18	.7	75.80	24.20
−2.3	1.07	99.93	.8	78.81	21.19
−2.2	1.39	98.61	.9	81.59	18.41
−2.1	1.79	98.21	1.0	84.13	15.87
−2.0	2.29	97.73	1.1	86.43	13.57
−1.9	2.87	97.13	1.2	88.49	11.51
−1.8	3.59	96.41	1.3	90.32	9.68
−1.7	4.46	95.54	1.4	91.92	8.08
−1.6	5.48	94.52	1.5	93.32	6.68
−1.5	6.68	93.32	1.6	94.52	5.48
−1.4	8.08	91.92	1.7	95.54	4.46
−1.3	9.68	90.32	1.8	96.41	3.59
−1.2	11.51	88.49	1.9	97.13	2.87
−1.1	13.57	86.43	2.0	97.73	2.27
−1.0	15.87	84.13	2.1	98.21	1.79
− .9	18.41	81.59	2.2	98.61	1.39
− .8	21.19	78.81	2.3	98.93	1.07
− .7	24.20	75.80	2.4	99.18	.82
− .6	27.42	72.58	2.5	99.38	.62
− .5	30.85	69.15	2.6	99.53	.47
− .4	34.46	65.54	2.7	99.65	.35
− .3	38.21	61.79	2.8	99.74	.26
− .2	42.07	57.93	2.9	99.81	.19
− .1	46.02	53.98	3.0	99.87	.13

majority of persons from the general population and 27 percent of psy-chiatric patients, there should be little question about the need for treatment. Most reasonable managed care reviewers would agree.

Some Limitations of Norm-Referenced Comparisons

Determining the necessity of treatment by norm-referenced comparison is not without limitations. First, many instruments lack adequate norms, especially when it comes to diverse populations, such as persons of color, immigrants, and persons whose primary language is not English. Among other limitations, norms are expensive to gather, require updating to be contemporary, and must be relevant to each client's circumstances. Yet the norms should reflect a population similar to a client. Comparing a client to a norm that "sort of fits" limits the ability to interpret the score. For example, comparing a middle-aged, African-American mason with a sample of college sophomores would not be appropriate. Similarly, comparing the score of a client who needs short-term outpatient therapy with a norm of patients requiring inpatient hospitalization might very well lead to an incorrect conclusion that treatment is not warranted. Consequently, we stress the need to compare clients to relevant norms.

SELF-REFERENCED COMPARISONS

Another approach to establishing treatment necessity is with self-referenced comparisons. Scores are interpreted not in relation to a representative sample but in comparison to one's own scores. This technique is less well established than norm-referenced comparison, but it does avoid some of the problems found with norms.

For the purpose of establishing treatment necessity, self-referenced comparison allows clinicians to interpret a client's functioning at the beginning of treatment with how he or she was doing prior to the onset of the presenting problem. This may be accomplished by comparing the client's score on a rapid assessment instrument with how he or she remembers feeling earlier, say, a month or two before the intake or in general. The time frame should be of a period when the client was not distressed by the problem. Ideally, the time would be consistent with the duration criteria of the client's diagnostic group. For example, a client whose presenting problem is generalized anxiety should complete an instrument for how he or she felt six months earlier.

To illustrate, assume the client enters treatment complaining of anxiety. From among the numerous assessment instruments to measure anxiety, including 25 known rapid assessment instruments (see appendix D), you choose the Self-Rating Anxiety scale. You instruct your client to complete the instrument as the items reflect his or her current functioning. Later, perhaps at the end of the intake, the client completes the instrument again, this time with the instructions to answer each item according to how he or she felt before the problem began. This retrospective assessment, useful in documenting treatment outcomes, compares how the client currently feels with how the client felt prior to the onset of the problem. If the current and retrospective scores are noticeably different, the clinician and the managed care reviewer will probably determine that the client's anxiety is sufficient to warrant treatment.

Clearly, this approach is not effective for problems with a long and stable history—for example, personality disorders or clinical problems that are more a trait of the client as opposed to a state of functioning. In other words, presenting problems that have had a long history or are chronic and persistent show little difference between current and retrospective scores.

Moreover, many presenting problems require long periods of duration to be a bona fide DSM-IV diagnosis (e.g., two years for dysthymia). As such, many clients may not remember how they felt prior to the onset of the problem. For example, a depressed client may say, "It seems I've felt this way forever."

One solution to this dilemma is to use a self-reference comparison between a client's current functioning and how he or she *wants* to feel. This prospective assessment of what the client hopes for may be used later as an indicator of a treatment goal. In this case, the client would complete the assessment instrument according to current functioning and then complete it again from the perspective of how he or she hopes to feel at the end of treatment. A noticeable difference between a client's current functioning and what he or she hopes for at the end of treatment may be used to suggest the problem is sufficient to warrant treatment.

It is possible to combine retrospective and prospective assessments to arrive at a score for how the client felt before the problem began, how he or she currently feels, and how he or she hopes to feel after treatment. This information allows the practitioner to interpret the client's current functioning compared with how it was before the problem and with how he or she hopes it will be. The more the current score on a rapid assessment instrument differs from the other two, the greater the necessity for treatment.

An added advantage to using retrospective or prospective assessment scores is that they are useful for setting the goals of treatment, such as returning to the level of functioning prior to the onset of the problem (as ascertained from the retrospective assessment) or reaching the level of functioning at the end of treatment (as suggested from the prospective assessment). Either approach is frequently convincing to a managed care reviewer that there is a need for treatment and that the goals are obtainable. As we will discuss in chapter 6, these assessments are useful in monitoring a client's improvement, deterioration, or stability in treatment.

SUMMARY

One of the first elements of quality assurance and cost containment is to establish that treatment is necessary. This element of managed mental health care is designed to control cost by preventing fraud and waste.

Operationalizing the presenting problem may be accomplished through a variety of assessment techniques, including diagnostic and problem screening inventories, standardized mental status exams, and rapid assessment instruments. With the exception of the Multi-Problem Screening Inventory, most screening tools are rather expensive, time-consuming, and difficult to interpret. Although various diagnostic screening tests are available, not many are useful when the client already knows why he or she is seeking treatment, as most clients do.

Regardless of what assessment instrument is used, scores must be interpreted in order to evidence the need for treatment. This can be based on comparing the client's scores with scores from well-established norms (norm-referenced comparison) or against the client's own scores (self-referenced comparison). The use of a standardized assessment instrument is greatly facilitated when it has a cutting score to differentiate clinically significant scores from those that do not seem to require treatment.

When norm-referenced comparisons are not available, we recommend using self-referenced comparisons to contrast the client's functioning at the time he or she is seeking treatment with how this person was before the onset of the problem or with how he or she wishes to be at the end of treatment. The goal, of course, is to have noticeable differences between how well the client is doing at the beginning of treatment and how he or she was earlier or wishes to be.

We do not intend to suggest that a managed care reviewer will always find these approaches persuasive. Often, however, a reasonable reviewer will. Moreover, these approaches to establishing treatment necessity should be used as part of the intake interviewing procedures. They are useful in conjunction with arriving at a diagnosis and have the added benefit of providing referent points during treatment. This is information that most managed care programs expect will be available throughout the treatment process.

Chapter 5

Prospective Utilization Reviews

Authorizing Systematic Interventions

A fter determining if treatment is necessary, the second essential element of managed mental health care concerns the specific treatment intervention that is to be authorized. This decision is based on
the magnitude of the client's problem balanced against different levels
of services. This type of case management is designed to ensure that
important aspects of sound clinical practice are implemented in accordance with acceptable professional standards (Fauman 1992). Often
these aspects of acceptable practice are defined by the standards established by the managed care organization.

The evaluation of standards of practice may occur in terms of what
the clinician and the client intend to do to facilitate the client's
change. This information is also ascertained in a prospective utilization
review form. Alternatively, it may be requested in terms of what actually did occur during the course of treatment. This would be mandated
in the authorizing of a continuation of services (i.e., concurrent utilization reviews) or approval of reimbursement for services already delivered. (i.e., retrospective utilization review). We will discuss the practice
of concurrent and retrospective utilization reviews in the next chapter.

Many clinicians consider preauthorization by the managed care organization an interference with professional autonomy; others see it as
enhancing the goal of identifying potential problems with diagnosis and

treatment while also affording an opportunity to correct any inaccuracies in the clinician's assessment and treatment plan (Fauman 1992). Much of the material covered in this chapter pertains to prospective, concurrent, and retrospective utilization reviews. We will discuss much of this in the context of prospective utilization reviews because preauthorization helps ensure that the intervention contains components of effective practice. Additionally, concurrent utilization reviews are similar to prospective utilization reviews; they are prospective about the remaining aspects of treatment. Moreover, retrospective utilization reviews will need to delineate persuasively that the treatment did occur in an adequate manner. We believe it is best to determine this in advance of implementing the intervention, even if not mandated by a managed care organization.

The three elements of a treatment intervention in managed care settings are basic elements of sound practice:

1. Defining the clinical intervention in such a manner that the treatment plan logically relates to the client's presenting problem.
2. Structuring treatment so that it is goal directed, systematic, and planned.
3. Including definable components and techniques that facilitate the implementation, replication, and evaluation of the treatment.

These parameters will need to include the actual components of treatment—what the clinician and client will do to reach the goals of treatment. The parameters will also need to include the predetermined length of treatment.

In this chapter we will demonstrate how to establish treatment interventions that comply with the standards of prospective utilization reviews. We do not outline how to practice the actual interventions or even explain the different treatment modalities but rather show what might be expected of an intervention if it is to be acceptable in a prospective utilization review.

PROSPECTIVE REVIEWS AND PREAUTHORIZED INTERVENTIONS

Prospective utilization reviews, managed care procedures that authorize and monitor client services prior to treatment, may occur in an interdisciplinary clinical case management meeting in a capitated managed care setting or between an independent practitioner and a managed care reviewer. The review will assess the necessity of treatment and frequently will identify the actual intervention and how it will be implemented, including the authorized number of treatment sessions.

The preapproval and determination of the treatment may occur for outpatient services, such as a private practitioner working for a fee-for-service or a capitated program. Fee-for-service prospective utilization reviews may be conducted by a quality assurance agent with the program itself, such as with HMOs of networks of providers who manage a solo practitioner's client. Currently there is considerable variability in how this occurs and by whom.

The interventions that tend to be authorized by a managed care reviewer are those that relate directly to the client's presenting problem, are goal directed and well defined, and delineate what will occur over the course of treatment in clear and specified steps. A managed care organization requires information regarding the treatment through standardized prospective utilization review forms and for continuation of existing services or reimbursement. The purpose is to ensure quality of care. By refusing to authorize certain treatments or reimburse interventions that lack specificity and are nebulous, the second goal of managed care is addressed because funds are not allocated to questionable care. This is cost containment at its best. Consequently, the procedures to preapprove a treatment plan or to evaluate it during treatment and subsequently is another major way that managed care attempts to control costs and ensure quality.

The goal of predetermining the nature of the intervention is the assurance that the clinician is using an appropriate intervention that is up to date and has the potential to be efficient when implemented correctly (McCall-Perez 1993). This goal, based on having some idea of what seems to work, is quite elusive in much of clinical practice because the knowledge of treatment outcomes and client preference is often unavailable. The more realistic goal of managed care in authorizing specific interventions is to require preapproval of what seems to work best (Office of Technological Assessment 1994). This is also the goal of the managed care organization. Authorization is designed to direct the practitioner to specific interventions that are considered likely to work best or are the most effective of the known and available interventions.

To some degree this review limits a client's choices of what treatment techniques will be available for the presenting problem and whom he or she may see to treat it. However, to rely on the personal and professional experience of the clinician is also questionable. All too often the preference of many clinicians is to use a passive, insight-oriented verbal therapy with every client (Rabinowitz and Lukoff 1995). This one-size-fits-all approach lacks effectiveness for all clients, is time-consuming, and is quite costly, with outcomes that are of marginal value. This is especially so in comparison to interventions that can be done with less time and at lower cost (Wells 1994). Moreover, these unstructured and unsystematic approaches often lack empirical evidence of what seems to work with what specific client problem, and the belief in effectiveness is often based on the clinician's experience.

This view is challenged with questions about the validity of the research supporting a preauthorized intervention, and some have questioned the entire value of research (Tyson 1992, 1995; Witkins 1991). Reid (1994) observes that the selection and evaluation of certain components of effective interventions also include clinical judgment. In addition, such empirically based treatment components are better than those from other sources, especially when used in conjunction with such critical aspects of professional practice as clinical judgment, empathy, and intuition. In our opinion, it is not advisable to rely solely on empirically supported intervention or clinical judgments and practice wisdom in determining what will most likely work with a particular client. The effective practitioner judiciously relies on both.

There are numerous different forms of prospective utilization review (probably as many as there are managed care companies). Some are quite general and ask only a few questions about diagnoses, goals, and treatment plans. Others are much more detailed (see, for example, Mattson 1992). At a minimum, all are generally concerned with the course of the illness, the severity of symptomatology, and patient disability (Wilson 1992).

Most prospective utilization reviews for preapproval of the intervention will look at the treatment goals, the objectives, specific interventions (including the number of sessions necessary to reach the goal), and information about collateral services. The prospective utilization review form in appendix B attempts to ascertain this with items displayed in figure 5.1. In general, questions of this sort are frequently used by managed care organizations to determine if the intervention is sufficient for authorization.

Part of the assessment includes information about earlier clinical services so that previously unsuccessful interventions are not needlessly repeated. Additionally, such information may be used to determine if the presenting problem is in fact a preexisting condition and thus not covered by the payor or capitation program.

The purpose of determining the treatment intervention in advance is to improve the chances that an effective intervention will be implemented efficiently. In essence, managed care organizations are intent on ensuring quality by judging what is and is not an acceptable treatment plan. In managed mental health care, treatment plans that are likely to be authorized are often called *preferred practices* (Giles 1991). These interventions have some degree of empirical support for their effectiveness with certain client problems. They are well-defined clinical interventions with clear and replicable components that may be implemented in a specified order.

DEVELOPING INTERVENTION PROCEDURES

Prospective reviews are designed to ensure that the treatment procedures reasonably relate to the client's problem and the delineated goal or goals. This is accomplished through the authorization of preferred practices—those interventions with some established recognition of effectiveness. Often the preauthorization review will expect the clinician to delineate the treatment in a step-by-step manner. These preferred practices range from standards, guidelines, and options to protocols and manuals. There is no general agreement on the usage of these different terms; often they are lumped together under the category of "practice guidelines."

In a general sense, practice guidelines are delineations of elements of an intervention with well-defined and well-organized components with an appropriate fit to the client problem and treatment goal. Guidelines are a set of strategies developed to assist the practitioner in clinical decision making (Zarin, Pincus, and McIntyre 1993). They are intended to document what is known and what is not known about the treat-

Figure 5.1   Determinants of Intervention

History of Treatment

Was the client ever treated before for this or a similar problem?

____No ____Yes

If yes, what type of clinical services were provided?

Please summarize the outcome of previous treatment or clinical services.

Please indicate if medication was provided before, and include the type, dosage, and duration of the medication. _____

Current Request for Clinical Services

Summary statement of the presenting problem for which you are requesting treatment:

What is the short-term goal of treatment? That is, objectively define what you hope to achieve if treatment is authorized.

Please describe the treatment plan for reaching the short-term goal, including the specific steps you will follow in implementing it.

How will you determine (i.e., assess/evaluate or monitor) the client's success in reaching this short-term goal?

What is the long-term goal of treatment? That is, objectively define what you hope to achieve if treatment is authorized.

Please describe the treatment plan for reaching the long-term goal, including

the specific steps you will follow in implementing it. _____

_____

_____

How will you determine (i.e., assess/evaluate or monitor) the client's success
in reaching this long-term goal?

_____

How many sessions are you requesting? _____

How many minutes will each session last? _____

Will outside services be provided? ____Yes ____No

   (a) If yes, what services? _____

_____.

   (b) Who will provide these services?_____

_____.

   (c) When will these services begin and end? _____

_____.

_____

ment of particular clinical problems. Although the American Psychiatric Association published specific recommendations for practice as
long ago as the mid-1800s, guidelines now are developed chiefly because of fourth-party oversight of mental health treatment (Zarin, Pincus, and McIntyre 1993).

Managed care organizations are most likely to authorize practice
guidelines that are outlined in a step-by-step fashion. This not only
ensures that the implementation can be easily assessed by the managed care reviewer, but that the implementation was done accurately.
When a step-by-step protocol is not possible, such as with some family
therapy approaches, clinicians are advised to build into the protocol
techniques with some degree of proven effectiveness or professional
recognition.

PREFERRED PRACTICES

Standards, guidelines, and protocols are elements of effective treat-ment that are generally integrated into many of the preferred practice approaches required for authorization in managed care prospective uti-lization reviews. The terms *standards, practice guidelines*, and *protocols* refer to some degree of specified procedures for implementing an inter-vention that is preferable to other interventions, at least in the opinion of someone in the managed care organization. Of course, preferred practices are no guarantee of treatment effectiveness. It is often hard to get clients to change, even with good interventions. The goal of pre-ferred practice, then, much like the general components of treatment effectiveness, is to ensure quality by increasing the likelihood of a suc-cessful outcome.

One cogent view of structured intervention distinguishes standards, guidelines, and options (Eddy, 1990). Standards, guidelines, and op-tions vary in the degree of specificity of what is expected to be included in treatment. Most are derived from some amount of evidence from empirical research. They also vary in terms of the degree of acceptance by the majority of the mental health providers.

In general, standards, guidelines, and options are attempts to "define the parameters within which appropriate clinical care may take place" (Applebaum 1992, p. 341). They serve many purposes, including direct-ing clinicians to effective and efficient interventions, facilitating consis-tent implementation, and ensuring reimbursement under the gover-nance of managed care. From the perspective of managed care, these parameters of practice interventions help ensure optimal treatment based on the most up-to-date empirical evidence (Applebaum 1992).

Standards

Standards are those elements of treatment that most practitioners be-lieve must be followed in every case. Thus, they are essential elements of an intervention, and exceptions to following them are rare. In fact, failure to follow a standard of practice may be considered negligence and may result in a potential claim of malpractice.

Standards are much more common in physical health care than in mental health care. For example, in a standard eye exam, a glaucoma test is typically considered to be a standard of care, in part because of the low cost of the test balanced against the value of the medical information.

In contrast to physical health care, mental health has much wider variations in what a practitioner is expected to do in each case because standards are determined by sufficient knowledge and unanimity of knowledge of the desired outcome of an intervention or the undesired outcome for standards that prohibit specific action (e.g., sex with a client). What is necessary from one theoretical orientation may be super-fluous to another. This variation is quite defensible from the perspective of the "respectable minority doctrine," a legal position that recognizes the lack of uniformity in mental health treatment (Reisner and Slobogin 1990). Nevertheless, as behavioral science advances, less variability is considered tolerable (Klerman, et al. 1992), and failure to adhere to a standard is difficult to defend professionally, ethically, or legally.

Practice Guidelines

Practice guidelines are more flexible than standards and give way to in-cluding more clinical judgment. Guidelines are parameters of treat-ment that probably should be followed in most cases (Eddy 1990). As the word suggests, a guideline is just that—a guide. They are based on known outcomes preferred by the majority of practitioners and clients (Eddy 1990; Littrell, 1995). It most likely will require adaptation to the particularities of the client's problem, circumstances, setting, and other factors. Practice guidelines are currently being developed by a variety of organizations (e.g., the American Psychiatric Association), and many managed care organizations.

The practice guidelines with probably the most persuasive authority are those available from the American Psychiatric Association. Three guidelines are available now—for eating disorders (APA 1993a), major depression (APA 1993b), and bipolar disorders (APA 1994b)—with numerous others in the developmental stages.

Options

Options, the third level of parameters of treatment, are neutral in terms of recommendations for practice but may be applied to a case (Eddy 1990). Options are often determined by the clinician's professional training, theoretical orientation, and practice experience. They often lack established knowledge of effective outcomes, so their use is arbitrary and primarily theoretical. Sometimes options have little evidence of effective outcomes, although a client may prefer the option. Examples are popular trends that appeal to large audiences, such as inner-child work and narrative therapy.

Options are frequently based on one's theoretical orientation, even if it is not accepted by the majority of practitioners. Options, in effect, recognize the different interventions available to practitioners that may be useful in a case. Each practitioner is free to decide if it will be appropriate for a particular client's problem or treatment goals.

Clinical practice has a long way to go before empirical knowledge is established by sufficient guidelines or standards. Consequently, options are rather pervasive today.

Using Preferred Practices

As a consequence of using preferred practices, the provider, the client, and the managed care organization all understand what should occur during the process of treatment. This information will be relied on to assess quality and consistency in implementing the treatment intervention. This can hardly be said for such general forms of treatment as "psychotherapy," "ego-oriented dynamic treatment," or even "behavior therapy." From the perspective of managed care, such nebulous treatment plans fail to inform anyone about what will be done in the course of treatment, and they do not provide a standard to compare the implementation.

General statements in clinical practice do not allow the managed care organization to know what the particular intervention will be, if it is an appropriate procedure for the client's needs, or if it was implemented consistently and efficiently. Structured treatments, in contrast, provide this information to a greater extent. A preapproved preferred practice approach communicates the actual elements of the intervention and how they are to be implemented. Sometimes these components of the intervention are well established, sometimes they are not, especially when more exploratory interventions are necessary because the level of knowledge in the field is not available to guide practice more precisely. One example of well-established and accepted interventions are those useful in the treatment of anxiety disorders (Thyer

1987). An example of less established and less available interventions are those useful in working with a person with a borderline personality disorder (Corcoran and Keeper 1992; Linehan and Kehrer 1993) or other personality disorder.

OPERATIONALIZING INTERVENTIONS

Much like determining treatment necessity, getting a treatment authorized is a concern of operationalization. How is the intervention operationalized in observable terms? Researchers would consider operationalizing as the independent variable. Treatment is considered an independent variable partially because the intervention occurs independent of and should contribute to the actual change. The client's change is dependent on the frequency, duration, or intensity of treatment. Client change in a problem or attainment of a goal is the dependent variable.

Regardless of the degree of acceptance by the greater professional community of mental health providers, most managed care organizations have a fairly narrow range of interventions they believe are useful for specific client problems (Giles 1993). Consequently, when a clinician's work is governed by a managed care organization, he or she will have to delineate as thoroughly as possible what will occur in treatment, for what purpose, and in what manner. This explanation is facilitated by developing treatment plans that incorporate as many relevant and effective components of practice as possible. In other words, a practitioner is in a better position to advocate for a client and the necessary treatment if he or she has developed a specific intervention with techniques that have been shown to be effective (e.g., modeling).

Developing treatment that will be approved is facilitated by keeping abreast of the literature on treatment effectiveness and by following treatment guidelines. Giles (1993) lists fifty-six practice guidelines, although many on the list are clearly options.

PRACTICES THAT SEEM TO WORK

Managed care reviewers authorize practices based on what seems to work, with these determinations based primarily on the research literature on psychotherapy process and outcome. This information is available from reviews, some with a long-standing presence in a field

(Garfield and Bergin 1986) and others from professional journals that focus on quality reviews (e.g., *Psychological Review*).

In the past twenty-five years or so, literature reviews have provided practitioners with information about what specifically to do. These reviews are advanced by asking more practical questions than whether treatment worked. As Wood (1978) notes, to ask whether clinical practice works is the wrong question because it provides few useful answers to practitioners. A more valuable line of questioning asks, "What works, when, how, and with what client problem?" The answers to these and similar questions enable practitioners to incorporate empirically substantiated components of treatment into an intervention with a particular client, avoiding those that seem less successful.

Wood (1978) has identified six general components of quality practice:

1. A clear definition of why the client is seeking treatment.
2. A functional understanding of what gives rise to the problem that brings a client into treatment, maintains that problem, and facilitates its change.
3. Established goals to address the problem.
4. A contract agreed on by the client for obtaining the goals.
5. A plan or strategy for how the goals will be obtained.
6. A means of evaluating the effectiveness of the intervention in reaching the goal and resolving the problem.

Reid and Hanrahan (1992) additionally note that effective interventions are explicit about the particular problem to be addressed, have explicit goals, and were well organized in a step-by-step manner to reach those goals. These interventions contrast with the more nebulous interventions of "psychotherapy," "counseling," "casework," or just "behavior therapy," which earlier reviewers concluded did not make a difference.

Reviews based on professional assessments of the research literature are useful for isolating effective treatment components for inclusion in an authorized managed care intervention. Reviews are available for specific types of therapy (Thomlison 1984), client problems (e.g., Markowitz 1994), and just about every area of the social and behavior sciences.

As clinicians review research, they need to select appropriate treatment. Hanrahan and Reid (1984) propose a number of criteria to facilitate this decision making, including the genuineness of the treatment effects (i.e., the ability to conclude that the intervention actually caused the change), the importance of the effects in terms of the clinical significance of the observed change, and the ability to generalize the conclusions of the effects of that intervention to the clinical setting, client problem, treatment goal, and ability to reproduce or replicate the intervention. Hanrahan and Reid discuss these criteria in more detail, including questions to consider in the evaluation of research articles. At a minimum, we suggest four important questions when evaluating an article for incorporation into practice:

1. Was there reason to believe the treatment led to the client change?
2. Was the observed change meaningful and clinically relevant?
3. Was there sufficient similarity between the clients in the study and one's own client to warrant using the intervention?
4. Is the intervention delineated with sufficient detail to enable replication?

Each of these questions must be answered affirmatively if a research article is to be of much use in a specific intervention. If one or two questions are answered "no," this does not mean that the intervention will never be useful, but it will suggest that the research is not strongly persuasive. In such cases, and even with sound and robust research, a practitioner must rely on his or her clinical judgment in selecting effective interventions, especially those that seem to be more "option" than "guidelines."

Additional and more specific information about what seems to work has become available from research on research. This meta-analysis, or the analysis of analyses, contributes dramatic patterns of outcome and clinically significant results that can guide practitioners in developing a managed care intervention (Lipsey and Wilson 1993).

Meta-analysis is a research approach that converts the dependent variables of any study into a standardized score, known as an *effect size*. As the name suggests, an effect size is a quantitative indicator of the magnitude of the effect of an independent variable (e.g., a type of therapy) on the dependent variable (e.g., a client's problem). It is essentially a standardized Z score that ranges from about −3 to +3. This is the same standardized score we used in chapter 4. An effect size based on a Z score allows a clinician to know how one group performed in comparison to another group, such as a no-treatment control group or another comparative therapy. Just as a Z score of 1.0 indicates a client is more distressed than 83 percent of the comparative sample, an effect size of 1.0 means the treatment group performed better than 83 percent of the comparison group. Thus, the value of meta-analysis is that it allows a determination of treatment effectiveness in comparison to no treatment or some other treatment.

In meta-analysis, the effect size of a large number of studies becomes the dependent variables (i.e., a variable with a range of scores from about -3 to $+3$). These dependent variables may be submitted to statistical manipulation with independent variables in order to determine which seems to cause the effect, or at least contributes to the effect.

Numerous meta-analysis reviews have been conducted on the impact of clinical practice, including different forms of psychotherapy (Andrews and Harvey 1981; Shapiro and Shapiro 1982; Smith and Glass 1977; Smith, Glass, and Miller 1980); social casework (Videka-Sherman 1985); marital therapies (Hazelrigg, Cooper, and Bordin 1987; Shadish et al., 1993); and specific clinical techniques, including systematic desensitization (Berman, Miller, and Massman 1985); relaxation techniques (Eppley, Abrams, and Shear 1989); and rational-emotive therapy (Engels, Garnefski, and Diekstra 1993). Meta-analysis reviews are also available on what seems to work with particular disorders, such as the chronically mentally ill (Hogarty 1989; Videka-Sherman 1988); geriatric depression (Scogin and McElreath 1994); panic disorders (Clum, Clum, and Surls 1993); and a variety of behavioral health conditions (e.g., adolescent smoking prevention, Bruvold 1993). There are also many meta-analysis studies on psychotropic mediation, such as antidepressants (Davis, Wang, and Janicak 1993); clomipramine, and fluoxetine and exposure therapy (Cox et al. 1993).

From the perspective of the clinical practice, much valuable information may be derived that may facilitate a better understanding of what seems to work. This information can influence the development of treatment interventions useful for practice in the context of managed care.

Meta-analytic studies support the general components of effective interventions, for example that a particular intervention must be applied to a particular problem (i.e., one size does not fit all). As Corcoran and Videka-Sherman (1992) summarize, "Perhaps the most consistent finding from meta-analysis . . . applies to well-defined interventions" (p. 21). This notion is not limited to quantitative reviews from meta-analysis but is consistent with other efforts in the empirical practice movement (Barlow, Hayes, and Nelson 1984; Reid 1994). In general, treatments with specificity tend to be more effective than unstructured, ad hoc interventions.

Five components of an intervention seem to relate to positive client outcomes:

1. Preparing the client for active participation in the process of change.
2. Using client exploration.
3. Assigning homework.
4. Requiring active instead of passive participation by the practitioner in the change process, including the use of modeling, advice, and systematic reinforcement.
5. Establishing time limits in terms of the number of sessions offered.

ESTABLISHING GOALS

One of the first steps in developing "best-practice" or preferred practice is to determine a match between a particular client problem and an intervention that is the best one available. "Best available" means one that has been demonstrated to work on certain client problems (Compton and Galaway 1989). For example, physical health care promotion may be advanced by a cigarette cession program with established procedures (Bruvold 1993).

In essence, managed care mandates some specific intervention while refusing to authorize others. This requirement poses both problems and challenges in the selection of an effective intervention. The clinician must ensure that the recommended and authorized intervention is adaptable to the person with whom he or she is working.

The selection of an appropriate intervention will be guided by the client's goal or goals of treatment. In fact, virtually all utilization reviews ask for a clear statement and cogent goal and objective. The goal and the objective are the basic map for the course of treatment in determining where the client wants to go.

One simple and straightforward approach to establishing a goal is to ask the client at the intake interview, "What do you want to accomplish by the end of treatment"? As Wells (1994) discusses, the therapeutic challenge and benefit of this approach is the refinement of knowing what the client wants and reasonably expects from a planned intervention. A clinician who is clear about the client's initial goal will be better able to develop an effective and tailor-made treatment plan.

Knowledge of the client's goal also facilitates the managed care organization's understanding of the procedures that will be used to reach the specified goal. The goal must be specific and challenging, and selected mutually by client and clinician. Consequently, it is essential that the managed care reviewer does not exclude the client in the goal-setting process. One reason is that client participation yields therapeutic benefits (Anderson 1989; Simons and Aigner 1985; Videka-Sherman 1985).

In addition to simply asking the client, a clinician may find a more formal goal-setting procedure to be useful. Goal setting is facilitated by using Goal Attainment Scaling (GAS) procedures (Kiresuk, Smith, and Cardillo 1994). The GAS is a method for monitoring a client's progress in reaching a goal (Kiresuk and Sherman 1968), as we will illustrate in chapter 6. At the early stage of treatment, however, it also serves the purpose of helping clinician and client develop a specific goal (Corcoran and Gingerich 1992). The GAS procedures structure the clinician's interaction with the client such that both determine what behavior (regardless of whether it is a feeling, thought, or action) is to be changed. This task is facilitated with work sheets for the clinician and the client (see appendix E). In other words, the GAS helps clinician and client focus concretely in answering the question, "What do you want to accomplish by the end of treatment?"

The hoped-for outcome of treatment—goals—can be expressed in at least five levels:

1. What is expected at the end of the intervention (scored as 0).
2. What it would be like if the outcome of treatment was somewhat better than expected (scored +1).
3. What it would be like if the outcome of treatment was a lot better than expected (scored +2).

Since treatment may not make a difference and the client may get worse, the GAS delineates this possibility. Thus:

4. What the outcome would be like if it was somewhat less than expected (scored −1).
5. What it would be like if it was a lot less than expected (scored −2).

The consequence of using the GAS for goal setting is not only a clear and concise goal but a potentially valuable tool for monitoring treatment progress.

This scheme is reflected in the form in figure 5.2, to be used with clients. The boxes in the first column, under the heading "Scores," are for the five levels of outcome: a lot more than expected (+2), somewhat more than expected (+1), expected level of outcome (0), somewhat less than expected (–1), and a lot less than expected (–2). The boxes in the second column are for setting out the actual description of the five potential levels of the goal. This form should be completed

Figure 5.2 *Goal Attainment Scale*

Client problem: ______________________________

Treatment goal: ______________________________

Score	Observable Description	Observation of Performance By Client	Observation of Performance By Relevant Other
+ 2			
+ 1			
0			
- 1			
- 2			

early in the treatment process, possibly right after determining the treatment necessity and ideally during the first session. The descriptions of each level of the goal should be brief but concrete. A guideline is to write the descriptions so that a third party can observe the level of performance. Well-written descriptions will help establish clearly defined goals and facilitate evaluating and scoring the level of goal attainment. Needless to say, some goals and problems are observable only to the client, such as intrusive thoughts or depressed feelings.

Clinician and client should complete the GAS by providing descriptions for each significant goal that is relevant to treatment. A separate form is used for each goal.

Determining and scoring the level of goal attainment at various points over the course of treatment are facilitated by the last two columns of boxes, designed so the observer may record the event used to rate the level of goal attainment. This version of the GAS is designed so the client and some other relevant person (e.g., a partner or staff member in a residential program) can record the descriptions of the behavior that reflects client performance and goal attainment. Describing the actual event is useful because the outcome may not fit exactly with the original description of the goal; thus, clinician and client have additional information about how the particular assessment of the goal was made.

PRIORITIZING GOALS

Often the limitation of a client's insurance coverage or the range of services authorized to enrolled members of a capitated program will prevent the clinician from addressing all the problems and goals identified by the client. This is often the case for clinical practice and is especially prevalent for clients whose services are reviewed by managed care. In fact, it is not uncommon for a managed care organization to limit treatment to one or two goals, so prioritizing goals is important.

The priority of a goal may be influenced by its importance to the client, the severity of the problem addressed by the goal, or the potential for successfully reaching the goal within the limits of the authorized intervention (Austin, Knopp, and Smith 1986). The clinician and client might discuss whether to take the most difficult goal first, or the one that corresponds to the most severe problem, or the one that will facilitate additional growth and development after treatment ends (Gelso and Hazel-Johnson 1983).

By using such an approach to goal setting, the clinician and client establish the objective of the intervention. In contrast to a goal, which is fairly general, an objective is more specific and measurable in terms of who will do what, how, where, and when. The development of objectives is preparation for a prospective utilization review. Moreover, clinician and client now have a clearer sense of the client treatment needs, and the clinician is in a more informed position to advocate for the client with a managed care organization.

Regardless of any efforts at goal development or which of the goals is given the highest priority, the managed care organization probably will attempt to insist that the most severe problem be worked on first, provided it is covered for the client. In this sense, the clinician must be prepared to provide a rational basis for the position reached with the client. The clinician may need to be prepared for extensive advocacy for what seems to be in the best interest of the client.

One issue of goal setting unique to managed care is when it should occur. In our opinion, the specification of a goal should occur in advance of any contact with the managed care organization. This schedule helps to preserve the integrity of the developing clinical relationship, while preventing undue influence or pressure from a managed care organization to accept the procedure it recommends.

Waiting to interact with a managed care reviewer until after clinician and potential client have established some general sense of the treatment goals has the advantage of validation. In this sense, the opinion of the managed care reviewer also provides a referent point. Professional judgment may be compared with the recommendation from the managed care organization in order to see if there is general agreement.

TREATMENT PROTOCOLS

Regardless of whether the context of treatment results from standards, guidelines, or options, the challenge to the clinician is to develop a treatment protocol that will increase the likelihood of a successful outcome. In general, the goal is to establish a direction to the treatment process that combines the current knowledge of the field with the peculiarities of the client to formulate the best treatment. A treatment protocol is essentially the step-by-step organization of what will occur throughout the entire clinical process. A protocol facilitates the implementation of the intervention. Moreover, it enables the clinician to communicate efficiently with a managed care organization about what will occur (prospective utilization review) and what is occurring (concurrent utilization review) or what did occur (retrospective utilization review).

As all practitioners know from experience, many clinical problems do not have bona fide interventions of proven effectiveness. In fact, most treatment of client problems lacks proved interventions recognized by the majority of practitioners. This, however, will not prevent a managed care organization from mandating specific interventions or treatment protocols. The challenge is to develop a treatment plan, or protocol, that is the best treatment—that is, one with the highest probability of successfully helping a client change his or her problem and attain the treatment goal.

The published literature in the behavioral and social sciences is no longer limited in the availability of practice guidelines, as it once was. Additionally, most managed care organizations have established their own guidelines for practice, although many are developed from information other than the published data or are based on more limited criteria of effectiveness. Thus, the clinician must be judicious in accepting the authorized interventions without professional judgment. A clinician should not treat a client if his or her professional judgment concludes that the preauthorized intervention is either inappropriate for the client's problem or treatment goal or cannot accomplish its objective in the time allotted.

Most treatment protocols are developed for a particular disorder or presenting problem and must give way to individual differences between clients. Consider clinical depression, one of the most common reasons for seeking treatment. Clearly psychotropic medication has had a very encouraging track record of effectiveness, especially when combined with some forms of psychotherapy (APA 1993b). Even so, a large percentage of clients complaining of depression are nonresponsive to antidepressant medication. Others develop tolerance or adverse side effects. Still others refuse medication because they are unwilling to take drugs, and others are unlikely candidates for antidepressants because of other health care concerns, such as pregnancy (Markowitz 1994). Consequently, some form of psychotherapy is probably going to occur. In the view of a managed mental health care organization, treatment will likely be restricted to well-developed protocols with well-defined and clear parameters.

The development of such a protocol would be facilitated by one of three manual-based psychotherapies considered by Markowitz (1994) to be useful in treatment planning: a cognitive-behavioral approach (McCullough 1992), a social skills approach (Becker, Heimberg, and Bellack 1987), or an interpersonal approach (Markowitz and Klerman 1993). Most of these protocols have time limits, emphasize performance and homework assignments, and seek to enhance a client's sense of control over life's events. Most aspects of these elements must be tailor-made for each client. Not surprisingly, most of these elements are similar to parameters identified as effective from the empirical literature. Additional structured interventions are available from Biglan and Campbell (1981), Van den Berg (1992), and Young, Beck, and Weinberger (1993).

A number of books will prove helpful in developing a treatment protocol that offers a high probability of effectiveness. They are displayed in table 5.1. Many of these books contain procedures for a variety of disorders (Barlow 1993; Shelton and Levy 1981). Giles (1993) provides a list of fifty-six practice guidelines, most of them specific interventions addressing a specific problem. There are also manuals for the treatment of particular disorders, such as three from the American Psychiatric Association already mentioned, along with the 2,800-page *Treatment of Psychiatric Disorders* (Gabbard, 1995). Some volumes emphasize single theoretical orientation, such as Sifneos's (1992) dynamic-oriented interventions. Most of the treatments are based on the principles of cognitive behavioral therapy. A few are rather professionally parochial and needlessly limited to a single discipline (Craighead et al. 1994). Most of these books are valuable in efforts to develop more effective treatment procedures.

The benefits of using these works, although admittedly few practitioners have the time or resources to master them all, is that to varying degrees they will help in the development of treatment protocols. These protocols will need to include the parameters of effective treatment and delineate in a step-by-step fashion what will occur throughout the course of treatment. A consequence of such a treatment plan is not only

Table 5.1　Sources for Protocol Development

Barlow (1993). *Clinical Handbook of Psychological Disorders: A Step-by-Step Treatment Manual.*
Becker, Heimberg, and Bellack (1987). *Social Skills Training Treatment for Depression.*
Bloom (1992). *Planned Short-term Psychotherapy: A Clinical Handbook.*
Corcoran (1992). *Structuring Change: Effective Practice for Common Client Problems.*
Craighead, Craighead, Kazdin, and Mahoney (1994). *Cognitive and Behavioral Intervention: An Empirical Approach to Mental Health Problems.*
Fischer (1978). *Effective Casework Practice.*
Garfield and Bergin (1986). *Handbook of Psychotherapy and Behavior Change.*
Giles (1993). *Handbook of Effective Psychotherapy.*
Giles (1993). *Managed Mental Health Care: A Guide for Practitioners, Employers, and Hospital Administrators.*
Kendall and Braswell (1986). *Cognitive-Behavioral Therapy for Impulsive Children.*
LeCroy (1994). *Handbook of Child and Adolescent Treatments.*
MacKenzie (1995). *Effective Use of Group Treatment in Managed Care.*
Norcross (1986). *Handbook of Eclectic Psychotherapy.*
Pinkston et al. (1982). *Effective Social Work Practice.*
Reid (1992). *Task Strategies: An Empirical Approach to Social Work Practice.*
Shelton and Levy (1981). *Behavioral Assignment and Treatment Compliance.*
Sifneos (1992). *Short-Term Anxiety Provoking Psychotherapy: A Treatment Manual.*
Thyer (1987). *Treating Anxiety Disorders.*
Wells (1994). *Planned Short-Term Treatment.*
Wells and Giannetti (1990). *Handbook of the Brief Psychotherapies.*

---

a higher likelihood that the managed care organization will authorize its use, but the protocol will guide implementation of the intervention.

All treatment protocols must have considerable flexibility. They should be guides, not prescriptions.

LENGTH OF TREATMENT

Many treatment protocols are short-term interventions. If not, they almost always have time limits. Treatment, however, does not have to be short term. Under managed care, an intervention must first fit within the parameters of the benefit package (Austad and Hoyt 1992). It makes little sense to develop a long-term, insight-oriented treatment plan if the client will be authorized for only ten or twelve sessions, especially if some other form of treatment can accomplish the same outcome within the session limitation.

Treatment governed by managed care is not necessarily short term, but most of it is. However, an alternative model of managed care treatment is intermittent psychotherapy throughout the life cycle. Here treatment is intended to help people with problems at different points in life. In this sense, treatment is not ongoing but a series of discrete, planned interventions for different clinical problems at various points in life (Wells 1994). Visits to the clinician occur only when needed and end when the client successfully copes with the crisis or developmental episode. The role of the clinician is similar to that of the family physician (Austad and Hoyt 1992).

Such an approach affords the potential of an intergenerational psychotherapist, which would be particularly useful with persistent and severe disorders and for conditions with known genetic links, such as bipolar affective disorders. A clinician who works with the client at various stages throughout life would make possible the establishment and maintenance of an ongoing therapeutic relationship, one that is not as easily established in some brief treatments.

THE LIMITATIONS OF GUIDELINES AND PROTOCOLS

Treatment guidelines, or protocols, are not without criticism and limitations. Unfortunately, many times managed care organizations develop and authorize interventions as if they were standards instead of guidelines or options. Practice policies, such as those formulated by managed care organizations, can be difficult to use because they are developed for groups of clients instead of an individual client (Eddy 1990). As such, a preferred practice approach by a managed care organization may fail to take into consideration the subtle but critical difference of a particular client in contrast to the group of clients with similar clinical problems. This is especially so with clients from diverse populations. When the practice guideline imposed by managed care is the same as the clinician's treatment plan, then services are being duplicated—precisely the waste that managed care is attempting to eliminate.

There are additional limitations (Eddy 1990). First, there is a risk of an increase in the number of mistakes that are made because a protocol is designed for many clients, while treatment is an individualized intervention between one client and one clinician. When the preferred practice is incorrect or inaccurate, the harm to an individual may be huge.

Second, because the procedures are designed for groups of clients instead of an individual, they may not fit the client's problem or treatment goal. This uncertainty also increases the likelihood of error in the application of the treatment procedures.

Third, preferred practice may fail to consider variability among clients, even with clients who represent homogeneous groups. For example, young, Anglo, male alcoholics are not all alike, and they necessitate some differences in their treatment. The inevitable differences between clients, as well as between treatment settings, may limit the appropriateness of some aspects of a developed preferred practice.

These three limitations, and there are no doubt more, suggest that clinicians must actively maintain control over the development of the specific treatment plan for each client, even if it requires argument with a managed care organization. The responsibility—and liability—for the treatment remains with the clinician.

Consequently, as Eddy (1990) argues, there is a need for flexibility by policymakers in determining what is considered the best practice, with the treatment determined collaboratively with the clinician. Clinicians need to be flexible as well; they may need to tailor the authorized intervention to fit the subtleties of the client's problem and treatment goal.

Because of these potential problems, we suggest establishing the treatment goal prior to contacting the managed care reviewer. Any protocol will need to address this goal, and the clinician is in a position to adapt the recommended one with a protocol that fits the client's circumstance.

Additionally, some practice guidelines are limited in their current form because of a lack of convincing empirical evidence. Many are limited in their generalizability from the research group to the diverse population or to a particular client. They are frequently disregarded as "mechanistic" or "cookbook therapy," which further threatens the clinician's judgment. Consequently, there is a real need to modify the preferred practice to fit the tailored needs of individual clients. As Kiser and associates (1991) illustrate, treatment protocols can be developed by a treatment team in such a fashion as to include the theoretical proclivity of a clinic, program, or practitioner. The result is a higher probability that all clients with similar needs get similar interventions. Treatment protocols contribute to clinicians' ability to provide quality care while allowing the evaluation of whether the treatment was delivered in the established manner. In other words, protocols help facilitate managed care's goal of ensuring quality of care.

CONCLUSION

The second step in managed care cost containment and quality assurance goals, the preauthorization of interventions that are more likely than others to result in the desired change, may occur in a team meeting prior to channeling a client toward a particular clinician, as would be the case for enrolled members in capitated managed care. Alternatively, it may result from an interview or a form to complete in advance of treatment authorization.

The inevitable outcome of this process is an intervention that is likely to be goal oriented and include treatment components that are known to be effective plus some systematic procedure for implementing the intervention. These structured interventions must be developed from the perspective of each client's life circumstances and tailor-made to fit his or her needs. They must not become rigid steps to follow in a cookbook approach to clinical services. They must be derived from and guided by professional judgment and practice experience. Without these critical elements, the effectiveness of preauthorized interventions will likely diminish.

Chapter 6

Concurrent and Retrospective Utilization Reviews

Evidencing Treatment Outcomes

So far we have considered managed care in advance of treatment. This aspect of managed care attempts to fulfill the goals of cost containment and quality assurance by making certain that only those clients in need of services receive them and that only relatively efficacious services are provided. Both of these functions are frequently fulfilled with some form of prospective utilization review, regardless of whether the care is managed by a capitated program or an independent organization. We will now consider managed care's use of concurrent utilization reviews—the evaluation of the quality of ongoing treatment, often with the purpose of authorizing the continuation of services—and retrospective utilization reviews—the evaluation of services that have been provided in order to determine if they were sufficient to warrant reimbursement.

Much of what accountability in concurrent and retrospective utilization reviews demands is facilitated by the practice evaluation model of single system research. Practice evaluation provides useful clinical tools to collect quantitative information about client change, primarily in the form of observing changes in the client's problems and progress toward attaining the treatment goals. We will demonstrate these skills through the three rudiments of practice evaluation: (1) operational definitions of the client's problem and goals (much as with prospective utilization reviews, (2) assessing change over time, and (3) interpreting the observations of a client's performance in a clear and convincing manner.

RETROSPECTIVE COST CONTAINMENT

So far much of the discussion of cost containment and quality assurance has been conducted as if they were separate concerns. In fact, they are not. Cost containment and quality assurance are dependent on each other, and that dependency is nowhere more apparent than with retrospective utilization reviews and reimbursement. Costs are contained by refusing to pay for treatment that is not of an acceptable quality.

The quality of services is evaluated in terms of the product of treatment and the process of implementing the treatment—that is, the actual implementation of the intervention and its impact on the client. The questions asked by a managed care program are: "Was the treatment implemented in an acceptable manner?" "Did the acceptably implemented intervention produce the expected outcome?"

Some managed care programs use the answer to the first question as a threshold test: if the treatment was implemented correctly and with acceptable procedures, the practitioner will be paid for the services. Other managed care programs treat the implementation and outcome together, with the degree of adequately implemented interventions and successful outcomes determining a differential amount of reimbursement.

This interaction approach of adequate implementation and outcomes guides decisions about the amount of reimbursement. When the treatment is implemented in the manner that is expected by all the parties involved (the managed care program, the practitioner, and the client), the practitioner can anticipate full payment for the services. (And remember that this fee has probably already been reduced.) Most managed care programs willingly pay for well-done treatment with the desired outcome (Patterson 1990).

Similarly, the reasonable managed care program is aware that not all clients are alike and that not all clients are going to change as hoped. Thus, a practitioner who evidences an adequately implemented treatment but less than expected client outcome will not necessarily be denied reimbursement. As suggested by the example in figure 6.1, the managed care program and practitioner may have an agreement that in such circumstances the practitioner will be reimbursed at a rate less than 100 percent—perhaps 75 percent of the total costs of services.

The problem occurs when the intervention is not adequately implemented. One approach—the threshold approach—is to refuse to reimburse the practitioner for those services. This means that if the intervention was not implemented as agreed upon during the pretreatment authorization, the clinician receives no reimbursement from the third-party payor. Another approach is to reimburse at a rate less than would have occurred if the treatment had been adequately implemented. As the example in figure 6.1 illustrates, less than adequately implemented interventions may be reimbursed at 50 percent or 25 percent of the regular (albeit reduced) fee. As the reimbursement rates in the figure suggest, managed care programs value the well-performed intervention probably as much as the actual client outcome. After all, the reimbursement is for a particular service, which itself is no guarantee that the client will change. If the service is less than adequately delivered but the outcome appears to be positive, the intervention alone most likely was not the reason for the change. Consequently, some managed care programs would refuse to reimburse at the full amount, with the justification of paying the therapist for what he or she did and not for other, unknown influences.

Similarly, a reduced level of reimbursement—perhaps to the point of none at all—would be forthcoming if the intervention was not acceptably implemented and the outcome less than expected or negative. Some managed care programs recommend denying reimbursement in this situation as a cost-containment and quality assurance practice. Certainly few of us want to pay for something that we think is of poor quality and fails to accomplish the desired outcome. Other managed care programs use the assessment scheme of the interaction of quality assur-

Figure 6.1   Outcome-based Reimbursement Rates

Outcome		Unacceptable	Acceptable
	Positive	50 percent	100 percent
	Negative	25 percent	75 percent

Adequacy of Implementation

ance with cost containment with ranges of reimbursements, such as 0 to 25 percent for inadequately implemented treatment with negative or unexpected results or 50 to 75 percent reimbursement for an adequately implemented intervention with a negative or unexpected outcome.

There is some appeal to the ranges of reimbursement. However, like even dichotomous decision making (that is, adequate or inadequate implementation), this judgment is based on how well the practitioner can show evidence of the process and product of treatment. Stated differently, even if a clinician does a good job of implementing an intervention and obtaining the desired outcome but is unable to articulate it to a managed care organization, in all likelihood he or she will not be paid the expected or desired amount.

Under the managed care program reimbursement schedule illustrated in figure 6.1, or any other method to control costs by restricting reimbursement, the demonstration of quality is integral to cost containment or getting reimbursed for services provided. It is one of the ways to find the cheese at the end of the managed care maze.

WHEN REIMBURSEMENT IS DENIED OR REDUCED

When reimbursement is denied or reduced due to the lack of evidence of the adequacy of implementation or successful outcome, the clinician is left with a question of what to do about the expected fee for services. There seem to be at least three alternatives in this situation.

One is to quarrel with the managed care reviewer about the adequacy of the intervention, the quality of the outcome, and the reasonable expectation of reimbursement. We recommend this as the first measure and in fact we think the material in this book—if followed correctly—should help in this situation. Moreover, since a duty to advocate is emerging as a result of managed care, clinicians should be fairly comfortable with negotiating appeals.

Second, a clinician may accept the lost payment, become disgruntled with managed care in general and the particular managed care program, and possibly attempt to avoid doing business with the organization ever again. This alternative is not very appealing. Aside from the emotional sentiment, the refusal to do business may have an adverse effect on the clinician's practice. The managed care contract may guarantee a certain number of cases or include a noncompete clause that restricts practice for a limited length of time and in a particular geographic area. Moreover, walking away from managed care contractual obligations may be legally impossible. On the other hand, no clinician should expect pecuniary losses along with the added burden of managed care's reduced fees. The frustration thereby engendered is adverse to quality client care and defeats one of the very purposes of managed care—quality assurance. And finally, if a clinician avoids managed care clients altogether, the system loses the services of a sound practitioner. To bite the bullet is an alternative with high costs and few benefits.

The third alternative is to hold the client responsible for the cost of the treatment. This option is the least acceptable alternative and the one with the greatest potential liability. In some states, this option may be unlawful according to consumer protection laws. Consider how the scenario appears to an objective, neutral observer who is outside the treatment relationship, such as a plaintiff's attorney, a judge, or possibly even a jury. Here is a professional in a trust relationship (in legal terms, a fiduciary relationship; Kutchins, 1991) who has contracted with a managed care program regarding evaluations of treatment procedures and reimbursement rates. The practitioner, not the client, negotiated and accepted the terms and conditions of the managed care contract. The fourth-party evaluator is no agent of the client but one with whom the practitioner has had a meeting of minds about who will eventually evaluate the quality of care and determine if the level of quality of care is or is not sufficient to warrant payment. In simple terms, the service was not worth the cost from the perspective of the fourth party with whom the clinician agreed to allow to determine the quality of care. Now the practitioner hands the bill to the client to pay. This was not the agreement at the beginning of treatment (the only point at which informed consent is legally permissible). Moreover, the determination of quality insufficient for reimbursement was made by a set of external standards agreed to by the practitioner.

To attempt to get around the financial loss of income by charging the client may be a current customary practice, but at a minimum it is without informed consent. It is also passing the cost on to a consumer after the practitioner knows it is of questionable quality, and of questionable quality by an organization the practitioner agreed to allow to assess the quality. Unquestionably, this situation gives rise to issues of consumer protection laws in many states and possibly fraud in the common law. All of the eventual legal wrestling may be reinforced with the original quality assurance review material, which may be considered evidence that the treatment was below the standard of care, that is, proof of negligence and malpractice.

This practice of charging the client after the fact also gives rise to ethical questions within a profession's standards. In social work, for example, one of the codes of ethics concerns reasonable fees, which would be questioned if the intervention was seen as of poor quality. There is nothing reasonable about charging a fee for a service that is not at the level of quality everyone expected.

For these reasons—consumer protection laws, malpractice, and professional ethics—the alternative of holding the client responsible for treatment where reimbursement is denied or reduced seems an unwise decision. We recommend that practitioners avoid attempting to have clients pay for the treatment when a managed care program has reduced the reimbursement or denied it.

Consequently, the practitioner whose treatment is not reimbursed is at least in a position to quarrel with the managed care program for payment, but sometimes may be faced with accepting the lose of income and dealing with his or her resentment about managed mental health care. Alternatively, there is also the perspective of doing a satisfactory job of evidencing adequately implemented interventions and successful outcomes prior to the potential problem of a reimbursement dispute in the first place. This, of course, is our recommendation, and we hope this book will prove helpful in maneuvering this maze.

In summary, both concurrent utilization reviews and retrospective utilization reviews address the dual purpose of cost containment and quality assurance by limiting payment for services that were not accurately implemented. When care has been delivered at an insufficient level, no one is pleased. The provider may stand to lose time and money. The client may become frustrated with the insurance carrier. And the difficulty is also borne by the managed care reviewer or benefits manager who must explain to both the client and the clinician that the quality of care was below its expected level, even if the client reports and the clinician concurs that the client is doing better. This aggravation affects the pecuniary relationship of all three and may seriously undermine the relationship between clinician and client, who may begin to wonder how helpful the clinician truly was if the managed care company has questioned his or her effectiveness.

Because of these difficulties, many managed care organizations have moved away from only retrospective utilization reviews to using all three review processes—prospective, concurrent, and retrospective—to provide a much more coordinated and thorough managed care process. The combination of these three utilization procedures is also seen as a more effective way to conclude treatment successfully. Some managed care companies have also decided to use shorter time intervals for concurrent utilization review before evaluating the quality of care. This is done in order to revise necessary treatment plans, to reduce the potential financial loss to all involved, and to avoid some of the conflicts with clients and providers. For example, treatment may be evaluated after every three sessions, with authorization and payment discontinuing if the process or outcome is not at a sufficient level of quality. Any adjustments in treatment may be made at that time to help ensure quality.

We believe that more and more managed care organizations will move toward using prospective, concurrent, and retrospective utilization review procedures and shorten the interval between reviews. This means, of course, that providers can expect an increasing involvement of managed care throughout the treatment process and thus must develop efficient tools in order to bear the burden of managed care.

BENEFITS OF CONCURRENT UTILIZATION REVIEWS

In many respects, what is expected for concurrent and retrospective utilization review is simply a continuation of the expressed managed care purposes of containing costs and ensuring quality. The distinction between these two types of review is not always that clear. Both procedures are fairly similar and take on a variety of overlapping formats, from standardized forms, to telephone interviews, to in-depth-reviews of the clinical records. For example, with concurrent utilization reviews, some or most of the treatment has occurred, and the request may be for just a few more sessions in order to finish some critical work or goal attainment. This same period may be used by a managed care reviewer to fine-tune the intervention. A homework assignment might be added or a technique discontinued based on the client's progress. In contrast, utilization reviews of persons with chronic mental conditions may be made to determine the effectiveness of continuous, long-term treatment. In this respect, the concurrent utilization review is very much like a prospective utilization review in that the continued need for treatment is assessed and a new course of treatment may be structured. With retrospective utilization review, all treatment has occurred, and the evaluation of the quality of care is in advance of payment. Additionally, concurrent utilization reviews and retrospective utilization reviews are similar in that the managed care organization is simply trying to determine whether the standard of care and outcomes of treatment are at an acceptable level. This determination may be made for some or all of treatment.

Concurrent utilization reviews have certain advantages that are not afforded to retrospective utilization reviews. They are used to assess four elements of quality of care: (1) justification of those services initially authorized; (2) the continued appropriateness of the service plans being provided; (3) the accuracy of the clinician in implementing the approved treatment plan; and (4) the client's progress toward attaining the measurable goal (APA 1992). Much like prospective utilization reviews, the guiding principle of a concurrent utilization review is to determine why a continuation of services is necessary. Moreover, the assessment of these elements (especially the continued appropriateness of the service and the clinician's accuracy of implementation) enables the managed care organization and the clinician to adjust the intervention if it is no longer appropriate for the problem or if it should be implemented differently.

These advantages do not accrue to retrospective utilization review since treatment has already occurred. The retrospective utilization review is essentially the final evaluation of the quality of the services provided. It is similar to the prospective and concurrent utilization reviews in that it contains the same elements of justification, appropriateness, accuracy of implementation, and client progress. Since treatment has already occurred, there is little opportunity for corrective feedback.

REVIEW PROCEDURES

Managed care organizations differ widely in how they assess the quality of care. Some continue to rely on telephone interviews. Some even review a client's entire record. Most, though, continue to rely on some standardized form completed by the clinician.

Typical examples of concurrent and retrospective utilization review forms are presented in appendixes F and G. Like the prospective utilization review form, some of the content relates to identifying information about the client and your credentials as a clinician. Figure 6.2 reflects those aspects of the concurrent utilization review used to assess the quality of care provided to date and the need for a continuation of services. Figure 6.3 reflects those components of a retrospective utilization review used to assess the quality of services that have been provided.

Like the prospective utilization review, the concurrent utilization review form continues to reflect a problem-oriented focus. Items A11(a)–(c), as displayed in appendix F, are particularly important if the services are to continue, because most managed care reviewers expect some difference. That is, it should be made apparent that the client's condition is not the same as it was when treatment was originally authorized. If the problems and the symptoms have not changed, most managed care reviewers may well ask, "If things haven't gotten any better, why will more of the same make a difference?" or, "If you were not able to accomplish what you set out to do, what will enable you to succeed this time?"

These are difficult questions to answer, especially when a client regresses or gets worse, or a new problem develops. When the client's condition has deteriorated, the clinician should provide a written explanation as part of the concurrent utilization review, even it is only a brief one. The explanation may note the emergence of a new psychosocial stressor or other circumstance that exacerbates the problem. These circumstances may require a letter of explanation that goes beyond the space limitation of most concurrent utilization review forms.

In general, the level of scrutiny is slightly more stringent for a concurrent utilization review than for a prospective utilization review because the managed care organization may have reservations about routinely offering more of the same services in the absence of noticeable progress. It may question why the clinician was unable to complete the treatment successfully as planned or inquire why more of the same treatment is warranted in the event of the client's deterioration.

Consequently, clinicians need to give considerable attention to items A12(a) through 12(c) and item C8 which in general assesses the client's presenting problem and what progress is still required. Item C8 is particularly important because it will be necessary to indicate what

Figure 6.2   Unique Features of Concurrent Utilization Review

---

Client's presenting problems:

(a) 1 _____

(b) 2 _____

(c) 3 _____

What was the date of onset of each presenting problem?
(a) Problem 1: _____ (b) Problem 2: _____ (c) Problem 3: _____

Please identify current symptoms observed for each problem for which you are requesting authorization of services:

(a) Problem 1: _____

_____.

(b) Problem 2: _____

_____.

(c) Problem 3: _____

_____.

Contrast the client's current functioning in each of the following areas with his/her functioning at intake.

(a) Psychological: _____

_____.

(b) Social: _____

_____.

(c) Occupational/educational: _____

_____.

How did you assess the client's problems, symptoms, and functioning?

_____

_____

_____.

Please provide the following DSM diagnoses:

(a) Axis I: _____

(b) Axis II: _____

(c) Axis III: _____

(d) Axis IV: _____

     Stressors: _____

(e) Axis V: (GAF) _____

Description of Treatment to Be Continued

Summary statement of the presenting problem for which you are requesting a continuation of treatment:

_____

What was the short-term goal of treatment? That is, objectively define what you hope to achieve if further treatment is authorized.

_____

_____

Please describe the additional treatment plan you will use to reach the short-term goal, including the specific steps you will follow in implementing it.

_____

_____

How did you determine (i.e., assess/evaluate or monitor) the client's success so far in reaching this short-term goal?

_____

What was the long-term goal of treatment? That is, objectively define what you hope to achieve if further streatment is authorized.

_____

Please describe the additional treatment plan you will use to reach the long-term goal, including the specific steps you will follow in implementing it.

_____

_____

continued

How did you determine (i.e., assess/evaluate or monitor) the client's success so far in reaching this long-term goal?

_____

What progress is still required to warrant continuation of services?

_____.

What is the prognosis?_____.

How many additional sessions are you requesting? _____

How many minutes will each session last?   _____

Were outside services provided? ____Yes ____No

    (a) If yes, what services?   _____

    _____.

    (b) Who provided these services? _____

    _____.

    (c) When did these services begin and end?_____

    _____.

Will more outside services be provided? ____Yes ____No

    (a) If yes, what services?   _____

    _____.

    (b) Who will provide these services?_____

    _____.

    (c) When will these services begin and end?   _____

    _____.

_____

will be accomplished in a relatively limited number of sessions. If anticipated progress is not persuasively argued, it is probable that additional sessions or different services will not be authorized.

It is also important to give serious consideration to any realistic dif-

Figure 6.3 Unique Features of Retrospective Utilization Review Form

---

Client's presenting problems during the course of treatment:

(a) 1 _____

(b) 2 _____

(4) 3 _____

What was the date of onset of each presenting problem?
(a) Problem 1: _____ (b) Problem 2: _____ (c)Problem 3: _____

Please identify the symptoms observed for each problem you are requesting authorization of payment for services:

(a) Problem 1:_____

_____.

(b) Problem 2:_____

_____.

(c) Problem 3:_____

_____.

Contrast the client's current functioning in each of the following areas with his/her functioning at intake:

(a) Psychological: _____

_____.

(b) Social: _____

_____.

(c) Occupational/educational: _____

_____.

How did you assess the client's problems, symptoms, and functioning?

_____

_____

_____.

continued

Please provide the following DSM diagnoses:

(a) Axis I: _____

(b) Axis II: _____

(c) Axis III: _____

(d) Axis IV: _____

Stressors: _____

(e) Axis V: (GAF) _____

Type of Treatment Provided
Summary statement of the presenting problem for which you provided clinical services:

_____.

What was the short-term goal of treatment? That is, objectively define what you had intended to achieve in treatment.

_____

Please describe the treatment plan you used to reach the short-term goal, including the specific steps you will follow.

_____

How did you determine (i.e., assess/evaluate or monitor) the client's success in reaching this short-term goal?

_____

What was the long-term goal of treatment? That is, objectively define what you had intended to achieve in treatment.

_____

Please describe the treatment plan you used to reach the long-term goal, including the specific steps you will follow.

_____

How did you determine (i.e., assess/evaluate or monitor) the client's success in reaching this long-term goal?

_____

Why was treatment necessary?_____

What was the prognosis? _____.

For how many sessions are you requesting payment? _____

How many minutes did each session last? _____

Were outside services provided? _____Yes _____No

    (a) If yes, what services? _____

    _____.

    (b) Who provided these services? _____

    _____.

    (c) When did these services begin and end?_____

    _____.

---

ference in short- and long-term goals. At a minimum, it will be important for the provider to refine the goals in terms of feasibility or relevance. A completely new and different goal may be necessary. In these cases we suggest determining in advance whether the managed care organization expects a new and different prospective utilization review instead of a concurrent utilization review. Many do, and will require the additional documentation before authorizing the requested sessions.

As for retrospective utilization reviews, the general expectation of managed care is that the intervention was successfully implemented, the client's problem has ameliorated, and the treatment goal has been attained. These issues are assessed by the retrospective utilization review; the items unique to this purpose are displayed in figure 6.3.

METHODS FOR EVIDENCING CHANGE

The retrospective utilization review and much of the concurrent utilization review seek to evaluate the quality of care that has occurred but has yet to be reimbursed. The critical issue here is to illustrate that the intervention has been at a high level of quality and that the client has improved and reached the goal of treatment.

The task of evidencing change is a relatively straightforward process and has been greatly facilitated by advances in practice evaluation, the single-case research methodology of documenting the course and outcome of treatment (Gingerich 1990). It is part of the current emphasis on accountability in practice through research techniques, which academicians in social work and psychology, in particular, have long argued for (Barlow, Hayes, and Nelson 1984; Jayaratne and Levy 1979).

Single case designs, also known as single system designs, have grown dramatically over the past two decades. Single case research has progressed from research techniques of questionable respectability used primarily by behaviorists to a variety of practical tools available to evaluate the course and outcome of treatment. Single case research designs basically organize the presence and absence of treatment to enable comparison of a client's performance during these periods. For example, is the client doing better, worse, or about same? Because some of these research designs are more rigorous than others, empirical clinical practice has emerged as a way to integrate research and practice (Briar 1973; Jayaratne and Levy 1979).

These same rigorous designs that allow for a meaningful discussion of integrating practice and research have greatly improved the reasonable conclusion that a particular intervention leads to a client's change. That is, they have increased the validity of asserting causal statements of clinician effectiveness with clients (Bloom, Fischer, and Orme 1995). Asserting causality has also been furthered by the development of psychometrically sound assessment tools and statistical procedures that have improved the accuracy of what was observed and inferences about how it occurred.

Because of the rigor that enabled the integration of research and practice, many questioned the feasibility of routine use by most practitioners (Rukdeschel and Farris 1981). Some contend that the logical positivism of science is incompatible with practice (Piêper-Hieman 1987; Witkins 1991). At a less extreme position, Thomas (1978) has asserted that the purpose of research, to develop knowledge by means of experimental controls, is less useful in practice settings where the purpose is to facilitate clients' change. Similarly, single case methodologies are appropriate for studying isolated and restricted aspects of treatment but may fail to consider the broad range of the complexity of social services or clinical services (Kagle 1982).

The routine use of single case procedures has not been forthcoming, in part because the single case design tools are fairly incompatible with the job of seeing clients day in and day out. Some of the impediments to routine use by practitioners were first addressed by Levy (1981), who discussed limits on the clinician's time. This illustration of an impediment is made even more meaningful in the context of managed mental health care. It is not uncommon for an HMO or an EAP to schedule eight 45-minute sessions with 15 minutes between each for paperwork over the course of a workday. Taking time to conduct a single case evaluation (including administering, scoring, and interpreting and graphing scores) may not be feasible. And there are other barriers to using single case research techniques in practice. Gingerich (1984) and Mutschler (1984) discuss the difficulty of getting clients and agencies to cooperate with the process, including completing assessment tools. In the light of the limited time between clients in some programs, there is less time to waste and less room for error.

These impediments to incorporating single case procedures into routine practice have not been very persuasive to academicians and empirically minded practitioners, who have responded to the majority of the barriers to routine use and adapted single case designs for routine use in practice (Corcoran 1985; Nelsen 1981, 1993). Few practitioners use the entire array of techniques in the research process, but many find certain tools quite useful (Blyth 1983; Gingerich 1984; Welch 1983).

Most practitioners in a managed care setting will find aspects of single case methods valuable for the purpose of developing objective indicators of client problems and treatment goals and for monitoring the process of treatment. Along with specified and clearly defined interventions, much of what is expected from managed care may be facilitated by single case methodologies (Osman and Shueman 1988).

THE PRACTICE EVALUATION MODEL

The use of those single case methods that seem best suited for routine practice, whether managed by a fourth party or not, has been conceptualized in the practice evaluation model (Gingerich 1990). This model of single case research is worthwhile to practitioners because it produces little interference into routine activities. More important, it will help determine how the client is changing.

Practice evaluation conceptualizes three phases of the single case research process that correspond to treatment: (1) the specification of target behaviors to be changed and identification of realistic goals; (2) the development of practical ways to observe change systematically and repeatedly; and (3) a meaningful way of organizing the observations in order to inform the practitioner, the client, and a managed care reviewer.

Much of what we have already advocated in response to managed care preauthorization review is an integral part of practice evaluation. Establishing treatment necessity with standardized assessment instruments is an example of setting up an observation system that can be used systematically over the course of treatment. This is also the case for goals established in response to prospective utilization reviews. We will now show how to use these skills, and other ones, to meet the needs of concurrent and retrospective utilization review. The research tools that are necessary for practice evaluation are designs, observation systems, and interpretation.

Designing the Treatment Process

Much of what is demanded by managed care is observation of change over time, including goal attainment. The field of measurement, known as psychometrics (Nunnally and Bernstein 1994), is the use of a number to understand the frequency or intensity of duration of the client problem, goal, or some other relevant variable. This information is simply a scientific method to be used in conjunction with—*not* a substitute for—intuition, clinical judgment, or practice wisdom (Jordon and Franklin 1995). A clinical measurement tool to describe either the client problem or the treatment goal is essential for providing feedback to all parties. Measurement tools must be reliable and valid, which means they must consistently and accurately assess some attribute (Fischer and Corcoran 1994a). By using measurement of a problem or goal, a practitioner can be precise in definition and better able to communicate about the course of treatment to a managed care reviewer. This communication is enhanced with four types of clinical measurement tools: goal attainment scaling, rapid assessment instruments, individualized rating scales, and the general assessment of functioning.

Goal Attainment Scaling. Goal attainment serves to establish some structure to treatment and may be an index of change and treatment outcome. By using goal attainment procedures, and the scoring procedures in particular, the provider may monitor goal attainment periodically throughout treatment. The client's performance is observed and recorded in the appropriate space on the GAS form shown in figure 5.2. Clinician and client now have some information on potential change to discuss over the course of treatment. Because the GAS requires some time and effort, we suggest monitoring goal attainment two or three times during treatment, at the end, and as a follow-up assessment. (Additional useful suggestions are provided in Kiresuk, Smith, and Cardillo 1994)

Most likely, higher client compliance will be achieved when the task is part of a series of homework assignments. Homework assignments are designed to facilitate the goal attainment and the generalization of the treatment effects to environments outside the clinical setting. Making GAS monitoring an integral part of the treatment process may also contribute to effectiveness (Kiresuk, Smith, and Cardillo 1994; Shelton and Levy 1981).

The GAS also provides convincing evidence of client change to submit to a managed care organization. This use of it offers two convincing sources of interpretation. First, the clinician can address the progress over the course of treatment and look for general trends, such as a gradual trend toward achieving the goal. Alternatively, there might be sudden evidence of goal attainment or performance greater than expected. Second, GAS scores provide observations of the final outcome of treatment with assessment at termination at some follow-up period (say, about ten to twelve weeks later). As a final outcome, scores are not necessarily compared to each other but judged in terms of whether the client seems to have reached his or her goal. That is, they measure whether the purpose of treatment was accomplished.

GAS observations are valuable therapeutic information to discuss with the client throughout treatment, especially as part of the termination. And they serve the purpose of providing convincing data for a managed care organization. Moreover, clinicians who routinely gather this information eventually will have a sufficiently large set of observations to inform their practice. They will have empirical information on what treatment seems most likely to result in reaching what types of goals or is successful with particular types of clients or presenting problems.

Rapid Assessment Instruments. Another way to observe client change over the course of treatment is with rapid assessment tools. As a monitoring device, the same rapid assessment instrument that persuasively evidenced the need for treatment is a propitious way of showing successful treatment as scores that reflect a lower frequency, duration, or magnitude of a problem. Scores of this nature would indicate that treatment was successful and is no longer necessary.

Rapid assessment instruments are particularly suited for monitoring practice for the purpose of quality assurance. The standardized instruments are client-administered self-reports of the problem. They are relatively short and may have refined subscales that take little time for the client to complete. These assessment tools are easily and quickly scored and may be useful feedback for the client as well as the provider and a managed care organization. There are a number of other advantages— and disadvantages—to using rapid assessment instruments (Fischer and Corcoran 1994b).

Managed care's emphasis on observing change resulting from specified interventions is a strong incentive to use rapid assessment instruments. Perhaps obtaining a particular score on them had been determined as an index of the treatment goal. In this respect, a rapid assessment instrument may be beneficial as an indicator of progress toward or achievement of the treatment goal.

Say that you are treating an adolescent with bulimia. Several rapid assessment instruments are available for this problem (see appendix D). You might find that the use of the bulimia test (Thelen et al. 1991) is helpful in establishing the need for treatment by showing that the client's score is similar to a clinical sample or significantly higher than is found in the general population. As a tool for monitoring the problem over the course of treatment, this rapid assessment instrument may be administered at the middle and end of treatment, or at intervals required for concurrent utilization reviews. You might instead have set the goal of having your client score within a certain number of points of the mean score for the general population.

Alternatively, you might need to monitor the client's problem more frequently—maybe weekly. A different rapid assessment instrument might then be necessary, such as the Eating Questionnaire (Williamson et al. 1989). It is better, however, to use the same instrument throughout the course of treatment in order to facilitate cooperation from the client and produce less confusion for the managed care reviewer. Clearly you should be familiar with various rapid assessment instruments and select them carefully.

Rapid assessment instruments can also play a valuable role in concurrent and retrospective utilization review as one means of addressing quality assurance. This is ascertained with items of the utilization review forms displayed in figures 6.2 and 6.3. Items numbered A12(a)–(c), C4, C7 in the appendix may be assessed by a rapid assessment instrument which taps the particular construct domain.

Even if a rapid assessment instrument was not used during a prospective utilization review to establish treatment necessity, it may be worthwhile in concurrent and retrospective utilization reviews. In fact, the most common use of these instruments is as an objective indicator of the client problem at various times throughout the course of treatment. Since clinician, client, and the managed care company are all concerned with change, rapid assessment instruments often afford strong evidence of change in the frequency, intensity, or duration of a problem.

Even short rapid assessment instruments are somewhat time-consuming to complete, score, and interpret. Consequently, Gingerich (1990) recommends considering the rapid assessment instrument as a social validation of progress in treatment that should be used judiciously. It may not be needed more than at the beginning, middle, and end of treatment and as a follow-up assessment.

We do not necessarily disagree with this limited use of a rapid assessment instrument, but many of them are sufficiently short and amenable to more frequent repeated use. Those listed in appendix D generally have fewer than fifty items, and many have even shorter subscales. For example, the Auditory Hallucination Questionnaire (Hustig and Hafner 1990), which measures psychotic symptomatology, has only nine items. It would be feasible to use it weekly. A similar use of these instruments is available when the instrument is composed of subscales, which can be used to assess some of the nuances of a client's problem. The subscale items can be used alone for truly rapid assessment, completed just before or in the first few moments of a therapy session. This repeated use of a rapid assessment instrument produces scores useful for monitoring progress on a regular basis—perhaps weekly or more often. For example, a client could observe himself or herself daily or a couple of times a day in different settings. This proves very informative for environmentally dependent problems, such as anxiety or interpersonal problems.

We advise, as others have (Hudson 1982), not administering a rapid assessment instrument or any other assessment of a client's problem immediately after the session. To do so tends to inflate scores artificially due to the immediate impact of a good session. Since many clients leave a treatment session feeling better than they did before, scores tend to suggest more improvement than may be valid.

Individualized Rating Scales. Sometimes clinicians need measures that are not readily available. Perhaps they are too expensive, or maybe none is available for the purpose. In this situation, individualized rating scales of the problem or symptom may be developed.

Individualized rating scales enable clinicians to observe a variety of client behaviors, especially those that are covert and observable only by the client. In fact, along with rapid assessment instruments, individualized rating scales are one of the few ways for observing treatment that focus on how a client feels or what he or she thinks. Like rapid assessment instruments, an individualized rating scale may be developed to observe a client's cognition, affect, and action. It can measure these dimensions of human behavior in terms of frequency, intensity, or duration, although it tends to be used primarily to rate the intensity of a problem.

Individualized rating scales are useful for monitoring progress because they are single items on which the client rates a problem, complaint, or goal. These instruments are especially valuable when weekly or daily observations are needed and when used in conjunction with goal attainment scaling and rapid assessment instruments. The flexibility and utility of these scales is so great that they have been called an all-purpose measurement tool (Bloom 1975). Although there are a number of different types of individual rating scales (Bloom, Fischer, and Orme 1995; Fischer and Corcoran 1994), we will discuss two: anchored rating scales used by the client or a relevant other and the target complaint scale.

Anchored rating scales provide a quantitative index of a client's thinking, feeling, or action by rating performance on a continuum that is anchored with descriptions of what is being rated. The descriptions must be written in clear and concise terms that are observable to the client (Corcoran and Gingerich 1992). Two examples of anchored rating scales are illustrated in figure 6.4 for a client whose presenting problem is depression.

Anchored rating scales are fairly easy to develop. Appendix I contains a work sheet to facilitate their development.

Let us illustrate how you would develop an anchored rating scale. First, you and your client must have a clear and complete description of what is being rated. Next, you establish a range of scores to correspond to the ratings—perhaps 1 to 5 or 1 to 7, although some authors recommend 1 to 9 or 10 (Bloom, Fischer, and Orme 1995). The range of ratings should be determined by how capable your client is in distinguishing or discriminating the attributes of the behavior to be rated. This, of course, is influenced by the cognitive ability of the client. For example, children may be able to distinguish only three or four attributes of a behavior, necessitating a range of 1 to 3 or 1 to 4.

After you have the range of scores, the next step is to anchor the end points with descriptions of that which is being rated. It is also helpful to develop a couple of descriptions for the middle points of the scale, as is illustrated in figure 6.4. Midpoint descriptions are advantageous because they facilitate the rater's decision making when doing the rating and greatly improve the accuracy of the assessment.

When developing the various anchors, you may need to take the lead in writing the descriptions, especially if your client is very young, not wise about treatment, or has a limited capacity due to the presenting problem. In these circumstances, make certain that your client is actively participating and agrees with the final descriptions, which must be clear, complete, and observable (Corcoran and Gingerich, 1992).

The anchored rating scale is now available for use by the client or a relevant other. It should be used at various times over the course of treatment. The behavior is rated in comparison with the description found on the scale. As a single item index, anchored rating scales can be used frequently. This might include daily ratings, or even more frequent ones if the circumstance warrants, such as for monitoring mood. Such ratings afford valuable data to demonstrate client change for a concurrent or retrospective utilization review.

Figure 6.4   An Anchored Rating Scale for Depression

To what extent do you feel hopeless about your future?

1.	2.	3.	4.	5.
Not at all hopeless: "I feel hopeful about my future. It looks bright."		Feels hopeless about half the time.		Extremely hopeless: I feel hopeless about my future. It looks bleak."

How frequently do you think pessimistic thoughts?

1.	2.	3.	4.	5.
Not at all: "I rarely have negative or self-defeating thoughts."		Has pessimistic thoughts once or twice a week.		All the time: "I almost always think negative or self-defeating thoughts."

A slightly different type of anchored rating scale assesses the target complaint. Sometimes these individualized ratings scales are called target complaint scales (Bloom, Fischer and Orme, 1995; Fischer and Corcoran, 1994a). Target complaint scales are individualized ratings of the client's initial complaint, which is the focus of treatment. The anchors are either the severity of the problem or the degree of improvement. Like the anchored rating scale, the complaint must be written in clear, concise, and observable terms.

Like other individualized rating scales (and let's admit it, they are quite similar), target complaint scales can be used repeatedly and frequently. As a consequence, you and your client have indicators that can provide valuable feedback while treatment is in progress, as well as observations for managed care that evidences quality assurance.

General Assessment of Functioning. So far we have considered measurement primarily in terms of the client problem or treatment goal, with the client completing the assessment. Another observational system that serves the purpose of concurrent and retrospective utilization review is part of the original prospective utilization review: changes in the provider's observation of the client's general functioning.

Observations of client functioning should be made for the concurrent and retrospective utilization reviews and compared to the functioning at intake. Retrospective assessment of the client's highest level of functioning over the twelve months before treatment can be used to compare with the client's current functioning.

Organizing and Interpreting Observations

The second and third elements of the practice evaluation model are the organization of the intervention and procedures for interpreting the observations. These are the research tools of a design and data analysis.

The various ways of organizing an intervention and the observations of the client's scores on clinical measurement tools are different research designs. Research designs are the controls used to format the occurrence and nonoccurrence of treatment and to help the researcher determine what caused a specific outcome. In practice evaluation, designs are the way clinicians organize observations around the period when treatment occurred compared to when it did not in order to see if change has occurred. There are a number of useful research designs, although the most rudimentary ones serve well in demonstrating quality of care.

From the perspective of practice evaluation, the actual course of treatment determines the design. The most elementary view of designs is the comparison of scores over a period when treatment occurs or between periods when treatment occurs compared with when it does not. For example, when treatment is authorized for a certain number of sessions, the design is an *intervention-only design*, also known as a B design, and observations are recorded over the course of treatment (figure 6.5). It is quite limited; also there are more powerful ways to make comparisons of a client's performance, such as when treatment occurred compared with when it did not. For example, scores at intake on the General Assessment of Functioning or a rapid assessment instrument are a reference point for comparing the observations during treatment with a period when there was no treatment. This is known as the baseline, or the A, phase. When they are combined over the course of treatment, the product is a simple AB design. Sometimes a number of observations may be collected before treatment, so it is advisable to collect observations after treatment has ended in order to determine if the client's improvement has endured, deteriorated, or remained the same. Such ob-

Figure 6.5   An Intervention-Only Design

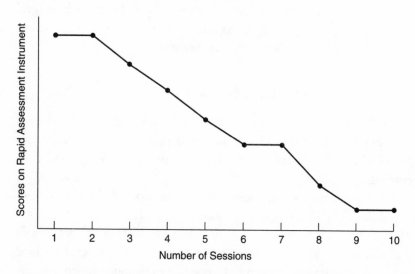

servations now afford a meaningful follow-up of treatment effectiveness, called an AB with follow-up design (figure 6.6). With this research design, observations are collected before, during and after treatment.

Observations collected before treatment begins may be gathered concurrently or retrospectively. Observations that are collected concurrently refer to those that are made at various points from the time of the first observation until treatment begins. These observations are quite

Figure 6.6   A Combination Intervention-Only and Baseline Design, with Follow-up

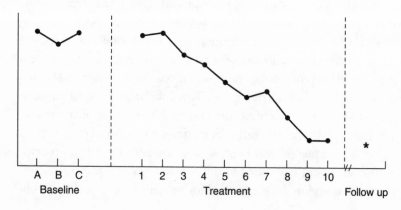

valuable but require that there be some time before treatment begins. The most likely time for these observations is while awaiting authorization of treatment. Of course, treatment may need to begin immediately. Moreover, it is arguable that therapeutic change actually begins with the intake assessment or even before, when the client decided to seek treatment. Because of these circumstances, the clinician may not be able to get more than a single observation or two—not much of a referent against which to compare the client's performance during and after treatment. If for no other reasons, a single observation may not be an accurate indication of the client's problem and may not be stable.

An alternative to collecting baseline observations before treatment begins is to collect this information based on the client's recollection, known as a *retrospective baseline*. The most familiar example of retrospective baseline data is assessment of clients' highest functioning over a twelve-month period.

Similar retrospective observations are available with a little creative use of a rapid assessment instrument or other assessments of the client's problem. It might be collected at the time of the intake, when a client scores a rapid assessment instrument in terms of how he or she was "last week," "last month," and "last year." Alternatively, retrospective baseline data might be gathered by instructing the client to complete the rapid assessment instrument in terms of the "worse" functioning, "general" functioning, and current functioning. These three observations provide a baseline for comparing the client's scores during and after treatment.

As an alternative, retrospective baseline data may be completed after treatment is finished; this is cumbersomely called a *postintervention retrospective baseline* (Howard 1980). Postintervention retrospective baseline data have a number of advantages over such data collected before treatment begins. Chief among these is that the client's self-report is not influenced by the distress that drove him or her to treatment in the first place. In such circumstances, a client may overstate or understate the intensity, frequency, or duration of the problem. Additionally, the client may not be able to observe the problem at the beginning of treatment. A client's problem might be substance abuse, which is noted for denial, or depression, when the client might be too despondent to assess the problem accurately, or just about any other presenting problem characterized by disturbances in judgment and perception.

Because of this, the client may be much more accurate in recollecting performance after treatment is complete than before it has started.

To summarize, we have only considered the most basic of the research designs that are available. The rudimentary designs include either a single intervention-only design, or a design that allows comparison with your client's functioning when there is no treatment. There are either baseline observations (retrospective and concurrent) or follow-up observations. Together these three phases provide you with a method of organizing your observations of prospective, concurrent, and retrospective utilization review to evidence your treatment effectiveness to a managed care organization.

Interpreting Scores

For the purpose of practice evaluation and managed care, the design is primarily a way of organizing the observations for making inferences about the client's change and treatment effectiveness. Much of what managed care expects from utilization reviews is documentation of change over the course of treatment. When used in this way, the observations of the client problem or treatment goal may very well illustrate improvement and goal attainment, or they may indicate failure to reach a goal or deterioration in the client's functioning. Many clients do not respond to even well-done treatment, and this may be the reason for requesting additional services during a concurrent utilization review.

The observations collected must be presented in such a fashion as to allow the clinician, the client, and the managed care reviewer to decide if change has occurred. In other words, the clinician must be able to analyze the data. Much like other research procedures that compare groups, such as an experimental and control group, data are interpreted by comparison. In managed mental health care, these comparisons are for the individual's scores before, during, and after treatment.

Data analysis with single case observations is quite different from other statistics in research, though there are a variety of very robust statistical procedures (Bloom, Fischer, and Orme 1995; Hersen and Barlow 1984; Jayaratne 1978). One of the most immediately available ways of interpreting observations is with visual analysis, although this type of analysis may not detect changes that could be found with various statistical procedures and may be somewhat misleading (Hartman et al. 1980). As Jayaratne (1978) notes, however, clinical significance requires more change than is required for statistical significance.

For practice evaluation in managed mental health care, visual analysis may be crude, but it is sufficient to infer if change has occurred to a clinically meaningful extent and is probably all that will be expected by a managed care organization. To do this type of interpretation, plot the scores from the client's observation system on graph paper, and then partition the graph into each of the phases of treatment: before, during, and after.

Visual analysis is greatly aided by the use of a standardized recording procedure, including computer programs. An example of a standardized pen-and-paper form is the Practice Evaluation Form, which is easily incorporated into routine practice and will provide a way to evidence change for quality assurance (Corcoran 1993; Corcoran and Gingerich 1994). A similar standardized records format useful for utilization reviews is displayed in figure 6.7 and appendix I. To use this form, hold it horizontally so the three boxes are at the bottom of the page. This displays the area for recording a summary of the presenting problem, a general assessment of functioning (GAF), the goal and objective, the treatment protocol, and measurements of the client's problem and treatment goal. A separate form should be used for each problem, goal, and intervention the client is working on.

This form may also be useful for preparing a prospective utilization review. In this case, the prospective utilization portion should be completed prior to contacting the managed care organization. The content should reflect as much of the treatment as possible.

Underneath the area for the critical information is work space for writing a summary of treatment. The lined area corresponds to the cross-sections of the graph, which will be used to record and analyze observations visually. Or the lines can be used to record salient progress notes or notes written exclusively to account for observations recorded in the graph. The beginning of each line is left with spacing to record the date, if appropriate.

The form is particularly useful for managed care because it allows a summary of treatment and a visual plot of observations. To use the graph, rotate the form so the summary information is to the left-hand side. The graph area, now at the top of the page, provides room for up to twenty observations. We have intentionally not numbered this area

Figure 6.7   Case Summary Sheet

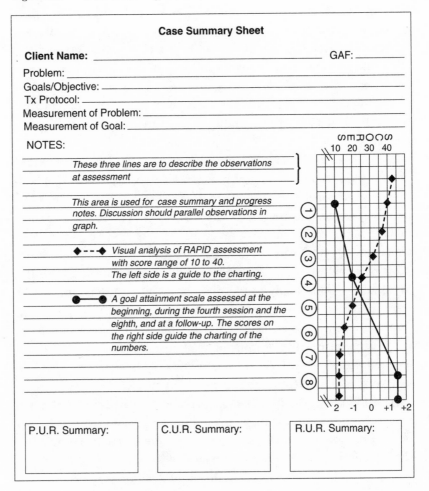

in case you want to use the entire area but do not have twenty observations. That is, you can use the entire area of the graph with only ten observations by numbering every other cross-section. You can decide how much spacing to use in graphing and should do so with the idea of how many lines you will need to record information about the observations.

This graph area is for summarizing the observations of the client's problem or treatment goal. As such, there is a way to use one graph for two different sets of observations—perhaps scores on a rapid assessment instrument and scores on the goal attainment. Use the left-hand margin of the graph for one range of scores, such as scores from 1 to 10 on a rapid assessment instrument, and the right-hand margin for a different range of scores, such as scores from –2 to +2 on a GAS. Plot your observations from left to right to reflect the course of treatment, but what number is represented by each cross-section depends on which observation system is being recorded. In figure 6.7, the left side is used to reflect a rapid assessment instrument with a range of 10 to 40, and the right-hand side is used to set the cross-section for –2 to +2 GAS. The observations were made weekly for an eight-session intervention.

The standardized case summary sheet is a supplement to—not a substitute for—progress notes. As such, it is an advantageous way to see an overview of treatment. It can be submitted to a managed care organization during a concurrent or retrospective utilization review as a summary of efforts to evidence treatment effectiveness. The boxed areas under the lines are available to record the interaction with a managed care organization. Three boxes are provided: one for a prospective utilization review (P.U.R. Summary), one for a concurrent utilization review (C.U.R. Summary), and one for a retrospective utilization review (R.U.R. Summary).

RECORDS REVIEW

Sometimes the managed care organization may demand an in-depth retrospective utilization review, perhaps by examining the client's entire record. Record reviews may be considered necessary for a variety of reasons, but tend to be restricted to very expensive cases (e.g., inpatient hospitalization). They might also be used when there is an unexpected increase in providers' claiming a specific diagnosis, especially if this increase seems to be in response to new rules and regulations about what conditions will be considered necessary for treatment. A records review may be demanded because the information will be used in the managed care organization's supervision of providers. Or it may be considered necessary as part of the overall determination of quality, either of a specific provider or one of a number who are randomly sampled to determine the effectiveness of a population of providers.

This potential exposure to all recorded information behooves clinicians to be judicious about what is included in the client record. We are not suggesting deception or intentional disregard for clinically significant materials, but not everything needs to be written down. For example, if your client smoked marijuana once in college, and possibly did not even inhale, there is probably little reason to include this information in your records if it is not directly relevant to the presenting problem. This type of information may come back to haunt the client personally, professionally, or even in terms of eventual health or life insurance coverage. This information not only might be irrelevant to the case, but frankly none of the managed care organization's business. If you do record it for some reason and the records are requested for review, then you have no way to screen this information from the managed care reviewer.

In preparing for a records review, we recommend that you organize your files in a manner that reflects the structure of the various categories of the utilization review forms used by the managed care facility. This organization is most likely one familiar to the records reviewer and may facilitate that person's understanding of your records. An introductory letter explaining your organization is also suggested. We suggest your records be organized by identifying client information, client treatment history, and treatment, including collateral services, progress notes, and miscellany. The standardized case summary sheet may be the first portion of the records.

CONCLUSIONS

This chapter has focused primarily on what you need to know and do to fulfill the demands of concurrent utilization reviews and retrospective utilization reviews. These two managed care procedures are quite similar because some or all of the treatment has occurred and the managed care organization is interested in determining the quality of that care.

The challenge of concurrent and retrospective utilization reviews is greatly facilitated with single case research designs, in particular the practice evaluation model. Practice evaluation reflects the majority of what is contained in managed care's notions of quality assurance by providing a framework for systematic observations, an organization of the intervention, including observations before, during, and after treatment, and a means of organizing observations to interpret the data visually.

There are, of course, a variety of ways of observing the client problem and treatment goal. We recommend using at least one measure of the client problem and one measure of the treatment goal. This may include many of the tools used earlier during a prospective utilization review in order to establish treatment necessity, as well as individualized rating scales and other rapid assessment instruments.

Finally, the demands of managed care may be facilitated not only with the practice evaluation model but with some standardized method of monitoring each client's progress and treatment goals. Such standardized procedures will not only prove useful for client summaries but are also for organizing records when a records review is mandated.

We would like to suggest you consider providing a standardized case summary form to accompany the concurrent or retrospective utilization review forms. Most managed care organizations are pleased when there are clear and objective definitions of the client's problem, treatment goal, intervention, and observation of change over the course of treatment.

Chapter 7

Culturally Competent Practice in a Managed Care Environment

Increasingly, Anglo-American service providers are finding that their clinic populations are racially and ethnically diverse. Yet many of the available services are perceived as inadequate or inappropriate for the needs of ethnic populations (Dana 1993). This chapter provides an overview of the common barriers that people from differing ethnic communities experience when attempting to use managed mental health services. We will focus on ethnic-specific issues related to the four major multicultural populations in the United States: African Americans, American Indians, Asian Americans and Hispanic Americans. Finally, we offer recommendations about how managed mental health care providers can offer culturally competent services to ethnic minority individuals, their families, and the managed care organization itself. Throughout this chapter we discuss physical health and mental health as one concept. In many ethnic societies, physical health and mental health are viewed as harmonious and interwoven concepts that cannot be categorized as one condition or another as it is in Western health care systems.

Research suggests that the majority of people with mental health needs do not receive services. This suggests that instead of cost containment by restricting coverage, there is a need for targeted populations or ethnic groups to have improved access to services—not less. If

143

managed care is to accomplish these goals, services must be culturally sensitive. Otherwise, clinicians may blame clients for not participating in services that are culturally inappropriate for them. Multicultural persons differ dramatically, one from the other and also within groups, with regard to their country of origin, language, culture, and degree of acculturation to the United States. They also differ in terms of health beliefs, attitudes, symptom expression, utilization of services, distribution of socioeconomic status, and the circumstances under which they came to the United States (e.g., immigrants or refugees seeking political asylum) (Nickens 1995; Shulman et al. 1995).

Because needs, goals, and ideas about mental health vary across and between ethnic communities, managed care organizations cannot count on one program model to fulfill the needs of diverse groups of employees or clients. The diversity of the workforce is a good example. Increasingly, there is an emerging workforce that is nonwhite and female. Between 1985 and 2000, eight out of every ten new entrants to the workforce will have been minorities, immigrants, or women (Motwani, Hodge, and Crampton 1995). Data from the Bureau of Labor Statistics indicate that between 1989 and 2000, 42.8 million people will join the U.S. workforce, but only 32 percent will be white males (Wagner 1991). The actual net growth of the U.S. labor force during that period will be: Hispanic females, 85 percent; Asian females, 83 percent; Hispanic males, 68 percent; Asian males, 61 percent; black females, 33 percent; black males, 24 percent; white females, 22 percent; and white males, 9 percent.

Although individuals with culturally distinct identities exist across many different subgroups in society, differences among dominant and ethnic minority groups have become especially recognized in recent years. Consequently, there is a great need for managed mental health care settings to employ providers who are culturally sensitive and culturally competent in dealing with multiethnic client populations.

As Dana (1993) suggests, cultural sensitivity is a precursor to cultural competence. He defines cultural sensitivity as awareness of another culture based on knowledge and first-hand acquaintance. This awareness is cultivated through professional activities (e.g., internships) and exposure (e.g., participation in ethnic-specific events). Cultural competence is the ability to provide services that are perceived by clients as relevant to their lives and to offer helpful interventions.

Even the concept of ethnic minority is a relative one and is used around the world to designate populations that are racially or ethnically different from the majority (Corin 1994). In this chapter, we will define ethnicity as the collection of group-specific behaviors that are mediated by those shared social values that are characteristic of a given group (Tajfel and Turner 1979).

COMMON BARRIERS

The United States is considered to have one of the most sophisticated and technologically advanced medical care systems in the world, yet it excludes many individuals because of cultural, cognitive, financial, and physical differences (LeClere et al. 1994). Many of the techniques that Western-trained mental health providers employ may be contradictory to the indigenous cultural values and social and family structures of ethnic clients (Ho 1987). These contradictions can be seen as common barriers in the way ethnic clients access and participate in the managed mental health care system. Common barriers that cut across all groups are philosophical, clinical, and organizational.

Philosophical Barriers

Jecker et al. (1995) point out that although all societies possess a concept of mental disorder, conditions that are considered harmful vary with the cultural values or beliefs of the individual and the community. Often the approach employed by mental health providers conflicts with the client's values and the values of the culture with which the client identifies (Jecker et al. 1995). One example can be seen in differing levels of client acculturation. A common barrier for many ethnic peoples, frequently overlooked by Western providers, relates to acculturation, or the ability to adapt to new aspects of cultural learning and behaviors in their environment. As people come into contact with a new culture, they undergo changes in cognitive style (e.g., language proficiency/preference, attitudes, knowledge of culture-specific traditions/customs, stress, and identification preferences), values (e.g., culture-specific value orientation), and socioeconomic status (e.g., including educational level and occupation) (Marin and Van Oss Marin 1991; Olmedo Martinez and Martinez 1978). The process of cultural learning and change is described as including an initial stage of crisis or conflict, followed by acceptance of an adaptation strategy (Berry 1980). Marin and Van Oss Marin (1991) note that the importance of examining acculturation is supported by studies that found that difficulty in acculturating has an impact on mental health, levels of social support, drug and alcohol use, and health behaviors.

Additionally, problems can occur when client and provider do not share a common moral framework or function with similar systems of meaning and modes of interacting (Jecker et al. 1995). Part of this problem rests with the values expressed by dominant white society that have become institutionalized through educational training programs. For example, the United States has an individual model of physical and mental health care that is often explained as one's choice. This model often precludes an examination of the circumstances of ethnic peoples, their family relationships, and the social context of their lives (LeClere 1994).

Through educational and professional training, mental health providers have been taught that their own belief systems or values are an important element in the provider-client relationship, yet they often lack the training and tools to investigate their own value base and the social and cultural values that matter to individuals from differing ethnic communities. Jeckner and colleagues (1994) argue that even textbooks, which often frame issues within Western tradition, omit discussion of relevant and conflicting values held by clients from non-Western cultures.

Clinical Barriers

Most mental health providers would agree that culture is central to the conceptualization, assessment, and diagnosis of mental health conditions (Rogler 1993). One way that cultural differences may become especially striking in psychiatric settings occurs at the time of diagnosis, when underdiagnosis or misdiagnosis may result.

With regard to underdiagnosis, Fuller (1994) reports that a significant barrier to care is the lack of recognition of many mental disorders by primary care physicians. Researchers have reported that many patients with psychiatric illness first present themselves to outpatient medical settings (Mollica et al. 1987). As a consequence, their psychiatric problems are often overlooked in medical settings by clinicians who are unfamiliar with mental health diagnoses and the symptoms of psychiatric disorder (Mollica et al. 1987). For example, missing the diagnosis of alcoholism may result in increased physical disability for the client (e.g., gastrointestinal hemorrhage). Multiple studies have demonstrated that patients with undiagnosed substance abuse and psychotic disorders have markedly increased medical and surgical costs— two to three times that of control groups (Fuller 1994).

Epidemiological data from large community studies found that 76 percent of men and 65 percent of women with the diagnosis of substance abuse or dependence also had an additional psychotic diagnosis (Kaplan, Sadock, and Grebb 1994). Additionally, the most common comorbidity involves two substances of abuse: usually alcohol and the abuse of some other substance. Substance abuse has also been reported to be higher among the unemployed and among some ethnic minority groups than among the employed or majority groups.

The risks associated with underdiagnosing are illustrated as well in the health status of ethnic peoples. For example, Nickens (1995) reports that some ethnic groups have higher death rates attributable to cancer, cardiovascular disease, chemical dependency (measured by death rates due to cirrhosis), diabetes, infant mortality, homicide, and HIV infection than whites. HIV is now the leading killer of Puerto Rican, Cuban, and African-American men and the second leading killer of Anglo-American men. With these kinds of health statistics, we can hardly continue to be conservative in diagnostic approaches.

Along these same lines, let us look at what happens when the pendulum swings in the other direction, to misdiagnosis. There is an ongoing debate in mental health research about the applicability of Western diagnostic criteria to non-Western populations (Feleppa 1986). And although the influx of non-Western immigrants and refugees into the United States has stimulated the development of new symptom checklists, psychological tests, and diagnostic manuals, most instruments have not been culturally validated. Managed mental health care providers are required to use the DSM-IV. With over 300 discrete diagnostic categories, it is no surprise that most mental health providers feel overwhelmed with the implicit responsibility to know it all. The formula becomes even more complex when clients present from ethnic communities and their symptom expression seems outside the range of DSM-IV criteria. The merits and obstacles of the DSM have been eloquently debated elsewhere (Kirk and Kutchins 1992); we will restrict our comments to issues of cultural competence.

Simply defining the criteria for a diagnosis will not make it appropriate or relevant to different client groups. Although some symptoms may be present across cultures, they may not be the symptoms strongly endorsed by the client. For example, Mollica et al. (1992) suggest that although core symptoms of posttraumatic stress disorder—increased arousal/hypervigilance, avoidance of stimuli associated with trauma and recurring dreams—may be universal, these symptoms may not be viewed by the client as distress related to the presenting problem.

Kirmayer (1994) suggests that many problems in other cultures that nosology attempts to construct as discrete disorders are not deviant or disorders but culturally constituted and sanctioned idioms of distress. He suggests that these expressions of distress are vocabularies for explaining and expressing a wide range of problems and cannot be added to any list of discrete entities (like the DSM-IV). For example, agoraphobia is relatively rare in many non-Western societies, but when it does occur (generally in women), it is often not considered a disorder. Many cultures perceive a woman's place to be in the home, and thus there is not the level of tension between the desire to stay home and the culture's expectation. In this case, neither the client nor the family may consider the condition as necessitating treatment (Wakefield 1994). Murphy and Helzer (1990) take this argument further and asks clinicians to consider whether the behavior they are assessing occurs in culturally sanctioned contexts (e.g., healing ceremony) and is confined to a particular occasion (e.g., during the ceremony). If so, then a conventional DSM-IV diagnosis may not be appropriate. For example, Murphy describes how a shamanistic healer was described by another Eskimo as being "out of his mind" in the middle of a seance yet was "not crazy."

Dana (1993) points out the bias in contemporary diagnostic systems and concludes that current diagnostic systems are problematic because of a Eurocentric male bias that conceptualizes social issues as pathological. This is illustrated in the pejorative use of "histrionic personality disorder" to describe angry women. Further, misdiagnosis has serious ramifications for certain ethnic groups. For instance, African Americans continue to be predictably diagnosed as schizophrenics by use of interview data from the Schedule for Affective Disorders and Schizophrenia (SADS) and the Global Assessment Scale (Dana 1993). As Dana

points out, misdiagnosis can affect the choice of treatment recommendation—criminal justice or mental health center—as well as the type of
intervention within the mental health system (medication or therapy).

Although progress has been made in the development of reliable diagnostic criteria, reliability may not equate to validity. Currently, epidemiological and clinical research uses the categorical approach to explain sociocultural factors. This fits comfortably within the scientific
paradigm, which focuses on the individual as the basic unit of society.
Critics of the scientific paradigm argue that it is virtually impossible to
sort out how much of cross-cultural variation is due to differing diagnostic procedures, differing approaches to mental health phenomena,
and different views of reality (Corin 1994).

Organizational Barriers

Ethnic minorities face two critical structural barriers when they attempt to participate in managed mental health care services: access
and staff qualifications.

Access. Access to mental health care has long been recognized as a factor in patient satisfaction, reduced hospital admissions, and increased
quality of life (Lehman, Rachuba & Postrado 1995; Pickett et al.
1995). Despite strong epidemiological data that illustrate the benefits
of access, many managed mental health care strategies have consisted
of discouraging clients from obtaining services through large deductibles, high copayments, and refusing to approve services. This approach may decrease short-term expenditures, but there is no evidence
that it has been effective in decreasing overall health care costs.

LeClere, Jensen, and Biddlecome (1994) cite five reasons that ethnic minorities, particularly immigrants, have difficulty in using the
health and mental health system: limited education, language differences, lack of knowledge of resources, cultural differences in health-
seeking behaviors, and variable socioeconomic status.

Level of education is a predictor variable in how well clients will be
able to incorporate health promotion information. Since a great deal of
the health care system is organized around the assumption of literacy in
English, some ethnic (as well as nonethnic) populations cannot access
health or mental health care services (Nickens 1995). Lower educa-

tional attainment decreases their ability to comprehend written information and instructions from physicians, health care facilities, and third-party payees and pharmacists.

Language and dialect are two related issues that influence ethnic peoples' ability to benefit from mental health services. For example, North American Indians have over 200 distinct languages (Fleming 1992). There are thirty subgroups of Asian–Pacific Island Americans who speak different dialects (e.g., Cantonese, Toishanese, Mandarin, Shangainese, and Taiwanese); (Yen 1992). For some ethnic peoples, adopting the English language has fragmented their first language and introduced semantic bias into their ability to express themselves in the English language. Fleming (1992) describes how native languages have particular terms that express kinship and relationships, yet there is no English equivalent. Adopting English may mean losing the linguistic symbols of culture and gaining new biases in health expression. The variety of languages and dialects within these cultures speaks to the challenge in developing written materials for public health education. Consequently, when developing mental health prevention curricula, the managed care organization will have to consider the native languages of its target population, a challenge greatly increased if the program has only Anglo staff.

Underutilization of managed mental health services is also related to lack of knowledge of existing services. Corin (1994) points out that people in the more fragile communities, such as recent immigrants and the elderly, are often reluctant to use mental health or social services. The reasons vary from feelings of personal shame and social embarrassment to not knowing what services are available and where. When services are used, they tend toward the most expensive one and the least specific: the emergency room (White and Means 1995).

There are also cultural differences in health-seeking behaviors of ethnic peoples that typically involve the use of self-treatment and family members in the treatment process. Westermeyer (1991) points out that self-treatment for psychiatric and medical symptoms with alcohol and other drugs of abuse can occur among immigrants who do not have effective access to health care, including mental health care. Research with Laotian refugee families has found that family members play an important role in how and when their relatives seek formal health and mental health care services (Vandiver et al. 1995). Many immigrant families value total family input and decision making when it comes to participating in the health care system. Not many managed care programs are sensitive to authorizing treatment protocols that include family, kin, elders, or clan members.

LeClere et al. (1994) identified three health-related functions of families of immigrant-refugee clients: (1) financial access to care is usually family based, such that the client may pay for medical care through pooled resources; (2) parents socialize children into particular patterns of health care involvement by demonstrating illness and help-seeking behaviors; and (3) relatives provide information, instrumental aid, and advice, which guides clients' health care decisions. Thus, the mental health provider seeking to coordinate managed mental health care services with an individual of immigrant status will need to be prepared to consult with all levels of kin: nuclear, extended, and adopted. This collective approach will both promote treatment compliance and serve to support the core values of the family system.

A final barrier to accessing services for ethnic peoples is related to economic issues. The socioeconomic status of many ethnic groups has extreme variability. For example, Japanese-Americans and Hmong refugees from Laos, as groups, occupy opposite ends on the economic ladder (Westermeyer 1991). As such, any generalities made about these groups would be inaccurate. However, some ethnic groups are more economically fragile than others. Epidemiological studies suggest that recent immigrants are more likely to be in poverty and face substantial economic barriers to obtaining physical health and mental health care than nonimmigrant populations. They have limited access to publicly funded programs that improve access to health and mental health care (LeClere et al. 1994).

Staff. Agency personnel also influence service utilization by multiethnic clients. One large-scale study of 14,000 clients in seventeen community mental health centers found that multiethnic clients saw more teachers, vocational rehabilitation counselors, and paraprofessionals and fewer psychologists and psychiatrists than did Anglo-American clients. A few of the reasons listed for client termination were attributed to frustrations, misunderstandings, language problems, and differences in priorities of treatment approaches (Sue and Zane 1987).

Managed mental health care organizations cannot overlook the importance of matching multiethnic clients' attributes with providers'. In many cultures, the age, race, sex, ethnicity, and credentials of the provider have a significant impact on the therapeutic relationship and require similarity between the client and the provider.

MANAGED CARE WITH ETHNIC COMMUNITIES

At the risk of oversimplification, this section reviews four ethnic–racial groups: African Americans, American Indians, Asian Americans, and Hispanic Americans. We provide a brief overview of common characteristics associated with demographic background, cultural values, barriers to care, and health promotion strategies, and make recommendations for measurement instruments. We selected these instruments because of their ethnic-specific focus, clinical utility, and construct validity. We have tried to present themes common to each group yet convey the rich cultural diversity of each.

African Americans

The term African American is used to denote people whose ancestry is linked to the continent of Africa, although black people have immigrated to the United States from numerous countries for the past four centuries. The 1990 U.S. Census reports that African Americans represent approximately 12.1 percent of the population, or 30 million inhabitants. Estimates are that the African-American population will increase by 22 percent, or 6.6 million persons, by the year 2000 (U.S. Bureau of Census 1990).

The economic status of African Americans can be examined from 1990 census data reporting that over 42 percent of this group were below the poverty line, with approximately 13 percent consisting of nonworking persons with little income. When stratified by class, the African-American upper class contains 10 percent of the population, and the middle class includes roughly 40 percent.

African Americans in the United States have a turbulent history, beginning with their forced deportation from their continent of origin centuries ago and slavery. African Americans today have a more contemporary history encased with experiences of slavery, racism, the civil rights movement, poverty, and a rich and viable community growth and increasing sense of ethnic and cultural unity.

Cultural Values. Butler (1992) describes African Americans' concept of self as tied to a group identity or an "extended self" that is confirmed by its functioning in a relationship and in harmony with the collective whole. Jackson (1986) points out that while there has been a history of oppression, there is a strong group identity formation. This is referred to as *Afrocentrism*, defined as a recognition of or relearning of ancestral roots. Another developmental term used to describe the psychological development of "becoming African" is *Nigrescence*, a concept that has its origins with advocacy leaders like Malcom X and Marcus Garvey (Dana 1993).

Ho (1987) points out that the cultural values of African Americans are influenced by their continent of origin and their identification with Anglo-American culture. However, like other ethnic groups, African Americans are expected to adopt Western or mainstream values and traditions. For example, mainstream Western values stress individualism, autonomy, ownership of material goods, mastery, efficiency, and future planning. In contrast, African-American values stress collectivity, affiliation, spiritualism, and respect for the elderly, as well as recognition of illness as emerging from natural, spiritual, or occult sources (Dana 1993; Ho 1987).

Health-seeking behavior among many African Americans consists of a mixture of traditional approaches (e.g., folk healers) and Western medicine. For example, individuals may use folk medicine to treat common afflictions, using the local clinic or hospital only in emergencies (Spector 1991). A physician may not be consulted routinely nor is he or she sought for prevention of disease.

Health-seeking behaviors for African Americans may involve the use of religious figures. Church affiliation and a pastor may be important in directing persons to formal and informal service providers (Dana 1993). The church has functioned as both a religious resource and a social service agency. Gary (1987) describes how African Americans' preferences differ in terms of how they seek out private practitioners and institutional or informal support systems. In a survey of black church attendance, he reports that Catholics prefer private practitioners, Baptists and Lutherans express only a slight preference for informal supports, and the majority of Holiness church members prefer informal supports. There still continues to be a web of religious networks that includes faith healers, prophets, advisers, missionary societies, prayer meetings, and preachers.

Learning styles of African Americans tend to reflect their worldviews and cultural ethos and that is the value placed on relationships. Consequently, the most effective learning styles for African Americans will utilize processes of modeling, mentoring, oral delivery, and apprenticeship while stressing the relational qualities between client and therapist. Successful learning is closely tied to clinician attitude and behavior, the social and political climate, and the content, quality, and organization of instruction (Butler 1992).

Barriers to Care. Mistrust of mainstream mental health systems and therapeutic mismatch are two common barriers for African Americans seeking mental health care. Historically, African Americans' mistrust of mainstream institutions stems from discriminatory and segregatory practices with formal physical and mental health care systems. The examples range from denial of treatment to misdiagnosis of symptoms and thus inappropriate treatment services. As Spector (1991) points out, it is a common (and valid) belief in the African-American community that those who receive care in public clinics or hospitals are often the subjects on whom students practice and on whom medical research is done. From the client perspective, he or she may be afraid of the procedures (e.g., medication injections) and the possibility of misdiagnosis or mistreatment. Further, African-American test data showing psychopathology often lack similar behavioral markers. Behavioral responses are rarely considered within the context in which they occur. As Dana (1993) explains, "Paranoia, especially when identified as Paranoid Personality Disorder, may not necessarily be pathological, since paranoia is a common, reality-based byproduct of African-American experience with prejudice and discrimination" (p. 99)

Therapeutic mismatch is another barrier to care for African Americans. Surveys of community households found that many individuals reported negative experiences with mental health personnel. Complaints were frequently leveled at providers whom they did not perceive as culturally competent and who treated them with disrespect and condescension (Spector 1991). Often, mainstream providers may not realize that for clients to attend appointments will often require missing a full day of work and arranging transportation, child care, and possibly elder care—all of which places additional burdens on people (typically women) who already may be at risk for mental health problems.

Health Promotion Strategies. Effective promotion measures must be taken to reduce diagnostic errors and increase therapeutic cultural competence. An initial step to reduce diagnostic errors is to use culturally sensitive assessment techniques. One useful tool is the Bio Psychosocial Cultural Assessment Checklist for DSM-IV Use (appendix J). The checklist combines the elements of the Axis I–V diagnostic categories with a checklist of culturally relevant questions for the interviewer to ask. Given the tendency to diagnose African Americans outside their sociocultural context, this checklist can be used as an interview guide in assessing and diagnosing using DSM-IV-compatible criteria. Note that the questions begin with establishing ethnic identity and then move into asking information about health. This is considered to be an effective entry point for discussion for most ethnic clients given the tendency to somatize emotional problems.

Many African Americans value the clinician who is aware of their cultural distinctness. For example, cultural sensitivity has been found to be correlated with being culturally competent (Pomales, Claiborn, and LaFromboise 1986). Elements of a good therapeutic match are related to provider availability and presence in the community, maintaining confidentiality, and provider awareness of racial identity issues. Providers with a humanistic orientation tend to emphasize values placed on person-to-person relationships. The emphasis is the working alliance or relationship between people, not the accomplishment of a specific task in a defined time frame (Ho 1987).

As African-American communities are experiencing a renewed interest in their ancestral roots, issues of racial identity may emerge, such as conflicts with partial identification with the dominant society. At lower levels of racial identity, African Americans express attitudes that are consistent with the idealization of the dominant culture and the devaluation of the African-American culture. Conversely, higher levels of racial identity are associated with racial pride, participation in the community, and recognition that all cultures have strengths and limitations (Grace 1992).

For providers who work with clients on issues of racial identity and self-awareness, three instruments can be helpful during the assessment phase: the African Self-Consciousness Scale (ASC), the Developmental Inventory of Black Consciousness (DIB-C), and the Racial Identity Attitude Scale (RIAS) (table 7.1). The ASC is a forty-two-item instrument that assesses black awareness, customs, and recognition of racial oppression; the DIB-C is a four-stage assessment tool that measures the

Table 7.1   Measurement Tools for African Americans

Measurement Tool	Purpose	Source
African Self-Consciousness Scale (ASC)	42-item scale based on Afrocentric theory of black personality structure; assesses: 1. awareness of black identity 2. recognition of survival priorities and affirmative practices, customs, and values 3. active participation in defense of survival, liberation, dignity, and integrity 4. recognition of racial oppression	Baldwin and Bell (1985)
Developmental Inventory of Black Consciousness (DIB-C)	Measures Nigrescence, or the process of becoming aware of African-American identity; four stages of consciousness are measured: Stage 1—Preconsciousness Stage 2—Confrontation Stage 3—Internalization Stage 4—Integration	Milliones (1980)
Racial Identity Attitude Scale (RIAS)	Used to measure racial identity (e.g., world-view shaped by values toward own ethnic group); four stages of identity are measured: Stage 1—Preencounter Stage 2—Encounter Stage 3—Immersion, emersion Stage 4—Internalization	Helms (1986)

extent to which racial and cultural stereotypical attitudes are internalized by the individual; and the RIAS examines cultural adaptation using four stages of racial identity. Each of these measures can provide the framework for assessing client issues and modes of intervention.

Overall, any intervention with an individual or family who is African American should incorporate a systems framework using the ecological approach. This approach focuses on the interface between the client and his or her environment. In this model, stressful problems in living are considered consequences of person–environment transactions rather than psychological deficits. Ho (1987) reports that many African-American individuals and families benefit from a problem-focused, present-oriented, activity-directed, short-term-therapy approach. The role of the mental health provider is to supply culturally relevant techniques specific to the needs of the client. Often the provider will take on the role of coach. Techniques helpful in a managed care setting would be for the provider to gather data using an ecomap that considers a family's environment and community. Figure 3.2 provided an example of a completed ecomap; a blank form can be found in appendix A. The process of intervention should focus on steps for immediate change that are tangible and realistic.

Ho (1987) describes four themes that can be helpful to providers in working with African-American clients: (1) strong kinship bonds, (2) orientation toward achievement, education, and work, (3) flexibility of family roles, and (4) a humanistic orientation, which stresses interpersonal relationships.

At the community level, mental health providers can be creative beyond the usual structural boundaries by working with the natural community networks. For example, traditional mental health services could team up with church-based social services as a means of accessing clients who normally feel marginalized by formal mental health service systems. Health promotion campaigns, including topics related to medicine and recognizing signs of depression, could be folded into the existing education groups at churches. Given the strong community presence and wide web of social services provided by many African-American churches, a mental health–social service delivery system that is church linked would be appropriate and could be delivered within the parameters of the church setting. Managed care serving mentally ill African Americans will find the social network integral to the continuum of care.

American Indians

The term *American Indian* is used interchangeably with *Native American* and *Indian* when referring to aboriginal peoples of the continental United States: American Indians, Eskimos, or Aleuts. A great diversity characterizes the 512 federally recognized native entities and in the additional 365 state-recognized Indian tribes (Orlandi 1992). There are 200 distinct languages currently spoken by Native Americans, which may be as distinct as Chinese is from English.

The 1990 U.S. Census data report just under 2 million American Indians and Alaska Natives in North America. They live predominantly in twenty-six states, primarily in the West. The states of Oklahoma, Arizona, California, New Mexico, and Alaska report the largest numbers of American Indians (Spector 1991). More than 50 percent of American Indians live in urban areas.

The historical experiences of American Indians are as painful and poignant as those of any other group. Trimble (1988) points out that the history of cultural contact between the tribes and European fur traders, soldiers, and immigrants proved to be a different experience for each tribe, yet all tribes experienced a wholesale cultural and physical dispersion of their people and lands. Their history is marked by multiple losses from war, forcible removable of children from families, loss of language, (re)education efforts through boarding schools, displacement of homeland, and attempts at obliterating traditional culture. To this day, conditions have not improved appreciably due to the incompatibility of Native American and Eurocentric views (Dana 1993). Despite wholesale attempts at ethnic cleansing by government and business-sanctioned efforts, American Indians are emerging with a resurgence of pride, dignity, and identity.

The 1990 census reports that 55 percent of American Indians have four or more years of high school, and nearly 8 percent have four or more years of college. This compares to the U.S. population at 66.5 percent and 16.2 percent, respectively. With regard to economic status, 13.0 percent were unemployed; the median income was $13,678, with 23.7 percent below the poverty line. This compares to U.S. population data at 6.5 percent, $19,917, and 9.6 percent, respectively. When compared to Asians and Pacific Islanders, American Indians seem to fare the worst.

Cultural Values. Although each tribe has its own value system, several common themes reflect a similar cultural value preference of American Indians: harmony with nature, present-time oriented, emphasis on collateral relationship with others, and an activity style that reflects a "being-in-becoming" mode. Humankind is seen as good, and dual religious practices (Indian tribal and Christian religions) are observed (Ho 1987).

American Indians have an extended self-concept that refers to their obligations to other human beings and to the native community (Dana 1993). This extended self-concept is an adaptive effort to maintain group identity and survival. In spite of various levels of assimilation into the larger culture through education and occupation, many American Indians retain strong ties to traditional cultural values.

The traditional American Indian belief about health reflects living in harmony with nature and having the ability to survive under difficult circumstances (Spector 1991). According to this belief, all people should treat their body with respect, just as they should treat the earth with respect. Navajos see illness, disharmony, or sadness as the result of displeasing holy people, disturbing the elements, or tampering with witches and witchcraft. The germ theory has little relevance with Indian beliefs. Diagnosis would be made by divination, and treatment—such as chanting, sweatbaths, stargazing, or herbal remedies—would focus on the external causative factor, not the illness itself (Spector 1991).

The expectations of a traditional Navajo reflect the culture's ideas about healing. It is a process of moving the ill person from a negative state of illness or imbalance to a positive state of harmony and health. Hopefulness and positive thinking are perceived as integral to healing; negative thinking is regarded as potentially deleterious. Navajos emphasize that if one thinks of good things and good fortune, good things will happen. If one thinks of bad things, a bad future will occur.

Traditionally, tribes have recognized a variety of individuals as healers or helpers: medicine men, shamans, and tribal elders. The person's relationship with the environment, the community, and the creator was linked to the role of the traditional healer. The mental health needs of parents and children were addressed through these natural helping systems (Cross 1987).

The learning styles of American Indians are quite diverse. The principle of observation has been central to the American Indian for centuries. In traditional Indian society, the oral tradition was the primary method of teaching values and attitudes. In oral storytelling, emphasis is given to the creation of complex relationships that use symbolism, anthropomorphism (giving human characteristics to animals), and animism (giving life and soul to natural phenomena such as rocks, trees, and the wind). Additionally, the use of metaphor is an effective method of teaching very complex concepts. Fleming (1992) reports that modern Indian children have superior strengths in the ability to memorize visual patterns, visualize spatial concepts, and produce descriptions rich in visual detail.

Barriers to Care. Barriers to care for American Indians are the lack of role models, poverty, and mismatch of therapeutic approaches. Cross (1987) suggests that many Indian parents have been deprived of opportunities and role models to learn adequate parenting skills, life skills, and some basic principles of child development. Consequently, they are reluctant to seek help based on the values of self-reliance and noninterference. When assessing for an appropriate intervention, the mamaged care clinician must keep in mind the larger context of cultural values, patterns of interaction, and history.

Noninterference also affects the ability of a community to identify role models to intervene with social problems. For example, although the Indian Health Service has made significant strides in providing inpatient facilities and outpatient clinics for the increasing problems of alcohol use, domestic violence, depression, anxiety, and coping difficulties, the problem has much deeper roots. A traditional viewpoint suggests that the problems emanate from the fact that American Indians have lost their opportunity to make choices, terms of practice of religion and medicine, as well as where and how they live. This is complicated by a lack of role models for correcting the problems.

The fact that one-third of the American Indian population lives in poverty does not bode well for their ability to participate in the physical and mental health care system. Isolated living serves as a further barrier.

American Indian culture is quite diverse, and many clients may resist certain aspects of the dominant culture, particularly a health care provider or therapist (Ho 1987). American Indians may underutilize white-dominated services due to feelings of disrespect experienced in clinic offices, organizational rigidity to time schedules, long waits, and demanding attitudes from mental health care staff. It is Indian practice to speak softly and respectfully while listening attentively. Poor interviewing skills and excessive note taking by clinicians interfere with the relational aspect of the encounter.

Health Promotion Strategies. As with any other ethnic population, a culturally relevant assessment should direct the intervention method. Historically, Western methods of assessment have been used with little research to support their efficacy (Cross 1987). The following suggestions have been found to be effective in working with Indian communities:

1. Assess whether the intervention goal fits within the client's cultural context or another attempt toward assimilation into European-American society. Assertiveness training may work well with mainstream clients but be viewed as invasive by Indian relationships.
2. Establish a helping climate by admitting your ignorance, keeping the doors open for discussion of cultural differences, and appreciating Indian culture and strengths of the Indian family. Emotional availability is enhanced by sharing a bit about yourself and knowing your own values and biases so that you may listen, observe, and learn nonjudgmentally. Avoid excessive note taking or forms that may distance you from the client and his or her concerns. Finally, it is important to observe local etiquette about what is polite and follow it.
3. Be prepared to establish your credibility with the client by demonstrating your ability to assist with obtaining concrete services (e.g., child care, arranging for basic needs such as food, shelter, clothing, legal services, filling out forms and applications) while at the same time assisting family members in developing their own support networks.
4. Participate in "context stretching" exercises by helping clients understand their problems from a broader perspective through exploring issues of racism, bicultural experiences, and government policies.
5. Provide family interventions that include extended family and seek to understand who is in the family system and what roles they play.
6. Participate in advocacy services in which client and family rights are upheld, and work to foster changes in attitudes and cross-cultural practices within agencies and personnel.

One measure that a provider could use with these strategies is the Rosebud Personal Opinion Survey (RPOS). Originally used with the Lakota Sioux, this survey measures social acculturation, values, language, and education (table 7.2).

Cross (1987) describes a group intervention, Indian Self Actualization, whereby Indian clients are encouraged to evaluate their behavior in relation to Indian and non-Indian values. By examining their values and where they come from, clients move forward in understanding their individual strengths and weaknesses. This has the secondary benefit of externalizing the problem while still assigning personal responsibility for correcting the problem. Cross notes that this group format, like others, works best when all participants are Indians. Groups are a natural assembly process for many Indians; consider the power of the "talking cir-

Table 7.2   Measurement Tools for American Indians

Measurement Tool	Purpose	Source
Extended Family Chart	Visual diagram to be used by provider to help the client determine the resources in the extended family	Cross (1987, p. 63)
Rosebud Personal Opinion Survey (Lakota Sioux) (RPOS)	Instrument to measure social acculturation, values, blood quantum, language usage, education, and occupation	Hoffman, Dana, and Bolton (1985)
Native American Acculturation Scale (NAAS)	Uses the case history as a basis for documenting acculturation using four behavioral criteria: 1. family/self 2. social/recreation 3. spiritual/religion 4. training/education	Brown (1982) as reported in Dana (1993, p. 128)
Structural Assimilation Scale (SAS)	Use of seven stages of assimilation (e.g., home ownership, employment, marital status; cultural assimilation measured by modernization/ assimilation and separatism items)	Chadwick and Strauss (1975)

cle" or the use of the sweat lodge and storytelling. Clinicians wishing to examine acculturation issues will find useful the Native American Acculturation Scale (NAAS). This instrument is designed to use a case history approach to document acculturation using four domains: family/self, social/recreation, spiritual/religion, and training/education.

For many traditional Navajos, staying healthy equates with existing in harmony with nature, thinking in a positive and hopeful manner about the future, with the goal being to live long enough to see the grandchildren's children. Clinicians should understand that for a health promotion and prevention education approach to be effective, the emphasis must be positive.

Ho (1987) illustrates the benefit of problem-solving techniques to promote health strategies. Bearing in mind that many American Indian families maintain a holistic, interdependent view of the world and their close interpersonal relationships, techniques for health promotion strategies should be based on how the family interprets its problems. Six techniques are compatible with American Indian cultural orientation:

1. Screening and relabeling the problem as social, moral, or organic
2. Mobilizing and restructuring the extended family network
3. Promoting family interdependence
4. Assuming role as educator and advocate
5. Restructuring taboos for problem solving
6. Collaborating with natural helpers (e.g., medicine person, paraprofessional, and therapist helper)

The instrument appropriate for measuring these techniques is the Structural Assimilation Scale (SAS), which assesses seven stages of assimilation, including home ownership, employment, and marital status. Cultural assimilation is measured by modernization, assimilation, and separatism.

Many Indian people have a historic distrust of written language (Cross 1987). Managed care clinicians will have to explain the purpose of paperwork (e.g., self-report measures) and explore clients' feelings about this method of gathering information. Given the communication preference of American Indians to view situations in present time, genograms, ecomaps, and a transitional cultural map are helpful tools for gathering information early in the therapeutic relationship. Gathering information for the genogram and ecomap should be approached slowly and spontaneously rather than as part of a formal interview process. The transitional cultural map appears very much like an ecomap but more accurately reflects the location of the reservations and the different tribal relationships of each family member. Additionally, measures of therapeutic completion can be ascertained by reviewing the problem-solving phase of intervention. An Extended Family Chart is a useful tool to help clients determine their resources in their extended family (see table 7.2).

Asian Americans

The term *Asian/(Pacific Island) American* refers to over sixty separate ethnic and racial groups and subgroups. Asian Americans represent thirty-two distinct ethnic or cultural groups comprising Chinese, Japanese, Filipino, Asian Indians, Korean, and Indochinese. Pacific Island Americans are mostly Hawaiian, Samoan, and Guamanian. Indochinese refers to the people from Vietnam, Cambodia, and Laos. In the United States, these people comprise Lao, Hmong, Iu-Mien, Thai Dam, and Khmu from Laos; Vietnamese and some ethnic Chinese from Vietnam and Cambodia; and Khmer from Cambodia (Van-Si 1992).

Many Chinese and Japanese have been in the United States for three generations or more, whereas most Southeast Asians were born overseas. Each group is very heterogeneous and evinces a great deal of variation in customs, values, level of acculturation and assimilation, languages, and social organizations (Kim, McLeod, and Shantzis 1992). As such, it does not make sense to group them together because each is distinct. Given the broad topic areas that each group lends itself to, we will limit the discussion to Asian Americans, with an emphasis on the Indochinese communities.

The 1990 census reported that 7.3 million Asian–Pacific Islanders (2.9 percent of the total population) live in the United States, primarily in New Jersey, Texas, Rhode Island, California, and Oregon (Dana 1993). Recent statistics indicate that between 1980 and 1988, the Asian population increased by about 76 percent, compared with 36 percent among Hispanics. It is estimated that with natural population growth, more than 1 million Indochinese have made their home in the United States, with the largest proportion, nearly 400,000, settling in California (Van-Si 1992).

Regarding the educational attainment of Asian Americans compared with other ethnic groups in the United States, Asian Americans have the largest proportion of college-educated students (34 percent), more than twice that for the U.S. population as a whole (16.2 percent).

The economic status of recently arrived Asian immigrant families is strained due to limited English proficiency and job skills and relatively large families. Kim et al. (1992) state that Southeast Asian refugees are three to four times more likely to be on public assistance than African Americans or Hispanic Americans. Additionally, many families continue to support other family members in their country of origin. Thus, when employment is available, family obligations limit existing financial resources. For those who are first-generation immigrants or refugees, Asian Americans may come from backgrounds that are largely agricultural but are influenced by industrialization and urbanization.

Van-Si (1992) provides a historic framework of the political moves that gave way to the Indochinese flight from Southeast Asia to the United States. In the spring of 1975, Vietnam, Cambodia, and Laos fell to communism. This created two waves of refugee immigration: pre- and post-1975. The first wave fled for political reasons and consisted of mostly urban, affluent, middle- and upper-middle-class, educated individuals who were Catholic and Buddhist. The second wave fled for economic reasons and fear of political oppression. They included rural, younger, less educated people who were mostly Buddhists and ethnic Chinese (Skinner 1980).

Many of the Indochinese who are in the United States today came under refugee status, which means that they fled their country under economic or political duress. They constitute a large population of severely traumatized people who have been exposed to torture, physical abuse, rape, illness, malnutrition, forced family separation, and relocation. Many of these experiences occurred in labor camps or during the process of escape, or both (Dana 1993). Despite this shared history, each regional ethnic group (Lao, Vietnamese, or Cambodian) maintains a distinct cultural identity.

Cultural Values. Asian traditional culture contrasts sharply with American culture, especially in the view of self, family, and community influences and toward health-seeking behaviors and learning styles.

Asian perceptions of self are divided into concerns for society and humanity and for self and immediate family. Familial loyalty is stressed over individual interests. Traditionally, the Asian family unit connotes strength and stability for all family members and plays a critical role in the development of children through adulthood (Kim et al. 1992). Family life for the Chinese and Japanese is typically described as patriarchal, with guilt, shame, and honor used to control family members. There is strict adherence to traditional norms, which includes familial decision making. However, as many families experience acculturation and assimilation into mainstream society, the absolute control of the family is being challenged, particularly by second-generation youth. Their self-worth is increasingly defined by dominant culture values (e.g., personal pride) and less by filial piety (e.g., subjugation of self for family or ancestors).

The values of many Asian Americans are captured in the combined teachings of Confucianism, Buddhism, and Taoist religions, which emphasize harmony and suppression of individuality and emotion in favor of conformity and mutual personal and financial dependence. Within these teachings, individuals experience a call for collective responsibility that is framed with a sense of fatalism and conservatism.

The belief systems of Asian Americans are derived from different philosophical and religious influences and organizations (especially Hindu, Muslim, Buddhist, animist, and "nativized Catholicism"); (Sundberg et al. 1995). Kinzie and Manson (1987) note that Asians are more likely than Westerners to see mental affliction as a source of humiliation and potential ridicule. They point out that a standard of secretiveness prevails about sharing emotional upset, especially for those who have been raped or tortured while in detainment camps. Disclosure to a fourth-party managed care organization is incompatible with this secrecy.

In traditional Chinese society, psychological illness is viewed as disgraceful, whereas physical illness is quite socially acceptable (Corin 1994). Physical complaints are, then, an acceptable way to express distress, demoralization, and unhappiness. Bizarre behaviors are often recognized as a medical problem and presumed to be some derangement of the body humors. These humors that govern health have both physical and emotional correlates, and thus there is little need for a special category of mental illness. Kirmayer (1994) suggests that "illness" may be a manifestation of social-moral problems or cosmological forces, and, thus, distressed emotions point to an organic imbalance.

This traditional view of health is still quite popular in contemporary Chinese medicine. A common diagnosis may be neurasthenia (nervous weakness), which refers to a host of social, emotional, and physical complaints. As a diagnosis, it neither conveys the stigma attached to mental illness nor implies personal accountability for the associated physical correlates of an emotional illness (Corin 1994). In the Vietnamese culture, it is not unusual for a patient to present to his or her primary care physician with complaints of "feeling tense or tired or chilly in the neck, shoulders, or back." This is to be interpreted as a general feeling of unwellness, which might be due to fatigue, depression, anemia, or the initial stages of cold or flu. There are, however, other symptoms that have been shown to be specifically indicative of anxiety and depression among Vietnamese: feeling chilly or hot inside (especially among Laotians and Cambodians), "chronic rheumatism" (an acceptable expression for anxiety and depression); "weakness of the kidneys" (an acceptable somatic expression for diminished sexual potency); and tending to be forgetful and unable to concentrate (Mollica et al. 1994).

Religion continues to play an important role in how Asian Americans view mental health. Obeyesekere (1985) offers another perspective of looking at mental illness through Buddhist eyes. From the Buddhist perspective, many of the key symptoms of depression are indicative not of pathology but of responding to the inevitability of suffering and loss. He suggests that some individuals who would be labeled depressed by psychiatric criteria are, in Sri Lanka, viewed as having acquired important religious insights. From this perspective, the "disorder," if it can be called that, resides not in morbid thoughts or cognitive distortions but in the struggle to hold on to transient experiences. The goal of spiritual mental health is not a strong ego but the dissolution of the self (Obeyesekere, 1985).

Health-seeking behaviors are highly influenced by perceptions of illness and culturally sanctioned treatment methods. As we have illustrated, mental illness in Asian culture is perceived to be caused by karma, spells, spirits, and or cosmic imbalances. There is a tendency for Southeast Asians to feel that medical symptoms are the only legitimate reason to seek help. Relief for mental health problems is sought through folk healers and community resources (such as family, Buddhist monks, or Catholic priests). The main mode of treatment would be physical or meditation, not psychotherapy.

The learning styles of Asian Americans are often an extension of their belief systems. For example, the cognitive learning styles of Asian Americans would accept a teaching method of medication information given by a person of professional status—preferably a professional who reflects the patriarchal family structure, such as an older male. Preferred learning styles are those that are directive, structured, logical for the situation, and moralistic. Tan (1967) found that Asian-American students preferred counselors who were trained in medicine or education and did not use self-reports or tests as part of their intervention efforts.

Barriers to Care. Stigma toward mental illness is a significant barrier to care for Asian Americans. The stigma is highlighted by the involvement of the managed care reviewer. Given the profound effects that family has on clients, many Asian families associate shame and stigma with the admission of mental illness within the family member (Yen 1992). A negative cultural view of mental illness promotes both denial and underutilization of available services. Other barriers arise from language differences and need for interpretation services.

Health Promotion Strategies. Considering that one of the fastest-growing immigrant and refugee populations in the United States is Asian (Berg and Jaya 1993), mental health providers in managed care organizations will need to be prepared to deal with the emerging physical and mental health needs of these individuals and their families. For managed mental health care programs to be effective, services must be based on indigenous mores and resources. This includes identifying local resources and building on them. For example, traditional healers and religious leaders may be trained and involved in prevention activities (Sundberg et al. 1995). In Asian communities, providers could work with the leaders of local civic associations and of local churches and the Buddhist temple. Local radio that is broadcast in the native language is an effective communication tool and can reach many at-risk clients who may be isolated from mainstream activities (e.g., elderly, young mothers or wives). This could be a helpful diversion from the excess use of emergency room services.

For providers who work with Japanese clients, the Ethnic Identity Questionnaire (EIQ) may be helpful to assess clients' preferences in community social relationships, child-rearing customs, family kinship, and sex roles. This is a fifty-item measure of Japanese preferences in several life domains. Knowing these preferences may assist the provider in developing culturally relevant mental health services (see table 7.3).

Obtaining accurate information of a trauma survivor's experiences and symptoms is necessary for properly diagnosing and providing effective treatment and positive therapeutic outcomes. Research evidence from work with Chilean torture survivors suggests that a triadic model, in which the clinician and patient relate to a third party (e.g., questionnaire or a tape recording), is most useful in providing a context for discussion of painful and sensitive events (Cienfuegos and Monelli 1983). There are several ethnic-specific instruments to assess depression and trauma. For managed care clinicians who work with Indochinese clients, three instruments are available to assess trauma, anxiety, and depression associated with posttraumatic stress disorder, a prevalent disorder among refugees: the Harvard Trauma Questionnaire (HTQ-30), a thirty-item questionnaire useful for identifying symptoms related to the refugee experience; the Hopkins Symptom Checklist (HSC-25), a twenty-five-item screening instrument to assess symptoms of anxiety, depression, trauma, and severity of psychiatric disorder; and the Vietnamese Depression Scale (VDS), a fifteen-item screening tool that assesses physical and psychological symptoms related to expressions of depression. Chinese clients who are recent immigrants may be assessed with the Chinese Depressive Symptom Scale (CDSS), a twenty-two-item screening instrument that measures depressive symptoms associated with past events, such as the Cultural Revolution. It is designed to be used with Chinese people in China but has utility for new immigrants as well. Each of these instruments is available in the native language and meets the requirements for psychometric reliability and validity.

Hispanic Americans

The terms *Mexican American* and *Hispanic American* are used interchangeably in the literature despite a diversity of opinion about which label is "correct." *Mexican American* implies that one's origins are from Mexico so it would not be appropriate when describing people from other countries. *Hispanic* has been used by the U.S. Bureau of Census to identify individuals whose cultural roots are in Mexico, Puerto Rico, Cuba, Central America, and, in some cases, Spain, and Brazil. Hispanic

Table 7.3   Measurement Tools for Asian Americans

Target Population	Measurement Tool	Purpose	Source
Indochinese	Harvard Trauma Questionnaire: Cambodian, Laotian, and Vietnamese Versions (HTQ-30)	30-item instrument to identify first-time trauma symptoms related to the Indochinese refugee experience associated with posttraumatic stress disorder	Mollica et al. (1992)
Indochinese	Hopkins Symptom Checklist 25:Vietnamese, Cambodian, Laotian (HSC-25)	25-item screening instrument for use with Indochinese refugees for the purpose of recognizing symptoms associated with anxiety, depression, and trauma; severity of psychiatric disorder	Mollica et al. (1987)
Indochinese	Vietnamese Depression Scale (VDS)	15-item screening tool that covers three sets of symptoms—physical, psychological, and symptoms related to expressions of Vietnamese depression	Kinzie and Manson (1987)
Chinese	Chinese Depressive Symptom Scale (CDS)	22-item screening instrument to measure depressive symptoms among Chinese people in China; measures psychiatric complaints of past events related to Cultural Revolution	Lin (1989)
Japanese	Ethnic Identity Questionnaire (EIQ)	50-item monolevel measure of Japanese preferences (e.g., personality, child-rearing customs, family kinship, community social relationships, discrimination, sex roles and others)	Masuda, Matsumoto, and Meredith (1970)

Americans are also known as Chicanos, Latinos, Mexicanos, Hispanos, Spanish-speaking Americans, Spanish Americans, and Spanish-surnamed Americans. We will use *Hispanics* because of its inclusive description of many cultures and ethnic backgrounds. The U.S. Bureau of the Census provides 1990 population data on the three major Hispanic groups: Mexican Americans or Chicanos (62 percent), Puerto Ricans or Puertoriqueños (13 percent), and Cubans or Cubanos (5 percent).

The Census Bureau reports there are approximately 22.4 million Hispanics in the United States, with concentrations of Mexican Americans in the Southwest, Puerto Ricans in the Northeast, and Cubans in the Southeast. There is an increasing population of Central and South Americans—approximately 2.5 million, or 13 percent of the Hispanic population—who are coming from the civil war–plagued countries of Guatemala, El Salvador, and Nicaragua (Padilla and Salgado de Snyder 1992). Using demographic projections, it is estimated that Hispanics will be the largest ethnic group in the United States by 2010.

Regarding the educational attainment of Hispanic-American adults over age twenty-five compared with the total U.S. non-Hispanic population, Mexican Americans, Puerto Ricans, and Cuban Americans have completed 10.8, 12.0, and 12.4 median years of school, respectively. These rates are substantially less than for non-Hispanic (white) populations.

The median family income of Hispanic Americans is, respectively, $21,325, $18,932, and $26,858 for Mexican Americans, Puerto Ricans, and Cuban Americans. These figures are less than the total U.S. non-Hispanic population ($33,142). Census information on Central and South American populations shows a median family income of $24,322. Many Hispanics live in large urban centers and hold unskilled or semiskilled occupations.

Padilla and Salgado de Synder (1992) provide an overview of the very different immigration histories for each of the three groups to acquaint readers with some of the historical context that Hispanic clients bring to the agency. A common feature shared by all Hispanic American populations is the fact that all came from Spanish-speaking nations and approximately 85 percent are nominally Roman Catholic (Dana 1993).

Most of the 14 million Mexican nationals who have come to the United States did so for economic reasons. Historically, the United States and Mexico have had an economic, if not exploitive, relationship regarding Mexican citizenry. Mexico controlled the American Southwest until 1848 and the Treaty of Guadalupe. For the next ninety years, Mexican residents living in the newly absorbed states lost their land through a series of land schemes, were forced into agricultural labor, and were denied equal educational opportunity. Some were "deported" back to Mexico during the Great Depression despite having U.S. citizenship. Others continue to be discriminated against in jobs and housing.

Current trends toward immigration can be traced back to the *bracero* program, a labor recruitment effort formalized after World War II. Cheap laborers were recruited from Mexico to work in agriculture and manufacturing on behalf of the war effort. After the war's end, labor needs were shifted to seasonal work, which has remained an economic pull to this day. Ironically, many Mexican Americans would have to trace their roots back as far as five generations before they would find relatives with links to Mexico, yet their culture and identity are firmly rooted in Mexican tradition. Today Mexican culture reflects a blend of the early Indian and the Spanish.

There are approximately 3 million Puerto Ricans in the United States, with over 3 million in residence in Puerto Rico. Historically, Puerto Rico had ties to Spain through colonization in the sixteenth century. As native Puerto Ricans (the Tainos Indians) were eliminated ("ethnically cleansed," using contemporary terms) by the Spanish and replaced with African slaves, the genetic blending of Spanish, African, and white melded into the Puerto Rican of today. In 1898, Spain ceded Puerto Rico to the United States following the end of the Spanish-American War and it became a U.S. commonwealth in 1917. Consequently, Puerto Ricans are able to move freely from the island to the continent. The profile of the Puerto Rican today may range from sugar cane worker to middle-class urban dweller.

Despite the ambivalent relationship that the United States maintains with Cuba, refugees continue to seek political asylum in the United States in record numbers each year. Historically, Cuba shares a similar history with Puerto Rico involving Spanish domination, African slave influence, and a distinct cultural identity. Major political upheavals have occurred in two waves: first in 1889 when the United States helped Cuba obtain its freedom from Spain, and again in 1959 when Fidel Castro overthrew the capitalist government run by Presi-

dent Fulgencio Batista. Shortly after the Castro revolution, large numbers of upper-class, professional Cuban citizens left the island and immigrated to the United States, settling mostly in Miami.

Cuban Americans today reflect a composition of upper-middle class to
working class. Most are typically bilingual, have a high rate of high school
(83 percent) and college (24 percent) graduation, and have the lowest
poverty rates of the three major Hispanic groups. The Cuban culture is a
blending of Spanish and African cultures. As Dana (1993) points out, for
many years Cuban Americans have retained a separate identity as an ex-
iled group but more recently have begun to form political ties with larger
Hispanic communities. Given Cuba's unique historical connection to
powerful nations such as the former Soviet Union, Spain, and the United
States, it is quite distinctive among other Latin nations.

Cultural Values. Hispanic Americans possess a rich, varied cultural identity. Their sense of self can be described as sociocentric; that is, the self
and self-interest are often subordinated to the welfare of the home and
the family, although this is moderated by the person's level of traditionalism versus modernism. For example, traditional people favor family
and kinship first; modern people may favor more egocentric decisions
and actions (Dana 1993). Hispanics may also define their self-worth in
terms of inner qualities or inner dignity, and they expect others to show
respect for the dignity. This concept, referred to as personalism, reflects
the view that every individual has some sense of personal dignity and
goodness and should be treated with respect (Ho 1987).

The view of self is also related to traditional sex roles. *Machismo*
refers to male physical dominance, sexual availability, and the role of
the provider who protects, honors, and is responsible for the welfare of
his family. *Marianismo* and *hembrismo* (known as femaleness) refer to
the spiritual superiority of women and their capacity to endure suffering; with references to the Virgin Mary, the concept includes sacrifices
and femaleness in the form of strength, perseverance, and flexibility.
Despite these well-defined gender roles, research has shown that male
dominance in marital decision making is absent among Hispanic couples (Marin and Van Oss, 1991).

Hispanic Americans place great importance on relatives as referents
and providers of emotional support. One of the key values of Hispanics
is familism and allocentrism (or collectivism). Familism is a cultural

value that involves identification with and attachment to the nuclear and extended families and strong feelings of loyalty, reciprocity, and solidarity among members of the same family (Triandis et al. 1982) Marin and Van Oss Marin (1991) describe allocentrism as a key Hispanic value that has been associated with high levels of personal interdependence, conformity, readiness to be influenced by others, mutual empathy, willingness to sacrifice for the welfare of the in-group members, and trust of the members of the in-group.

The cultural belief system toward health and illness is seen in the concept of spiritualism. Spiritual values involve the belief that the visible world is surrounded by an invisible world inhabited by good and evil spirits who influence human behavior (Delgado 1978). Since spirits can be invoked to do good or evil, attitudes toward health and illness reflect a striving for harmony. For example, to have good health and mental health requires a balance with God and harmony with family, friends, and the customs of the church. Illness, on the other hand, may be caused by soul loss, spirit intrusion, or anger of the gods or the consequence of punishment for sins.

Illness, then, is perceived to be rooted in external causes, which reduces much of the stigma associated with being considered *loco* (insane). In a general sense, some Hispanic-American clients may not separate etiology of illness into natural, supernatural, or superstitious origins. Consequently, they will try a variety of traditions, with Western medicine being the last resort at times.

Health-seeking behaviors are multifaceted for many Hispanic Americans. The concept of fatalism influences how some Hispanics engage in formal services. Hispanic Americans consider the spirit and soul more valuable than the body or worldly possessions. This value can be translated into the attitude of accepting tragic and unfortunate events as inevitable. It also has the benefit of externalizing the problem to fate as opposed to personal failure. Consequently, many Hispanics may not value the efforts of the mental health professional who encourages them to be involved in mental illness prevention programs. However, when physical or mental illness does occur, folk healing practices are considered an acceptable treatment method and may include *curanderismo*, a healing practice used by Mexican Americans that involves the use of herbs to treat illnesses caused by witches; spiritism, a healing practice used by Puerto Ricans that involves the use of herbal remedies to treat illnesses caused by evil spirits; and *santeria,* a healing and religious practice used by Cuban Americans that involves the use of shell reading, animal sacrifice, and herbs to treat illnesses caused by spirit intrusion. Dana (1993) points out that a common bond with all these practices is that the folk healer is a significant member of the social network of the ethnic community. Examples include *curanderos* (curers), *espritistas* (mediums), and *padrinos* (godfathers). They are practitioners of an ancient yet familiar form of medicine that involves diagnosing and curing through touch, the invocation of helper spirits, and the use of herbs and rituals. The mental health provider must find a way to value this resource and work with it.

The learning styles of Hispanic Americans will most likely favor an approach that is interpersonal, with elements that are nurturing, intimate, and respectful. Because of allocentrism or collectivism, Hispanics exhibit a pattern for preferred interpersonal relationships (Marin and Van Oss Marin, 1991). Similarly, Hofstede's research has shown that Hispanics value conformity and obedience and support autocratic and authoritarian attitudes from those in charge of organizations or institutions. Their tendency to be present oriented reflects an appreciation for the quality of the relationship as opposed to the punctuality of the occasion. In other words, being twenty minutes late to a meeting may not be as important as having a meaningful social exchange at the meeting. For many Hispanic Americans, a supreme value is respect in interpersonal relations. In designing treatment programs for Hispanic Americans, it is important to have services that acknowledge and respect the social power of the client and his or her values (especially as related to religion) yet permit face-saving during times of disclosure of sensitive material.

Barriers to Care. Factors that serve as barriers to seeking or receiving care for Hispanic Americans include language differences, a sense of shame attached to mental illness, socioeconomic level, and institutional barriers. Research has shown that Hispanic Americans suffer the full impact of culture poverty through cultural and linguistic barriers, adverse political and social acculturation, and severe economic stresses. As a consequence, Hispanics usually do not seek mental health services (Ho 1987).

Language proficiency—in Spanish or English—is quite variable for Hispanic Americans. For example, first-generation Hispanics may report being proficient in Spanish, but this may not be true for the second and third generations. Older Hispanic clients or recent immigrants may be dependent on English-speaking children or grandchildren to negotiate social activities, a role that creates significant conflicts between adults and children.

Mental illness is viewed by many Hispanic Americans as shameful and somehow reflective of the family's inability to care properly for its kin. Further, Hispanics may not consider mental health services as a solution to their emotional and family problems, especially when issues of language and poverty dominate as obstacles. Low socioeconomic status operates as a barrier in determining how well Hispanic Americans can even participate in mental health service systems. Since employment is a condition for many types of mental health insurance policies and unemployment is high among Hispanic Americans, many individuals will remain underserved. For those who are eligible through federal or state benefit programs, signing up for services may prove to be extremely difficult without the advocacy efforts of caseworkers.

Health Promotion Strategies. Hispanic Americans maintain a strong and vibrant presence in the United States. Clinicians and managed care systems seeking to increase service accessibility to this growing and diverse population must recognize several key service needs. Of the three main groups described in this section—Mexican Americans, Puerto Rican Americans, and Cuban Americans—there exist tremendous intergroup and intragroup differences. However, each group has its share of newly arrived, immigrant-American and immigrant-descent individuals and families. We encourage providers to think of services across this stratum first and then consider appropriate intervention strategies within these groups. Additionally, all service interventions should incorporate the client's first language.

Newly arrived immigrants need information, referral, advocacy, and such concrete services as English-language instruction. Providers can work with indigenous community leaders to identify these individuals. The assumption is that early intervention and assistance will lower the risk for adjustment and coping problems that can lead to or exacerbate mental illness. For mental health providers who work with recently immigrated individuals and families, two assessment instruments may be helpful: the Acculturation Rating Scale for Mexican Americans (ARSMA) and the Hispanic Acculturation Scale (HAS). The ARSMA is a twenty-item instrument designed to examine behaviors that represent cultural origins (e.g., language preference, ethnic identity, and generation as well as ethnicity of friends). The HAS is a twelve-item questionnaire used for screening traditional culture and acculturation level. Both instruments attempt to assess level of acculturation as treatment services are being assessed (see table 7.4).

Immigrant-American individuals—those who were born in the United States but whose parents are immigrants—are characterized by cultural conflict with their foreign-born, traditional parents. Individuals may need help in resolving generational conflicts, communication problems, and role clarification. In some cases, the provider will have to be sensitive to the political and social issues within the community of blended immigrants. For example, a mental health provider working with Cuban Americans in Florida would be wise to understand the class issues that exist between immigrants and refugees who arrived in 1960 versus those who arrived in 1980. The first group represented more of the upper class, whereas recent immigrants represent the blue-collar or working groups. Knowing the circumstances of the immigration and how long ago will be important factors in instituting culturally sensitive interventions. For clinicians working with Cuban Americans, the Cuban Behavioral Identity Questionnaire (CBIQ) will be helpful. The CBIQ is an eight-item measure of acculturation between Cuban Americans and non-Cuban Hispanic groups. The Life History Schedule (LHS) is a twenty-four-item instrument for Mexican Americans that examines multicultural values, worldviews, and traditional versus modern belief systems.

Immigrant-descent individuals—both parents were born in the United States but previous generations may have immigrated from Mexico and Cuba—are usually acculturated, speak both languages at home, and may participate in mainstream social services, mental health services, and traditional services. Clinicians who wish to learn more about the personal and socialization history and degree of past multicultural participation can use the fifty-seven-item Multicultural Experience Inventory (MEI).

Table 7.4   Measurement Tools for Hispanics and Cuban Americans

Target Population	Measurement Tool	Purpose	Source
Cuban Americans	Cuban Behavioral Identity Questionnaire (CBIQ)	8-item measure of acculturation between Cuban-Americans and non-Cuban Hispanic groups	Garcia and Lega (1979)
Hispanic Americans	Acculturation Rating Scale for Mexican Americans (ARSMA)	20-item monolevel instrument to examine behaviors that represent Hispanic cultural origins (e.g., language preference, ethnic identity and generation, ethnicity of friends and contact with Mexico)	Cuellar et al. (1980)
Hispanic Americans	Life History Schedule (LHS)	24-item measurement that focuses on three areas: 1. development and expression of cultural flex in different life periods 2. ability to arrive at multicultural values and worldviews 3. ability to combine multiple belief systems (modern and traditional values)	Ramirez (1991)
Hispanic Americans	Hispanic Acculturation Scale (HAS)	12-item questionnaire used for screening traditional culture/acculturation level using three factors: 1. language use and ethnic loyalty 2. electronic media preferences 3. ethnic social relations	Marín et al. (1987)
Hispanic Americans	Multicultural Experience Inventory (MEI)	57-item inventory that focuses on providers'/clients' personal history and behavior in three areas: 1. demographic/linguistic 2. socialization history 3. degree of multicultural participation in the past	Ramirez (1991

RECOMMENDATIONS

Clinicians involved in the many aspects of mental health service delivery to ethnic populations must be aware of different ethnic communities and what they require to benefit from interventions. We will provide a few recommendations for the managed care setting.

Role of Provider

Caring for the patient from a different ethnic group involves providing outcomes that the client can appreciate. Clinicians constantly need to ask the client and the family how they perceive the problem. Clinicians should solicit information about the client's ethical values and cultural orientation.

Jecker and colleagues (1995) recommend that clinicians in cross-cultural settings function as observational scientists, attending carefully to details and gathering information both by communicating directly with the client and speaking with important persons in the client's life. In clarifying their own goals, clinicians must be self-reflective, distinguishing the purpose they bring to a client encounter from the practice typically employed (Jecker et al. 1995). A caregiver from the dominant U.S. culture and a client from a very different culture can resolve cross-cultural disputes about treatment not by compromising important values but by focusing on the client's goals (Jecker, Caresse, and Pearlman 1995).

Types of Programs

Patient education techniques are part and parcel of all managed care programs. Families play an important role in influencing health-seeking behaviors. LeClere et al. (1994) remind us that families serve as social bridges between the formal medical care system and the individual in two ways: as facilitator and as substitutes for formal health care. Facilitators, as described by LeClere, are family and friends who precede the immigrant and provide both financial and cognitive access to formal medical care systems. As substitutes for formal care, the family provides advice and tangible support (money, traditional medicines). Both share caregiving and cultural alternatives to medical intervention, important functions of social networks.

Diagnostic Efforts

There is a growing recognition among mental health professionals that there needs to be a more culturally sensitive diagnostic system with culturally sensitive screening criteria. Efforts to reduce misdiagnosis in the cross-cultural arena are seen in one small section of the DSM-IV. In order to improve diagnostic specificity in cross-cultural assessments, the most recent DSM publication, the fourth edition, has added an appendix on cultural-bound syndromes and glossary. This appendix provides an outline of five categories to consider when assessing the individual's cultural and social reference group:

1. Cultural identity of the individual (e.g., ethnicity and preferred language)
2. Cultural explanation of the individual's illness (e.g., what are individual's explanation of symptoms in relation to the norms of the cultural reference group)
3. Cultural factors related to psychosocial environments and level of functioning (e.g., interpretation of stressors and available social supports)
4. Cultural elements of the relationship between the individual and the clinician (e.g., noting differences in cultural and social status between individual and clinician and how this may affect symptom expression, diagnosis, and treatment)
5. Overall cultural assessment for diagnosis and care (e.g., how cultural considerations specifically influence diagnosis and care)

With each of these categories, the provider is encouraged to write a brief narrative using utilization reviews.

The DSM-IV appendix also outlines twenty-five terms that refer to "recurrent, locality-specific patterns of aberrant behavior and troubling experiences that may or may not be linked to a particular DSM-IV diagnostic category" (p. 844). Culture-bound syndromes refer to localized or folk diagnostic categories that frame meaning for troubling behavior or experiences. The terms are generally limited to their society of origin and may not make sense to an assimilated person.

Using a biopsychosocial model of assessment like the DSM-IV can be quite appropriate for multicultural populations. Cross-cultural research suggests that assessments of psychiatric illness should begin with phenomenological descriptions of folk diagnoses or culture-specific symptoms, which can then be compared to Western psychiatric criteria (Mollica et al. 1992). Given that many cultures somatize psychological complaints as physical ills, the interviewer can comfortably solicit health information first. This will appear less threatening to the client and the family. Mollica suggests that the provider identify culture-specific symptoms, explore the impact of culture on the expressed illness response, and readily question the appropriateness of Western psychiatric diagnoses with non-Western clients. Providers using the DSM-IV can incorporate the use of the Outline for Cultural Formulation and Glossary of Culture-Bound Syndromes with a checklist of questions to ask. We have provided a cross-cultural assessment guideline in appendix J (Biopsychosocial-Cultural Assessment Checklist) of this book.

The conventional approach to assessing and diagnosing begins with identifying the problem and developing a client profile using Axis I through V. Briefly, Axis I refers to clinical disorders or other conditions that may be the focus of clinical attention, Axis II refers to personality disorders and mental retardation, Axis III refers to general medical conditions, Axis IV refers to psychosocial and environmental problems, and Axis V refers to global assessment of functioning (American Psychiatric Association, 1994a). All too often, managed care plans concentrate on Axis I and II diagnoses with little regard given to Axis III, IV, and V. However, by reversing the order of the axes and beginning with Axis III (General Medical Conditions), the provider can report medical or health conditions that may be relevant to understanding the individual's mental health. The medical aspect of the DSM-IV can be useful for some ethnic clients whose community's view of psychological illness is harshly stigmatized. This approach to reaching a diagnosis has the benefit of contextualizing the client's situation first and then working toward a diagnosis. Additionally, it enables the provider to utilize narrative approaches, a method that is more indirect and inviting to conversation than conventional methods that start, "What's the problem?" When starting off with Axis III, the clinician will discover that some medical conditions may or may not be directly related to the mental disorder but need to be assessed for their prognostic or treatment implications. For example, if hypothyroidism is a direct cause of depressive symptoms, then this would be coded on Axis I as 293.83, Mood Disorder Due to Hypothyroidism, with Depressive Features, with hypothyroidism listed again on Axis III. This combined coding becomes useful for certain groups known to have high rates of comorbid health conditions (e.g., undetected diabetes for African Americans).

Axis IV permits the provider to assess the Psychosocial and Environmental Problems that may affect the diagnosis, treatment, and prognosis of mental disorders. Both positive (e.g., job promotion) and negative stressors (e.g., longer work hours) can be highlighted as factors influencing the mental health status of the individual.

Axis V (Global Assessment of Functioning) is for reporting the clinician's judgment about the individual's overall level of psychological, social, and occupational functioning. The clinician can rate the client over several time periods (e.g., current functioning, highest level of functioning for at least twelve months).

Once the discussion of Axes III, IV, and V has occurred, and the Biopsychosocial-Cultural Checklist has been integrated through the discussion, the provider will be more likely to make an accurate diagnosis for Axis I (Clinical Disorders) and Axis II (Personality Disorders, or Mental Retardation).

Assessment

Ramirez (1991) identifies seven domains that the provider can use to assess the range of traditionalism to modernism that the client brings to the session:

1. *Gender roles definition.* Traditional environments stress distinct boundaries between males and females, whereas modern environments encourage more flexible roles.
2. *Family identity.* Traditional environments emphasize family identity over individual recognition, whereas modern environments encourage separation from family.
3. *Sense of community.* Traditional cultures foster notions of responsibility to the community, whereas modern culture promotes individualism.
4. *Time orientation.* People raised in traditional societies may view time with an emphasis on past and present orientation, whereas people who were raised in modern societies may be more future oriented.

5. *Age status.* Traditional societies value the wisdom of the elderly, while modern society values images of youth.
6. *Deference to authority.* Traditional societies emphasize conformity to standards and traditions with an emphasis on respecting authority, whereas modern societies are encouraged to challenge authority.
7. *Spirituality and religion.* Traditional societies acknowledge the importance of spirituality in explaining life circumstances, whereas modern societies are characterized by an emphasis on empiricism and secularism.

Most clients fall somewhere on the continuum, and clinicians will benefit from understanding their client's cultural orientation. Traditional orientations, emphasize close family and community ties; the emphasis is on cooperation, with spiritualism used as a way of explaining life. Modern orientations on the other hand, refer to lifestyles and belief systems that encourage individuation and separation from family and community; the emphasis is on individual competition and empiricism as a way of understanding life circumstances.

Organizational Concerns

Providers must pay attention to organizational structures that influence how clients participate in services. Fuller (1994) suggests that education, prevention, outreach, and greater involvement in the delivery and appropriation of health care resources are critical to making services accessible for people from differing ethnic communities. This becomes particularly relevant when delineating collateral services during utilization reviews.

Structural Concerns

An important strategy in improving care and reducing overall health care costs is ensuring ready access to cost-effective treatment services for ethnic populations. Health and mental health care institutions that regularly serve non-Western client groups have special responsibilities to make resources accessible and available. Jecker et al. (1995) describe how AT&T developed the Language Line to provide twenty-four-hour access to interpreters who speak 147 different languages. Another service is Language Banks, which are computerized lists of bilingual staff members. Human resources managers can provide intensive language training to staff to assist them in communicating with non-English-speaking populations.

Managed mental health clinicians need to recognize access issues for ethnic populations who present with physical and mental health problems. There are numerous differences among immigrant and refugee families and their willingness to appreciate information and prevention programs. Providers benefit from conducting needs assessments within the communities to ascertain what types of services are needed and by whom.

The essence of good prevention programs is knowing what is working in communities and building on that. Community surveys, conducted at local temples or churches, can be helpful to the clinician wanting to influence and understand health care practices for certain ethnic communities. Health education campaigns that utilize radio announcements have been found to be useful.

Corin (1994) recommends four ways that providers can adjust their actions to meet local conditions:

1. Programs have to be culturally and socially acceptable as well as appropriate. This means they must respect social definitions of privacy frontiers and the rules for giving and receiving support. Often the best ideas for prevention programs come from within the community.

2. Programs must build on community strengths and insights. Mental health services must not contribute to a collective sense of inadequacy or fragility by well-intentioned but culturally inappropriate actions.

3. Attempts to modify attitudes and behaviors should be based on an understanding of their cultural origins and significance, what function they serve, and the perceived position within the life of the community. For example, prevention programs in a Native American community would do well to emphasize a wellness philosophy that stresses family health as a result of individual actions.

4. The concept of at-risk populations (e.g., African-American young women) should be complemented by target conditions (e.g., poverty and substance abuse). Some programs may base their ser-

vice model on data that emphasize at-risk populations (e.g., African-American women who are pregnant and are substance abusers). Analyses that focus solely on typical at-risk markers, such as race, are neither appropriate nor useful in improving mental health care delivery (Shulman 1995).

Corin (1994) recommends that providers avoid dwelling on the individual, who cannot change his or her status (e.g., as a female and person of color), and focus on the environmental or social conditions (e.g., poverty) that may lead to increased risk of mental health problems (e.g., substance abuse). He suggests that attention be focused on the way in which specific or general health problems arise from a complex web of social and cultural determinants in an environment. Shulman (1995) extends this recommendation by suggesting that clinicians and policy analysts provide a broader inclusion of socioeconomic variables in the mental health services research analyses. For example, education, geographic proximity to clinic services, health status, immigrant or refugee status, employment level in the community, and location of regional health services are all variables that will be indicative of a community's mental health status and ability to respond to health promotion and disease prevention efforts. Shulman argues that by having a better understanding of these socioeconomic variables, providers can reduce undesirable differences in health care access and outcomes across populations, as well as develop health access policies that address correctable issues.

Training

Managed care organizations must train primary care clinicians in the early diagnosis and appropriate referral of clients with cormorbid conditions, such as substance abuse with gastrointestinal problems. Ramirez (1991) reminds us that values influence our socialization and teaching styles, which in turn affect the development of certain learning and problem-solving styles. If mental health education is to be effective, providers should make sure that health promotion strategies match the cultural orientation and learning style of the client. As clinicians tailor mental health practice curriculum programs to the issues clients face, they must match literacy and comprehension programs with the learning style of the client.

Personnel

The personnel available in a managed mental health organization are important to clients from differing communities. A fair procedure would be one that has a balanced representation of individuals from both Western clinical practice and the client's culture (Jecker et al. 1995). Corin (1994) makes the argument for hiring "like practitioners." His point is that since practitioners from the same culture share their patients' ideas regarding acceptable modes of symptom expression, they are predisposed to accept the physical interpretation of symptoms rather than to recognize individual or psychosocial origins of illness behavior. Westermeyer (1991) views the inclusion of immigrant staff in the health care system as a key tactic in a prevention strategy that encourages indigenous immigrant networks to integrate with the health care network. Treatment staff should include members of patients' ethnic groups to attract patients to treatment early and to maintain them in treatment.

Orlandi (1992) says that providers who are culturally sophisticated are (1) knowledgeable on the cognitive dimension (e.g., familiar with inter- and intraethnic differences), (2) committed to change on the affective dimension (e.g., able to express awareness and apply action to needed areas of change), (3) highly skilled (e.g., possessing appropriate techniques for skill building and problem solving), and (4) constructive in the overall effect of these qualities. In other words, being culturally sensitive means that both parties should refrain from assuming that their own ethical standard and cultural traditions represent universally valid truths (Jecker et al. 1995). It is not enough for the provider to be highly knowledgeable and fully committed to change; he or she must have the requisite skills to accomplish the change.

CONCLUSION

It is important to bear in mind that people develop learning and problem-solving styles that reflect the values and belief systems of their culture, their community, and their family (Ramirez 1991). Managed care systems need to foster a philosophy of respect that embraces the unique intellectual and cultural attributes of ethnic populations. For managed care to work with individuals from differing ethnic communities, considerable effort will need to be made to identify local needs and attitudes to ensure participation in program choices. These choices must be broadened to include diverse views of problems and their solutions. Without thoughtful representation and participation, many individuals and families will continue to be marginalized participants in the health and mental health care system.

Chapter 8

Ethical and Legal Issues of Managed Mental Health Care

Managed care has changed much of what is expected of a clinician. The entry of this new corporate control of what was once primarily a cottage industry has been accompanied by a variety of ethical and legal issues. In part, these issues arise from pitting people against profit. Many practitioners are troubled by the profit motive of a managed care organization, in contrast to their commitment to improving the quality of life of their clients—a commitment that provides a comfortable standard of living with median salaries of approximately $50,000, $49,000, and $81,000 for social workers, professional counselor, and psychologists, respectively (Ridgewood 1995).

These are comfortable incomes by many standards. Because they result from private mental health services the ethical dilemma is not so much a profit motive, but the shift of control of the finances from the clinician to a corporate entity. The economic impact of cost containment inevitably will translate into less care—either no treatment for those where it is not deemed necessary or shorter treatment for those who are authorized for services. We believe the ethical and legal issues must not be disguised as ones of money, profit, or financing. Rather, they must be seen in the context of practice. As such, ethical questions must be answered from the parameters of ethical and lawful clinical practice—not ethical and lawful business practice. This source of an-

189

swers will advance the managed care partnership with practitioners who are concerned with the best interest of the client. Unless we question the entire marketplace approach to mental health services, then the financial issues are, at best, of shift of control and profits.

Each clinician working in a managed care setting, or dealing with a client whose care is governed by a managed care organization, deals daily with many ethical and potentially legal issues. These issues are more difficult to resolve than in the past, prior to the advent of managed care, because there is now another party to the client-clinician-payor relationship.

Often the ethical and legal issues of managed mental health care are not recognized initially, which tends to compound the difficulty of handling the conflict properly. In this chapter we address a number of these issues including: conflicts of interest, confidentiality, informed consent, negligence, duties of the contract and the fiduciary, and financial obligations. Our intent is to elucidate some of the leading ethical and legal issues posed by managed care. Our goal is to provide helpful information for responding to ethical and legal issues of managed care. To us, the overarching guideline is to do what is in the best interest of the client.

DEFINING ETHICAL AND LEGAL ISSUES

Many of the challenges providers face from having clients' care managed by a fourth party are a combination of ethical and legal questions. For example, confidentiality is an ethical issue to every mental health professional; it is also a binding obligation and standard of care in the opinion of the courts (Weiner and Wettstein 1993). In this sense, ethical and legal issues differ in that ethical transgressions may be handled by professional organizations and state licensing. Ethics are often addressed through a professional organization and resolved with the established code of conduct. Professional ethics are the codification of what is considered right or just conduct for a person who voluntarily joins the association (Loewenberg and Dolgoff 1992). They are designed as guides to professional conduct and decision making (Sabin 1994).

Legal conflicts are those with the potential for judicial intervention or the threat of such an intervention (i.e., "I'm gonna call my lawyer and sue you!"). A legal issue is also different from an ethical one in terms of the threshold of harm that must be reached before there is action. That is, usually a legal issue is quite serious before it comes to the costly attention of the court system. Judicial intervention is designed to enforce a contractual obligation or remedy a wrong. It is predicated on damages—damages to society, as in the case of criminal action, or damages to an individual, as in the case of civil action. Legal issues of managed mental health care have resulted from common law, state statutes (such as mental health laws), professional licensing, and insurance regulations.

CONFLICTS OF INTEREST

A conflict of interest is a dilemma between two or more competing duties. For practitioners in managed mental health care, this is most likely between the duties to the client and those to the fourth party. This may be an ethical issue addressed in the professional code of ethics, or it may be a legal issue depending on common law or state statutes. The most blatant and ever-present conflict of interests from practicing in a managed care environment is the balance between delivery of quality care in the best interest of the client and cost containment in the best interest of the managed care organization (Sabin 1994).

Like most other ethical dilemmas, this one is not simple. After all, few practitioners are not also concerned with making a living from their practice. There are two aspects of managed care that seem to have pushed the profit issue to the threshold of a dilemma: it threatens a practitioner's standard of living by controlling practitioner costs, and many believe that managed care organizations are concerned primarily with profit, at the cost of adequate care for clients. In essence, for many practitioners the conflict of interest is between decreased hourly wages while increasing the demands of practice (e.g., paperwork), and a concern for best practice balanced against the managed care organization's emphasis on cost containment. How does a provider serve the best interest of the client in an era where "less is better"?

The conflict is seen in the obligation to serve the client with the best means available—beneficence—in contrast with society's best interest—communitarianism. In essence, should the least expensive cost to society be considered in the formulation of treatment decisions? (Wolf 1994). Sabin (1994) conceptualizes this to include an ethical conflict with society where a scarce and limited resource is being rationed in the marketplace. In Sabin's opinion, managed care has shifted the focus from being primarily the best interest of the client to the cost of that interest. Understandably providers cannot be concerned solely with what treatment may be in the best interest of the client without also considering the cost of that care to society; anything else is narrow and one-sided. In a society of limited resources in a marketplace economy, there are unfortunate trade-offs in access to services. Society, and thus everyone involved in clinical practice, must consider the cost of services, its impact on other services, and the availability of services for others in need. In essence, there is something to be said about factoring communitarianism into the cost formula of mental health. Should one group of peoples get expensive services to the exclusion of step-down services for others?

As Sabin (1994) discusses, few professional organizations give consideration to the conflict between providing the best care and the cost of that care to society. Sabin notes how this is addressed by the National Association of Social Workers but is absent from the professional code for the American Psychiatric Association, with the exception of a reference in the preamble. This contrasts sharply with the communitarian value in the United Kingdom's system, where the clinician's ethical duty is to provide both efficacious and economic treatment.

Consequently, professional organizations have provided little guidance around the communitarian ethical conflict of the best interest of the client and social justice. For the purposes of managed care, social justice is the distribution of mental health resources. Both the new system of care management and the old system of independent practitioners believe they know best how to distribute the access to this resource in a just manner.

Most likely the language of providers' professional ethics and values places the client in the paramount position independent of the cost of services. Without professional guidelines, it is difficult to solve this dilemma. Sabin (1994) suggests that it be resolved in part by informing the potential client of the existence of the conflict and collaborating with the client in managing that conflict. Moreover, it is advisable to bring this conflict to the attention of professional organizations at the local and national levels. Practitioners who voluntarily support and uphold the conduct of a professional organization have a legitimate expectation that their organization will help facilitate decision making in this type of dilemma. Professional organizations must not shy away from working cooperatively with managed care to address these and other issues. As Sabin (1994) summarizes, the professional code of ethics must continue to hold the best interest of the client first but strike a balance that recognizes both the stewardship of society and the fidelity to the client.

The conflict of interests is not limited to issues of the client's needs and the need for cost containment. It also includes conflicts between the provider's dual obligations to clients and the managed care company. Hall (1994b) calls this a conflict of allegiance. It occurs when providers are in fact agents of two different parties who might eventually have competing interests. This is especially problematic in the early stages of treatment, when a prospective utilization review is occurring. At this time, it is legally arguable that the provider has not formed a therapeutic relationship with the client and is thus an agent of the managed care organization. If an assessment does not reasonably lead to treatment, then the clinician's obligation to the potential client is minimal (*Oregon v. Miller*, 1985).

But quite possibly the provider has a higher duty to the managed care organization than to the potential client, if not directly than ostensibly. Still, it is probably best to resolve any conflict from fidelity and beneficence to the person seeking services and let the fourth party intervenor assert its own rights. In other words, by proceeding from the best interest of the client, the damages would be less than if the provider allowed the first priority to be a managed care organization.

CONFIDENTIALITY

Confidentiality is as much an ethical issue as it is a legal one. Like informed consent, it is derived from the principle of autonomy. Client autonomy refers to the governing principle that clients are independent in making their own decisions. Clients evidence autonomy by determining with whom they wish to develop a confidential relationship and what will occur in the course of that relationship. With the advent of managed care and electronic information management systems (Alpert 1993; Gostin et al. 1993), an independent fourth party may determine to whom a client will confide. By developing preauthorized treatment protocols, much of what may occur privately between a client and a clinician may be determined by someone else. In essence, then, managed care has the potential to determine in whom a client will confide. By restricting the focus of treatment, much of what the client may confide may also be determined by managed care. And yet almost every mental health textbook in every discipline considers confidentiality a hallmark of the therapeutic relationship and essential to successful treatment (Smith and Meyer 1987; Weiner and Wettstein 1993). There is even reason to argue that confidentiality is part of the legally defined standard of care (*MacDonald v. Clinger*, 1982). With managed care, the confidential client-clinician relationship has a managed care reviewer eavesdropping (Corcoran and Winslade 1994; Parsi, Winslade, and Corcoran 1995).

There are reasons that such deference is given to confidentiality. Confidentiality serves to protect the disclosure of private subject matter by recognizing a client's privacy interests and autonomous control over who should know that private information. As such, confidentiality serves an important public policy by facilitating the seeking of treatment by those who are in need of services. Failure to extend confidentiality would chill the actual use of needed services if the information discussed is not kept private. Moreover, without confidentiality, clients in need of service may shy away from seeking it, resulting in a more unhealthy individual, who eventually would cost even more to help.

Similarly, this public policy is served by extending confidentiality to the context of treatment—that is, the fact that someone is even seeking clinical services. As Smith and Meyer (1987) discuss, a person in need of services may avoid seeking therapy because of the stigma associated with being a "mental patient." Consequently, the very fact that someone is in treatment should be considered a private matter and confidential in order to encourage those who need help to get it. Managed care opens this private information to a fourth party, which may not have a duty to protect the client's right to privacy.

Legal Basis of Confidentiality

A client's right to confidentiality is legally based on the right to privacy. Confidentiality is the privacy right to determine who will know information that was private but has been disclosed. In a strict sense, information that has been disclosed to another is no longer private. As such, the issue switches from a privacy right to informational privacy.

Because confidentiality is based on a privacy right, it is afforded some constitutional protection. This protection, however, has limits since that which is to be protected is actually no longer private because it was told to someone else—e.g., a therapist. Confidentiality, then, has less protection than privacy.

The legal right to confidentiality was advanced primarily in *Griswold v. Connecticut* (1965) and the well-known *Roe v. Wade* (1973), which upheld the constitutional right to privacy, including privacy between a patient and a physician. These and other cases advance the doctrine that the Constitution creates a zone of privacy in which government may not intrude unless there is a compelling state interest (e.g., public safety and involuntary commitment). If there is a compelling state interest, the state may invade a person's privacy, but that invasion must be narrowly tailored not to extend beyond the compelling interest.

This would be the case for privacy but not confidentiality. As a less protected right, confidential information is easier for government to intrude into legally than occurs for privacy. To invade confidential information, the state needs only a rational basis for the action, which outweighs the individual's right to keep the information secret. This type of test of the constitutionality of a law is called a *balancing test*, whereby the state's interest is balanced against the individual's right. In contrast, a compelling state interest that narrowly tailors the action must be shown in order to invade privacy. This is a higher and more difficult test to pass in order for a law to be held constitutional. It is known as *strict scrutiny*.

Much of the current clarity on the right to privacy is articulated in *Whalen v. Roe* (1977), a New York case that challenged a statute requiring disclosure of a patient's identity if he or she was prescribed certain medications. Imagine what effect this statute would have if a provider were required to notify a state agency that a particular person had sought treatment, was being treated with a certain form of therapy, and that it was occurring on a regular basis. For a state to know who is taking what medication, how much, and how often is certainly an invasion of private information. The legal question, though, is whether this clinical information is protected.

The Supreme Court held the statute was not unconstitutional. It reasoned that the information was not strictly private, which allowed for the lower test (rational basis test). The Court held that New York State had a rational basis for invading the confidentiality and that this rational basis was greater than the individual's right to confidentiality. If a privacy right had existed (instead of a right to confidentiality), New York would have needed a compelling interest in knowing the information, and the action would have to be narrowly tailored to meet that compelling interest. Moreover, and more important for our purposes, the Court allowed for a lower constitutional test of the law because the state intended to continue to keep the information confidential. That is, the protection of the secret information would transfer to the state. Without the safeguard of securing this confidential information, Justice William Brennan argued in a concurring opinion, the issue would rise to one of privacy and require strict scrutiny in determining if it was constitutional.

In additional to constitutional protection, a client's right to confidentiality is protected by other legal theories, such as a fiduciary duty, a contract obligation, and the tort theory of negligence, which is commonly called malpractice. The application of these theories is seen in *MacDonald v. Clinger* (1982), in which the court recognized a duty not to disclose a client's confidential information. The breach of this duty was an invasion of privacy. This duty is based on the fiduciary relationship, that is, the client is in a position to trust the clinician.

The concurring opinion in *MacDonald* rejected the fiduciary duty, stating that confidentiality is part of the clinical standard of care. Consequently, confidentiality is protected by theories of negligence, and to breach the duty is malpractice. Additionally, *Roe v. Doe* (1977) advanced the protection of confidentiality in terms of an implied contract. In yet another case (*Home v. Patton*, 1993), which is parallel to many managed care settings, a physician was held liable for revealing confidential information to an employer. It is quite imaginable that capitated managed care offered by an employer runs the risk of unlawful disclosure of client information.

Confidentiality has various sorts of legal protection, and its importance to treatment is well recognized by professionals in mental health and the law. The legal protection of confidentiality becomes particularly complicated in the light of exceptions to the duty and the conflicting duty to protect others from a dangerous patient. Under these conditions, there may be an exception to keeping private information confidential. An example of this exception to confidentiality is seen in *People v. O'Gorman* (1977). In this case confidential information disclosed during a welfare eligibility interview was considered exempt from protection because it was the contemplation of a crime.

The duty to protect was first advanced in *Tarasoff v. Regents* (1976). The exception arises if the clinician knew—or should have known—that a client is dangerous. In California at least, the conflict between the provider's duty not to disclose and the duty to protect was settled in the much-publicized case of Eric and Lyle Menendez (*Menendez v. Superior Court*, 1992). Prior to this holding, once confidential information was breached, for whatever reason, it was no longer confidential and therefore not protected. This included confidential information disclosed in the course of fulfilling the duty to protect (*People v. Clark*, 1990). In *Clark* the information resulting in a duty to protect was later used in sentencing as evidence of premeditation.

In *Menendez* the courts reconsidered *Clark* and held that the duty to protect was independent of the patient's reasonable expectation of privacy (*State v. Miller*, 1985). In other words, confidential information does not have to remain secret to stay privileged. That is, the client retains the right to confidentiality if the disclosure was made by the client with the reasonable expectation that it would remain private. For Eric and Lyle Menendez, this meant that damaging evidence released under a duty to protect was not admissible in the trials of murdering their parents with a shotgun.

For clinicians, especially those in a managed care system, the *Menendez* case has a different importance. As noted by Corcoran and Winslade (1994), it reaffirms that the right to confidentiality is not easily dismissed. Moreover, disclosure to a third party, such as a managed care organization, does not destroy the client's reasonable expectation of privacy. Finally, the holding asserts that the dangerous person exception and duty to protect is an expectation superior to confidentiality but restricted to those persons who are in the zone of danger while pressuring the testimonial privilege of the confidential relationship.

This provides some comfort in knowing there is less frustration of the public policy interest by protecting a client's right to privacy and extending that expectation onto a managed care organization. If New York was allowed to invade the privacy interest of patients with a rational basis for needing the information (*Whalen*), and this was permissible in part because the information would remain secure, then it is reasonable to expect the same standards of managed care organizations.

Consequently, we believe clients and providers have a reasonable expectation of privacy when it comes to managed mental health care. If a managed care organization accepts confidential information, then it should do so with all the strings attached. That is, it must also adhere to a duty to keep the private information confidential. If a managed care organization has need of any information, it must accept the responsibility to ensure the information remains confidential.

There are at least two ways for providers and clients to be assured the information will remain secure. First, they can explicitly state this expectation in writing. Ideally this will be addressed in any contract with a managed care organization. If it is not, the provider must insist on additional clauses to address client confidentiality. Second, providers must explicitly discuss this issue with clients. This impediment to the potential therapeutic relationship probably needs disclosure in order for a client to consent to treatment. Without discussion of the impact of managed care on confidentiality, a client's consent is not based on complete information and is not informed consent.

There can be no doubt that managed care has restricted clients' autonomy and interferes with the confidential relationship. As Corcoran and Winslade (1994) point out, this includes the context and much of the content of treatment. Invasion into the context of treatment is seen in prospective utilization reviews, where the fact that someone is distressed enough to seek treatment is revealed to a fourth party. Invasion into the content of treatment is found in concurrent and retrospective utilization reviews, where client progress is monitored and evaluated.

The intrusion into confidentiality may impede the development of the trust relationship between client and provider, a quite unfortunate effect. As all providers know from daily practice, little movement occurs without a trusting relationship. Without it serious issues are not disclosed, emotions are often guarded, and treatment goals superficial and their attainment thwarted.

Client Records

Intrusion into the confidential content of therapy occurs when a provider shares information about a client's progress during a concurrent or retrospective utilization review and a records review. Protection of the client's privacy interest includes medical records (Parmet 1981;

Winslade 1982), whether the content of this record is disclosed directly (as occurs with a records review), or indirectly (as occurs when summarizing the information to indicate client progress).

It is important to bear this in mind when completing a concurrent or retrospective utilization review. The information being disclosed is the client's. The provider learned this information with certain strings attached, and this fact ought to guide what he or she reveals and records in the clinical records.

It would seem advisable to consider record keeping from the position of what is in the client's best interest. This means keeping the records in a fashion that holds private information private. This may be facilitated with concise and relevant notes and submitting to a managed care organization information relevant to the authorization of services. For example, it is not relevant that a client who is authorized for treatment of depression smoked marijuana in college. Not only is this information not relevant to the treatment, but it may adversely affect a client's employment, insurance coverage, or standing in the community. Consequently, providers should go to great lengths to provide managed care organizations only the most relevant information.

This same issue occurs when records are reviewed as part of a retrospective utilization review procedure. The clinician is no longer able to determine if he or she will disclose some private information or if that information is part of the records. The same principles of concise and relevant information should apply to keeping records. A decision to keep lengthy notes must balance their clinical utility against the risk of unacceptable disclosure of private client information.

There is one special caveat that concerns prospective utilization reviews and assessments. Providers should give careful attention to the security of the managed care organization when it comes to assessment and prospective utilization reviews in particular. While much of the provider's role as a clinician and a managed care provider is one of double agentry, this likely is not the case with an assessment, which is often not seen as a legally confidential relationship unless one would reasonably believe it would lead to one (*Allred v. State*, 1976). An assessment conducted for a managed care organization may create a greater duty as an agent of the managed care organization than as the confidant or fiduciary of the potential client. This may also be the case for private information disclosed early in a prospective utilization review. Is there actually a client to whom one would owe a duty if there has not been the authorization of services? During these preauthorization times, providers may very well be considered an agent of the managed care organization and not in a trust relationship with a client.

The courts have yet to address many of these issues in confidentiality and managed care. Consequently, we think it is especially important to discuss with your clients your dual role with managed care in advance of working with your first managed care client. This serves not only the privacy interest of clients, but the provider's obligation to protect that private information.

INFORMED CONSENT

Another major ethical and legal issue concerns client-informed consent. In order for any practitioner to proceed with an intervention, it must be with the consent of the client, and that consent must be informed. The question is whether clients consent to managed care and its participation in treatment. Did the client agree to have a fourth party participate in determining if treatment was necessary or consent to his or her provider's disclosure of private and confidential information?

Managed care has given pause to whether the consent that is given is truly informed, especially in the area of disclosing confidential information and the time when informed consent may be obtained. Confidentiality and informed consent are often complicated by state statutes on licensure and insurance law, where disclosure of confidential information need not require the consent of the client. As Winslade (1982) notes, few clients would understand the availability and complexity of disclosure law, and fewer yet would likely approve. Thus, while much of what we believe clients should consent to may not be legally necessary, all providers should still inform clients fully and get their permission to disclose the context and content of treatment.

There are three elements of informed consent: (1) a thorough understanding of the particular procedures to be used, (2) full knowledge of the risks involved in the procedures, and (3) knowledge of alternative procedures. For managed care and informed consent there are questions about whether alternative procedures are available and whether the consent is truly informed. The number of alternatives may be greatly reduced in terms of those that are available and paid for by a managed care organization. As Rodwin (1995) argues, informed consent should include informing the potential client of such restrictions. In other words, the duty to disclose should reasonably include the fact that the client's selection of provider and the nature of this relationship (its duration and intervention) may be restricted by a managed care organization.

Moreover, too many clinicians tend to defer to the suggestions from a managed care reviewer and may not fully consider the available treatment options. This suggests providers need to pay particular attention to what alternatives are available because this is not likely going to occur at the managed care level. If there is an alternative procedure, it is important to discuss it with the client, even if it is not one of the preferred practices of the managed care organization. In other words, the scope of the provider's duty is to consider all the available interventions, not just those authorized by the managed care reviewer.

Additionally, since we think that a managed care organization is less likely than the provider to consider viable alternatives, the provider will need to be prepared to advocate for the client. A provider who believes there is a better alternative treatment must not be idle and use what may be a less efficacious intervention. He or she must inform the client and be an advocate for the best intervention.

Informed Consent's Paradox

The time at which informed consent must be obtained greatly influences when to discuss the matter with the client. There is legal precedent for asserting that consent must occur before that to which one is to consent has occurred (*Roe v. Doe*, 1977). Informed consent must be prospective, not retroactive. This means consent given after the fact is not informed because of the potential influence of the trust relationship and all the dynamics of transference and countertransference that give rise to undue influence.

The requirement to consent prior to treatment creates a bit of a paradox. Consent prior to the developing relationship and the discovery of pertinent topics is consenting to content that is still unknown. How can a client consent to something that is not yet known? Such consent is truly uninformed.

This is quite similar to the problem with release of confidential information: one does not know to what one is consenting. How can a client consent to the disclosure of a repressed memory when it was not known at the time consent was obtained? It is not informed consent. In terms of a practice with managed care, how can a client truly consent to disclosing the progress in treatment when that progress is not known?

This paradox is addressed by the American Psychiatric Association (1987), though few other professional organizations have recognized or resolved this dilemma. The APA's solution is one of fidelity and beneficence. It recommends that providers conduct themselves in the best interest of the client. Thus, a solution to this paradox is to obtain as much informed consent as possible continuously. This includes delineating and thoroughly discussing with each potential client the eventual managed care procedures. We suggest doing this with clients with all aspects of the entire course of treatment: prospective arrangements, concurrent and retrospective utilization reviews, and possible record reviews and follow-up assessments. By continuously obtaining a client's consent, the provider is more assured that the client is informed about the interfacing role of the provider with managed care.

Secret Agents and Informed Consent

Because of contractual obligations with a managed care organization and the professional relationship with clients, managed care has created a double agent in the provider, who serves the best interest of the client and the pecuniary interest of the managed care organization's goals of cost containment and profit. This can lead to problems in informed consent.

The complexity of this double agentry is furthered by many managed care contracts that contain nondisclosure clauses. A nondisclosure clause restricts the discussion with clients of the limitations imposed by a managed care organization. In other words, the double agent must also become a secret agent. Any effort to resolve the conflict of a double agentry by client informed consent is out of the question. In the absence of a nondisclosure clause, obtaining informed consent from a client to participate in all aspects of the managed care (including the procedures, risk, and alternatives) should address most of the ethical issues. If the managed care organization requires a nondisclosure agreement, we suggest negotiating some alternative arrangement, perhaps by soliciting the help of other providers to address this issue and seeing that it is taken up by state and local professional organizations. Being a secret agent would thwart client autonomy and informed consent and must not be permissible as ethical managed care practice.

NEGLIGENCE

Most of the development in managed care law has been in the area of negligence. The tort of negligence is commonly called malpractice. This area of the law defines the legally binding conduct of practitioners in terms of their duty as a clinician, a breach of that duty, and resulting harm (Prosser, Wade, and Schwartz 1988). In terms of clinical practice, the duty is to provide treatment within a reasonable standard of care.

Malpractice is probably one of the foremost legal concerns to most practitioners. It motivates us to pay the premium on our professional liability insurance, and probably to be a little extra cautious with our clinical interventions (Furrow et al. 1991). Not surprisingly, most managed care organizations require providers to have malpractice insurance. Some even specify the amount of the coverage the insurance must provide in the event of malfeasance. Having malpractice insurance has always been a sound professional practice, and the advent of managed care has not changed that at all.

The legal development of malpractice and managed care tends to concern whether a managed care organization is legally liable for negligent practice. Should managed care be linked in the loop of liability? Or is managing care remote and attenuated from the act of delivering treatment? Should practitioners be able to assert an "it's not my fault" reasoning and shield their professional goodwill, reputation, and assets from a negligence claim?

The question of the duty owed by a managed care organization was first seen in *Wickline v. California* (1986). In this case the defendant sued the state of California for negligence due to authorizing only four days of hospitalization and not the eight requested by her physician. As a consequence of her early discharge, postoperative complications were exacerbated, resulting in the amputation of her leg. The court held that the managed care organization was not responsible because it did not participate in the medical decision to discharge Wickline. That decision, the courts reasoned, was a medical one, and by state statute only physicians may lawfully practice medicine. Moreover, the evidence suggested the decision to discharge was based on the medical evidence available to the physician and not just the cost-containment restrictions inserted by the managed care organization. Consequently, the responsibility and liability for the patient's care must remain the physician's. In other words, managed care may not be used as a shield to liability.

The court did not, however, discharge managed care from any liability, but deliberately asserted that the decision was to link managed care into the liability loop. The court stated that injured parties should recover "when care which should have been provided is not provided" and that the recovery should be "from all those responsible for the deprivation of such care, including . . . health care payors" (p. 670).

Wickline has direct implications for practitioners in managed mental health care. The court believed the action was an attempt to reduce the physician's liability by arguing he was complying with managed care authorization. The court, however, opined that the purpose and role of cost containment and quality assurance may not be used to discharge or disregard the physician's duty when making medical decisions. Medical decisions must be made on the available evidence. As such, the practitioner may not use the constraints of managed care as a cushion against being held accountable for the harm caused by those clinical decisions.

This "no-shield" doctrine speaks directly to all practitioners in managed care settings. Unquestionably, in the emerging view of the judicial system the course of treatment must be charted by sound professional judgment, and requirements of managed care may not impede that judgment. If such impediments occur, the provider's own liability will not be reduced. Consequently, the answer to one of the questions we raised earlier is that there is no defense to malpractice to claim, "It's not my fault. The managed care company made me do it."

While clearly not releasing the managed care organization from its own liability, other critical cases emerged from confusion over *Wickline*'s no-shield doctrine. The first upheld a judgment for denying coverage for psychiatric inpatient hospitalization. The denial of services was done, the court concluded, without adequate information and therefore without medical grounds for the resulting decision. This was negligent and with conscious disregard for the client, held the court in *Hughes v. Blue Cross of Northern California* (1988). *Hughes* indicates that while clinicians are not shielded from negligent decisions, neither is a managed care organization. With *Hughes*, the no-shield doctrine became applicable to both the clinician and the managed care organization.

In a similar case, Blue Cross of Southern California was sued for contributing to the wrongful death of a person who suffered from drug dependency and major depression (*Wilson v. Blue Cross*, 1990). The critical facts of this case were that three to four weeks of hospitalization were requested but only ten days were authorized by the managed care organization. The patient committed suicide within the three-week period when hospitalization was requested—an event that most likely would not have occurred if not for the negligent decision by the managed care organization. The appeals court was ruling on a lower court's pretrial motion to dismiss the case. It held there was sufficient evidence of a material question: whether managed care could be held liable for negligence, to allow the client to sue. In other words, *Wilson* furthers the conclusions of *Wickline* and *Hughes* that managed care may be held liable for decisions that harm clients.

Another view of negligence includes not just withholding care but its coordination as well. This is advanced in a recent case (*Marmar v. Health Care Plan of New Jersey*, 1995); the appeals court ruled unanimously that the HMO could be held liable for breaching a duty to coordinate care. This recognition of the emerging duty opens the door for countersuits by malfeasant providers to sue for contributions to malpractice judgments. It also opens the door for patients to sue HMOs more easily and established that the negligent action is not limited to denial of services, but extends to poorly managed services.

These cases have implications for providers' duty to clients in a managed care setting. As Applebaum (1992) argues, there seems to be an emerging duty to exhaust all the administrative procedures that are available. This means providers must appeal a decision to deny coverage or to limit the length of treatment when their professional judgment concludes that treatment is necessary. Failure to exhaust the appeals that are afforded to a client, and the provider as the client's agent, will not minimize the provider's liability or be evidence that the managed care organization was negligent.

ABANDONMENT

Failure to exhaust the available appeal procedures, and thus to terminate treatment, runs the added risk of negligent termination, a legal cause of action also known as *abandonment*. Abandonment is the legal claim of malpractice whereby the clinician improperly terminated treatment (Weiner and Wettstein 1993). It is the failure to provide needed clinical services in a case in which the provider has assumed responsibility for the client's care and knew or should have known that continued care was necessary. The most blatant example of abandonment occurs when someone learns his or her partner is having a sexual relationship with the couple's marital therapist. In such circumstances the marital therapist has abandoned the innocent spouse (*Mazza v. Huffaker*, 1983).

Practitioners working in a managed care setting run the risk of abandonment by limiting treatment to that authorized by the managed care organization. If a client needs more therapy than is authorized for reimbursement, the provider's duty continues regardless of the limit imposed by the managed care organization. To terminate the client's care simply because it was authorized for only a limited number of sessions may be negligent termination or abandonment.

The elements of abandonment provide practitioners with some guidelines for what to do when treatment authorization is not sufficient for the client's clinical needs. First, the provider's duty is to give the client all the care that is clinically necessary. Financial limitations are not factors in the formula of how far clinicians must go to provide a nonnegligent standard of care. Providers may not be responsible for providing continuous care to all clients, such as those who threaten them; however, for the routine client seen in a managed care setting, the clinician may not determine termination by the limits of a prospective utilization review or a concurrent utilization review's denial of additional services. The decision to terminate must rest on clinical evidence, not managed care authorization.

Surprisingly, no case law to date has reached the appeals courts based on an abandonment cause of action. This is partially because prospective utilization reviews are more directly related to a question of determining the standard of care, which is more easily evidenced as a simple negligence cause of action. Thus, many potential cases are argued first from negligent practice, with abandonment as an alternative theory. If a damaged client were to win on negligence, the abandonment claim becomes moot. Moreover, termination is more a question of concurrent and retrospective utilization reviews. Suits here are more often concerned with unlawful withholding of payment or questions of insurance law than questions of negligent practice. This may suggest that most practitioners continue to provide the treatment needed, though the managed care company may not authorize payment. To do anything less must assuredly be questioned as negligence or abandonment. This is not to suggest that clinicians are to simply lose income. They should pursue action for nonpayment by a managed care organization, but not terminate treatment.

We do not mean to give the impression that managed care only creates a potential liability problem of abandonment. In fact, many features of a managed care organization provide a defense against a claim of abandonment. Prominent examples include on-call coverage, emergency services, and vacation coverage. Additionally, authorizing treatment interventions that are well defined with time limits may provide defense against a claim of negligent termination. After all, the client should have participated in developing the treatment and consented to it in advance. Establishing in advance the time that treatment will end may be evidence of proper notice.

THE CONTRACTUAL DUTY

Clinical practice in managed mental health care has also been influenced by legal cases based on contract law. A *contract* is defined as a legally binding agreement, composed of mutual assent between two parties of an offer, acceptance, and consideration. The contractual elements of mutual assent are often found in state mental health codes, such as when a patient has a right to participate in the development of an individualized treatment plan.

Contracts for mental health services are legally binding (*Anclote Manor Foundation v. Wilkinson*, 1972), as are treatment contracts (*Roe v. Doe*, 1977). However, court decisions may steer a client away from a contract cause of action. For example, in *Lackey v. Bressler* (1987) a client sued her psychiatrist for negligently prescribing haldol and thorazine, which resulted in her development of tardive dyskinesia. One of Lackey's theories for her suit was a contract claim asserting the breach of an implied standard of care. The court rejected this position, asserting that a contract claim was not a recognized legal theory for recovery for negligence. It also does not allow punitive damages, allowing for recovery of only that which was bargained for (the benefit of the bargain). Restrictions on a breach of contract claim were advanced similarly in *Faigenbaum v. Oakland Medical Center* (1985). In addition to malpractice, the plaintiff filed a breach of contract claim in the development of her tardive dyskinesia. This contract claim was necessary because government immunity precluded the tort claims but not a suit for breach of contract. The plaintiff claimed the payment of money created an implied contract as a matter of law. However, the court refused to address this issue since it was not properly appealed. Although the court did not rule on the contract, it did delineate four obstacles to a contract claim, three of them relevant to this discussion:

1. The payment of money does not create a contract as a matter of law because there was a preexisting duty to provide care.
2. A contract claim would fail because the mutuality of obligations was not dependent on the consideration. That is, payment was not the basis on which the duties of the clinician were created. This means that since the obligation is to continue care even if a client cannot pay, it is likely that the contract claim will fail because of the lack of consideration.
3. Private practitioners who provide even minimal free services to a client could claim the absence of a mutual obligation, thus voiding the implied contract.

To claim breach of contract, a client must either show the total cost within the limits of the statute of frauds (usually around $250) or produce a written contract. A treatment contract, and probably the prospective utilization review forms, would be considered written contracts. Moreover, if a written contract delineates well-defined treatment procedures, as are found with practice guidelines and many of the activities of a prospective utilization review, it would be specific enough to meet the elements of a contract. However, treatment contracts, including those developed in conjunction with a managed care organization, are intended to be guides to implementing treatment, not rigid prescriptions. They are often modified throughout the course of treatment. Such revisions may be sufficient to void the original agreement or establish a mutual mistake or misunderstanding, all of which may shield a clinician from contract liability. In other words, although it is possible that the written treatment contract may satisfy the statute of fraud, most are not written with sufficient specificity and would fail for vagueness or mutual mistake.

In essence, the law of contracts seems more directed to the pecu-niary relationship—service contracts—than the treatment relation-ship—treatment contracts. In this sense it would seem that a service contract is enforceable in court. Treatment contracts seem to continue to be a guide to practice but most likely will not be the basis of legal ac-tion as related to actual clinical practice.

Service contracts include those agreements made with the fourth-party managed care organization. The most prominent case on man-aged care and service contracts concerns the clinician's contractual obligations balanced against the duty to provide a nonnegligent stan-dard of care. It may seem that the courts would hold that the duty a practitioner owes to a client is greater than a contractual obligation to a managed care company, but this may not be the case. The courts seem to assert that these are independent duties. This conclusion is seen in *Varol v. Blue Cross/Blue Shield* (1987), where a group of practi-tioners wanted to be released from the prospective utilization review restrictions imposed by a managed care contract. The clinicians claimed the contract was interfering with the quality of care. The case was dismissed due to federal preemption, which occurs when a federal law overrules a state law. However, the court did point out that providers who agreed to the terms and conditions of cost containment and quality assurance could not later claim preauthorization was re-sponsible for their negligent care.

Varol suggests that if a provider's care for a client is negligent but within the parameters of the arrangement with the managed care orga-nization, the provider remains responsible for any harm he or she causes. Moreover, the case indicates that if the provider believes that the cost-containment and quality assurance arrangement is resulting in negligent care, this is not a basis to void the contract. If there is a con-tract, the courts will not provide refuge simply because that contract causes the provider's practice to be below the standard of care. In other words, practitioners who agree to have a fourth party manage client care cannot later ask the courts to protect them from themselves.

210 *Maneuvering the Maze of Managed Care*

THE FIDUCIARY DUTY

Another legal area that may affect practice in the managed care setting rests on the provider's duty as a fiduciary. A fiduciary relationship is one of trust, when one person is at a disadvantage to the other. The disadvantaged person is dependent on the other and must trust that person to proceed in his or her best interest. Such is the case for a person who needs a lawyer, a stockbroker, or a clinician.

The fiduciary duty is derived from the obligation held in the patient-psychiatrist trust relationship. Case law extends this duty to other professionals. This was first seen in *Horak v. Biris* (1985), where a husband sued a clinical social worker for having sexual intercourse with his wife while they were receiving marital counseling. In the court's opinion, the social worker held himself out as having expertise in clinical treatment, and he mishandled the transference relationship. The mishandling of the transference was held to be a breach of the fiduciary duty.

The principle in *Horak* is also seen in the federal courts. In *Simmons v. United States of America* (1986) a suit was brought against the government for injuries sustained from sexual misconduct by a federally employed social worker. The plaintiff sought mental health services from 1973 until the middle of 1981. A psychiatrist attending to Simmons two years later testified that the deterioration of Simmons's condition was due to the inappropriate response to the "normal transference relationship" (p. 1364). Although the *Simmons* court stated that sexual relations with clients are unanimously considered malfeasant conduct (malpractice), the court also "regarded mishandling of transference as malpractice or gross negligence" (p. 1365). To support this assertion, the court cited numerous cases, including *Horak v. Biris*, and exemplified this by referring to numerous fiduciary relationships. The court also noted that sex with the client eventually results in "violated" trust (p. 1367) and that the therapeutic relationship was "a trusting dependency relationship" (p. 1371).

Although all of these cases of the fiduciary involved sexual misconduct by clinicians, the point is the judicial recognition of the fiduciary in clinical practice. Moreover, the dependency trust in the fiduciary relationship is not simply that a clinician will not have sex with a client but will actually work for the client's best interest. This duty would be imposed, it seems, even though there will be restraints set forth by a managed care reviewer. As Kutchins (1991) observes, by establishing the fiduciary obligations, the client holds the clinician "to a higher standard of conduct than is usually required in malpractice cases and can shift a major portion of the burden of proof to professionals to demonstrate that they acted appropriately." Appropriate action would reasonably include advancing the client's best interest over the interest of any third or fourth party, such as a managed care organization.

As you can see, the fiduciary duty is held in high regard and affects many aspects of practice. One example we have discussed is informed consent (Reisner and Slobogin 1990). It, too, is supported as a fiduciary duty. A clinician's failure to inform patients of the benefits, risks, and alternatives to a particular treatment not only violates the statutes and common law of informed consent but breaches the fiduciary relationship of trust and honesty.

FINANCIAL ISSUES

Since so much money is at stake with mental health and its management, it is not surprising that how providers handle financial issues is also influenced by the law of managed care. According to the law, the conflict of money must be framed within the context of sound *clinical* practice, not acceptable *business* practice. There are, nonetheless, financial conflicts that may not impede the clinical relationship but do affect the relationship with managed care.

One fairly apparent example is the ethical and legal issue of receiving financial incentives from a managed care organization to reduce costs by reducing the amount of care provided. It is not uncommon for an HMO or panel of preferred providers to increase or decrease the financial compensation based on cost-containment goals and profits for the managed care organization (Hillman, Welch, and Pauly 1992; Morreim 1995). For example, a costly provider may be dismissed from a preferred provider panel, or a managed care organization may not renew contracts of practitioners who exceed the cost-containment goals.

The case law we have considered so far suggests that such financial conflicts be balanced in favor of the client's expectation of quality care and without the provider's breaching any contractual obligation to a managed care organization. The parameters of managed care are such that the primary obligation is to the client. This is easily stated but, admittedly, harder to implement. Probably every day that their practice includes a client whose care is managed by a fourth party, providers feel the pressure to hold down costs by controlling the type or duration of services.

Some practitioners have attempted to ensure quality care with sufficient reimbursement by passing the discounted costs onto the client. For example, a practitioner whose standard fee for service is $100 per hour but is authorized to be paid only $60 may hold the client responsible for the remaining $40. This practice is highly questionable, and many managed care organizations include conditions in their contracts that prohibit it. The managed care organization contends that the provider agreed to a reduced fee, not to some unusual fee split between the third-party payor and the client.

This issue is critical for retrospective utilization reviews where the evaluation of quality may determine the level of reimbursement. When clinicians receive a reduced payment because the intervention was not implemented as expected or the client has not totally reached the goals of treatment within the specified number of sessions, should they charge the client the balance? The clinician may contend that services have been given to the client. It would be like driving a car for ten weeks, determining it does not get the gas mileage expected, and then wanting to pay the car dealer a lower sticker price.

This is a more critical ethical—and perhaps legal—conflict than is suggested by the frequency of the current practice. Granted the arguments presented above are reasonable. However, the argument against them is more compelling. A variety of legal theories would support the claim that to charge a client the balance between the usual fee and the reduced managed care fee is unlawful. For example, it is arguable that such conduct is fraudulent. Not only did the clinician agree to the reduced fee arrangement in the first place, but the determination that the standard of care was less than expected was made by an independent evaluator (the managed care organization). Moreover, it was the clinician—and not necessarily the client—who selected or approved of the independent evaluator and the methods of evaluation and reimbursement. Much like *Varol*, it is inappropriate to agree to a retrospective utilization review that determines the level of reimbursement and then claim it is not fair and hold the client responsible.

Finally, we note one other important financial conflict: the temptation to "play the game" in order to attract clients whose care is managed. The most blatant example is to overstate the severity of symptoms or diagnosis of the client's condition simply to obtain treatment authorization. A similar example is a provider's accepting a treatment protocol from a managed care organization but then treating the client as he or she intended to anyway. It would be fairly easy to show that such behavior is an effort to defraud an insurance company. As criminal behavior and intentional misconduct, in all likelihood malpractice insurance does not provide coverage for any loss or legal costs for the provider's defense.

"Playing the game" is at odds with the principle of honesty, which is so important to clinical practice (Lazarus and Sharfstein 1994). Just as honesty is paramount to the client-clinician relationship, so too it is critical to the relationship these parties have with an insurance company or a managed care organization. Most clinicians also agree that the therapeutic relationship should not be tainted by conspiring to defraud the third-party payor. Moreover, such deception expands the distrust and dishonesty in the mental health care system and most likely will eventually adversely affect one's practice (Lazarus and Sharfstein 1994).

THE PROVIDER'S ETHICAL AND LEGAL DUTIES

Clearly there are many more ethical and legal issues resulting from the advent of managed mental health care. In fact, this field is developing so quickly that it is difficult to stay abreast of the developments. Nevertheless, the ethical and legal developments to this point provide some guidance for practitioners—if not in terms of clear duties, at least in the sense of emerging duties (Applebaum 1992). Much of this can be summarized in six emerging duties.

There are, of course, many more important ethical and legal issues. A good list of them is presented by Wolff (1994). Also of interest are the December 1994 issue of *Behavioral Sciences and the Law* and the double issue of *Trends in Health Care, Law and Ethics* (1995), both dedicated solely to ethical and legal concerns of managed care.

1. The Duty to Protect the Client's Interests

This duty is actually the duty of fidelity. It allows providers to resolve conflicts of interests in favor of the client. Additionally, the duty to protect the client's interest includes his or her private and confidential information. Providers have a duty to keep private information confidential. Thus, they should provide clients the privacy they reasonably expect, including privacy of what is recorded about the client's treatment. This means providers should record and report only salient and relevant information.

When a concurrent or retrospective utilization review is conducted by a telephone interview, be certain the person to whom you are disclosing private client information is, in fact, with the managed care organization. Just because someone has identified himself or herself as a managed care reviewer does not make it so. To disclose information to such a person may irreparably destroy the client's privacy rights, resulting in the information's becoming public, not private. In the circumstances of telephone interviews, we suggest you tell the managed care reviewer that you will need to call back, or develop a security system based on confidential code numbers for the client.

Additionally, be certain that once private information is released, the managed care organization is committed to keeping it confidential.

This duty seems to be emerging with clarity. Clients have a reasonable expectation of privacy, and providers have a duty to keep that information confidential.

2. The Duty of Honest Disclosure

Providers have a duty to disclose to clients the facts about managed care. This duty is based on the provider's fiduciary duty and the client's right to informed consent. The provider's duty to disclose might require discussing the possibility of restriction of choices of intervention and practitioners and the obligation to disclose information to the managed care organization. Morreim (1991) argues that this duty to disclose also includes discussing the potential adverse effect of treatment of a client's employment, future insurance benefits, and other pecuniary consequences.

In essence, managed care has created a duty for providers to discuss every aspect of how a client's care is managed in order for him or her to be truly informed prior to any consent.

3. The Duty to Provide Complete Care

Providers have a duty to continue care and not to terminate treatment based on any decision other than that based on clinical evidence. Although managed care organizations may turn off the flow of funds, the provider's obligation to the client has not ended.

The duty to continue care may actually lead to a duty of managed care to continue payment. As Applebaum (1993) suggests, the duty to continue care is not sound public policy since no one can expect clinicians to provide unlimited services at no cost, especially if the only reason the clinician bears the burden is because the managed care organization wants to protect its profit. Both the provider and the managed care organization have to operate from the principle of beneficence and fidelity—that is, the best interest of the client.

The duty to provide complete care includes exhausting all administrative appeal procedures that are available for the client's mental health care. Morreim (1991) argues this as a need for advocacy for obtaining all available resources a client is legally and economically entitled to. The duty to advocate is thoughtfully delineated by Wolf (1994). She proposes that the need for advocacy arises when the potential results are likely to save clients from harm or likely to serve the client's goals. This duty shifts to informed consent and the duty to apprise the client when the potential benefit is not likely to prevent harm but might confer benefit. As such, this necessitates the publication of the procedures for selecting treatment protocols and the criteria used to evaluate all aspects of utilization review.

4. The Duty to Pay for Services

There are emerging duties imposed on managed care organizations as well (Applebaum 1992). One such duty is payment for reasonable and necessary services. Practitioners may see these duties as what they can expect from a managed care organization. For example, the provider's duty to continue care would lead to their legitimate expectation that a

third-party payor and fourth-party managed care company will continue to pay for necessary services.

5. The Duty of Coordinated Care

This is another emerging duty imposed on managed care organizations.
At a minimum, a managed care organization should be expected to
comply with its duty to provide reasonable care that takes the client's
best interest into consideration. Restitution is due when an entity fails
to fulfill this reasonable care standard.

This reasonable care duty would be applied to those who conduct
utilization reviews for a managed care organization. Providers should
expect the organization to meet this duty by having well-trained reviewers who reach decisions about care from sound professional standards, and not just containing cost for the profit goals of the organization. Another expectation is that the managed care organization is
reasonable in the way it treats providers and has reasonable review and
appeal procedures. As suggested by *Hughes*, the standard for determining treatment necessity must be within the standards of the professional community. Further, the authorization of care must not be negligent care, as advanced in *Wilson*. This duty goes beyond the denial of
necessary treatment to include the coordination of managed care.

6. The Duty to Supply Quality Providers

There is also the duty for managed care organizations to select appropriate
providers, not just those who are the cheapest. This means that those
who work with the same managed care organization or are part of a panel
of providers should be adequately screened for competence. In sum,
providers should expect their colleagues to be responsible practitioners.

CONCLUSION

As a general guide clinicians should resolve ethical and legal conflicts
within the parameters of their professional discipline and organizations.
Sabin's (1994) comparison of the American Psychiatric Association
and the National Association of Social Workers is a good example of
how professional organizations can take a meaningful stand to balance

the interests of the individual and of society. Jellinek and Nurcombe (1993) also suggest that providers define their professional standard of practice in terms of what they will and will not do under pressure from an external managed care organization and to comply with professional guidelines on managed care (NASW 1993).

Managed care organizations are not opposed to this form of advancement. This is seen with the cooperative relationship between managed care and the American Academy of Child and Adolescent Psychiatry (Graham 1995) which has broadened the scope of conditions covered by managed care, and promoted constructive advocacy based on scientifically supported interventions. Managed care organizations, too, are committed to quality of care, albeit balanced against cost containment.

Chapter 9

Promoting Client Participation in Managed Mental Health Care

M uch has been said recently about working with clients' strength and empowerment to enable them to accomplish self-determination and a reasonable quality of life. In one sense, empowerment means the person in need of clinical services is able to accomplish his or her goal in a just and nurturing environment. This same objective is obtainable in the structure of managed mental health care. There are two important ways we will consider to promote client involvement and participation in their total treatment process: as an informed and active consumer whose treatment is managed by a fourth party and as an agent of change in their treatment, which includes active participation in homework assignments and self-change programs.

This chapter assumes that clients are actively involved in both the management of their care and the actual intervention. Through active participation, clients are more likely to be informed in order to consent and more likely to succeed in obtaining a positive outcome of treatment (Shelton and Levy 1981; Videka-Sherman 1985).

CLIENT PARTICIPATION IN THE MANAGED CARE PROCESS

There are a number of reasons to believe that active client participation is important to clinical practice, regardless of whether managed

219

care is a fourth party. This is seen in Videka-Sherman's meta-analysis of thirty-three intervention techniques. The question asked was how much outcome was associated with each of these components. Among her findings were that techniques that facilitate the client's active role in the treatment process are associated with positive outcomes.

It makes sense to consider how clients may participate in their managed care treatment. This might include every aspect of the utilization review process, from preauthorization through retrospective utilization reviews and client satisfaction surveys. Each aspect of ensuring quality and containing costs affords unique opportunities for clients to make autonomous decisions about their treatment. Some patients, especially the chronic mentally ill or those requiring hospitalization, may not have the capacity for this type of participation. Many, however, will be able to, especially in light of the rather elementary information that is requested (Jackson 1987; Patterson 1990). As evidenced in the prospective utilization review forms, much of the information requested is known primarily by the client, and any account from a clinician would be secondary at the least, opening the door to the increased chance of distortion or error. Client involvement, then, would seem to have an impact on effective services while promoting the principle of autonomy and self-determination.

Preauthorization Participation

Prior to authorization, the person seeking a provider's professional services is not necessarily a client. He or she is simply a potential client. Most likely, there is not yet a trusting, therapeutic relationship. Thus, if two people (the provider and the potential client) are faced with disclosing information to a fourth party, it would be better for the client to do so. In all likelihood, the clinician will not be able to turn all of the demands of a prospective utilization review over to the potential client but should defer to him or her whenever possible, perhaps by having the potential client complete a prospective utilization review form. Much of what is expected from the clinician by a managed care organization may be obtained directly from the client. We have provided the utilization review form that ascertains information that may be reported directly to a managed care organization or used in the completion of utilization review forms.

Engaging the client in the entire treatment process, including candid discussion of the problems and symptoms and diagnosis, promotes a greater understanding of his or her mental health condition. And certain information needed, in fact, can only be divulged by the client, such as thoughts and feelings. Items A12(a–c), A13, A14, and C5 from the utilization review forms are examples of information that is best provided by the client.

When a clinician must continue the utilization review process, he or she must be fully informed and as involved as possible. Usually the clinician and client can complete the utilization review form together, or the client can review it prior to returning it to the managed care organization.

A bonus to having the client participate is that it helps to foster cooperation for other aspects of managed mental health care. This is a good time, then, to review other opportunities to promote participation by discussing the role and importance of various assessment tools, treatment planning and intervention techniques, treatment goals, anticipated utilization reviews, the follow-up satisfaction survey, and the potential of a records review.

Prospective utilization reviews often request information to approve a treatment plan for the potential client. The client's active participation in disclosing this information greatly increases the likelihood of the clinician's success not only in maneuvering through the managed care maze but in getting meaningful client change. This process informs the client and prepares him or her for how change will occur. Videka-Sherman (1985) reports that this type of socialization for the intervention correlated with effective outcomes for outpatient, community-based treatment and hospital-based settings. Clients are uniquely capable of summarizing their problems and goals, and frank conversation with the clinician about the intervention is more likely to obtain the desired outcome.

Informed Consent and Confidentiality

In addition to any availing therapeutic effect of client participation, active, thoughtful enrollment also facilitates true informed consent and may promote the protection of confidentiality (Corcoran and Winslade 1994). Having a client interact with a managed care organization provides for a clearer understanding of the treatment procedures and thus promotes the first two elements of informed consent: knowledge about the procedures and risk. This will not, of course, relieve the provider of responsibility to obtain informed consent prior to beginning treatment. There is comfort, however, in knowing the client has been afforded the opportunity to manage his or her own care to some degree. In all likelihood the third element of informed consent—disclosure of alternative procedures—will need more thorough discussion with the client. In this sense, anticipation in developing the treatment protocol helps promote some aspects of consent that is informed fully and in advance.

When the potential client interacts with a managed care reviewer during the determination of treatment necessity, the information used to reach a decision is disclosed by the client. In this respect, active participation in utilization reviews fosters the client's privacy rights because the client determines what gets disclosed to whom. Because computer information systems are entwined in a worldwide web, clients should reserve the right to limit disclosure of physical and health information to a managed care reviewer. (Alpert 1993; Gostin et al. 1993).

Participation in Concurrent Utilization Reviews

There are a number of ways for clients to get involved in concurrent utilization reviews, including completing or helping the provider complete forms. The client's perspective provides an important view of progress in terms of the problem, obtainment of the goal, and the need for continued treatment.

Client involvement is also critical in monitoring the problem and goal over the course of treatment. Participation is fostered by preparing the client for this role, including familiarizing him or her with the process of scoring and graphing rapid assessment instruments and the goal attainment scale. The client's compliance with these managed care needs is enhanced by using the information as part of the treatment process.

Finally, both the provider and the managed care reviewer will find it useful to pay attention to changes in the client's functioning. This information was useful in obtaining authorization for treatment (including retrospective baseline data) and is now useful in concurrent reviews. Information openly shared with the client in advance of a concurrent utilization review provides an overview of progress. Clients may find it useful to record their GAF scores to reflect their observations a year in advance of intake, at intake, and at a concurrent utilization review. This information allows clients to keep a finger on the pulse of treatment and thus be a knowledgeable contributor to utilization reviews.

Participation in Retrospective Utilization Reviews

By the time of a retrospective utilization review, the client should be fairly familiar with managed care and some of its procedures. Hopefully, the client has also reached the goals of treatment, so the problem requiring treatment has been resolved. The client should have completed parts of the initial request for services, delineated the goal and participated in the formulation of the treatment protocol, and assessed the frequency, intensity, or duration of the problem or goal.

In essence, the client should be fairly familiar with much of quality assurance. A final evaluation may find the client the best source for answers about whether short- and long-term goals were reached. They also provide a check for the accuracy of the clinician's account of how the intervention was implemented.

Participation in Follow-up Assessments

Clients can participate as well after treatment has ended, most likely through a mailed survey or a brief telephone interview. The follow-up may evaluate the client's current functioning with some standardized tool, such as a rapid assessment of physical and mental health status (Steward, Hays, and Ware 1988).

We cannot stress enough, and the professional literature has been saying so for years, that it is sound practice to follow up routinely on every case (Bloom, Fischer, and Orme 1995). The information gained strengthens the provider's standing with the managed care organization and is useful in his or her own professional development. And should reimbursement questions arise regarding quality control, persuasive evidence is at hand for the appeal procedures.

Including a follow-up will take time. First, it will take time to track down clients, score the information, and record it in the client's record. Additionally, many clients will telephone to discuss the follow-up. This is an ideal opportunity to conduct a quick assessment with the portions of the mental status exam relevant to the original presenting problem. This must be acknowledged to the client and the results shared with him or her.

Providers should prepare their clients for the likelihood of receiving a client satisfaction survey in the mail or in the form of a telephone interview, especially clients who are enrolled members of a capitated managed care organization.

Client satisfaction is important information that should be considered in the provider's assessment of treatment. One potential means of integrating client satisfaction is to have clients complete a satisfaction survey at the final treatment session and include another survey with the follow-up rapid assessment tool. The scores at the end of treatment can then be compared with the satisfaction at a follow-up period.

This information provides a sample of scores that may be compared to other providers working for the same managed care organization. These data can be used to determine if clients are on the average more or less satisfied than other clients served by the managed care organization. With time and sufficient clients, providers will have enough data to determine if there are differences between the types of clients they see and different types of interventions they use. In order for this to occur, however, it is imperative that the client participate.

CLIENT PARTICIPATION IN THE CHANGE PROCESS

The second major way to involve clients in managed mental health care is as a participant in the change process. There are two ways of doing this that are suited for managed care: homework assignments and self-change projects.

Homework Assignments

These assignments, frequently called behavioral assignments, are tasks that are assigned for the client to complete between sessions in order to facilitate goal attainment (Shelton and Levy 1981). They are suited for almost every outpatient setting and should be considered an integral part of treatment, not just a supplement. Shelton and Levy, in fact, argue that behavioral assignments should be the primary component of treatment. As Videka-Sherman (1985) noted in her meta-analytic study of social work interventions, homework assignments correlated positively with treatment outcome in outpatient settings. More effective outcomes, it would seem, are associated with more use of homework assignments.

Behavioral assignments have been applied to most client problems. A survey of eight popular behavior therapy journals from 1973 to 1980 identified 500 articles. Homework assignments were found for twelve client problems: anxiety, nonassertiveness, depression, insomnia, obsessive-compulsivity, obesity, physical illness and rehabilitation, sex disorders, sex dysfunctions, stuttering, social skill deficits, and smoking. Homework-based interventions are also available in Shelton and Levy's book (1981) on anxiety, depression, marital problems, addictive behaviors, obesity, chronic pain, sexual dysfunctions, shyness, nonassertion, and parenting skills.

Among the many advantages to assigning client homework between sessions is that they help generalize the change that is occurring in the treatment sessions to the client's natural social environment, such as with family or colleagues. Some problems, in fact, require that the effort to create change occur outside the treatment setting; examples are insomnia and problems with sexuality. In these circumstances, homework assignments become an essential aspect of the intervention. Homework assignments accelerate the rate of goal attainment by increasing the amount of time and effort dedicated to change, and they help maintain the change that has occurred after treatment has ended. Finally, benefits include access to private client behavior (e.g., moods, eating habits), which contributes to the efficacy of treatment while promoting clients' autonomy and self-control (Shelton and Levy 1981).

Homework assignments, when used, become a major focus of the treatment process. The provider needs to discuss how the assignment went when the client implemented it to communicate how important the therapeutic activity is and to enhance the likelihood of client compliance. A portion of time must also be set aside at the end of the session to prepare the client for the next assignment. Generally about twenty minutes of the session will focus on the assignments.

When used over the course of the entire treatment, assignments should become increasingly challenging. A simple rule we find useful is to rank-order the assignments that are in the treatment protocol and assign the easiest ones first. They should also be organized so they successfully approximate the final treatment goal. For example, assignments designed to facilitate a mother-daughter relationship may begin with a simple communication exercise and develop into a more complicated collaborative task (Corcoran 1992).

Preparing Assignments and Clients. Behavioral assignments are effective, in part, because they are well thought out and systematic. Rather than be developed on the spur of the moment or off the cuff, they should be developed to obtain particular goals and be integrated into the step-by-step protocol.

A good part of the success of the behavioral assignment is a well-prepared client. Reid (1975) developed a five-step format to prepare clients for implementing homework tasks:

1. Discuss the benefits of the assignment.
2. Develop a plan with the client as to when he or she intends to implement the assignment.
3. Evaluate the obstacles to the plan developed in step 2.
4. Conduct a behavioral rehearsal of the assignment.
5. Summarize the behavioral assignment for the client.

We think it is best to do the last step in writing and give it to the client as a behavioral cue to use when the assignment is implemented. A 3-by 5-inch note card is useful for this purpose.

The First Assignment. We assume that the managed care structure allows a limited number of sessions, so time is of the essence. Consequently, it is helpful to have the first assignment be one that familiarizes the client with assessing the problem and interacting with a managed care utilization reviewer. The first homework assignment should have the client assess the problem by completing a prospective utilization review, a rapid assessment instrument of the presenting problem, and a self-anchored rating scale, which should be completed as frequently as the condition warrants. We recommend that the potential client be given this task between the time of the intake and the authorization of treatment. Simultaneously, the provider should develop additional homework assignments to be used over the course of treatment.

At the first session, the information is used to establish baseline data for use in concurrent and retrospective utilization reviews. The client will be expected to monitor the progress of treatment with these assessment tools at various times throughout treatment. Moreover, he or she will chart the observations in order to determine if the problem and goals are stable, improving, or getting worse. Clients should be encouraged to record this information on a copy of the case summary form. The space for progress notes may be used for his or her interpretation of treatment.

Client Compliance. Homework assignments are not worth much if the client fails to perform them. Like self-change programs, it is challenging to get clients to follow though with new behaviors. For example, a client who has learned social skills to decrease social isolation may fail to demonstrate these skills in actual situations, or a client with behavioral control techniques for addictive behaviors may not use them. Homework assignments, then, face the challenge of facilitating client compliance.

There is much that providers can do to facilitate client compliance. One way is to begin each session with a discussion of how the previous one went, to communicate the seriousness of the assignments and thus point out how important it is to complete them.

Shelton and Levy (1981) recommend using a bilateral contract that delineates the tasks to be completed by the client and the clinician. A bilateral contract is a written agreement that summarizes what the client will do, when, and at what level of satisfaction. It also delineates an assignment for the clinician to complete over the same time period. If, for example, the first assignment was to complete a prospective utilization review and assessment tools, the clinician's obligation might be to contact the managed care organization and develop an initial treatment protocol.

The bilateral contract introduces a quid pro quo to the process of doing homework and thus fosters the active participation of a clinician. It enhances compliance by setting up mutual expectations of compliance—in a sense, an obligation not to let the other party down. Bilateral contracts clearly mean the provider must comply if he or she expects the client to.

Self-Change Programs

Self-change programs are structured, systematic interventions developed to change client behavior systematically. Instead of being implemented by a professional clinician, these interventions are implemented by the client. The behavior to be changed concerns how the client thinks, feels, or acts—for example, self-defeating thoughts and depressive symptomatology, anxieties and phobias, and any number of social skills necessary for functioning (e.g., dating skills).

Self-change programs are particularly suited to managed care because the interventions are highly structured and goal directed. They are extremely helpful as an integral part of the complete clinical intervention—sort of an ongoing set of homework assignments. At times, self-change programs may be the primary intervention, especially when the managed care organization has interventions restricted to four or five sessions. In these cases, the provider may be limited to developing and supervising a client's self-change program. There are many times when this is the preferred intervention, such as when the treatment of choice is participation in Alcoholics Anonymous. The self-change program may be designed to foster participation and to establish an environment resistant to relapse. Self-change programs are also a valuable way of distributing a health promotion program and disease prevention.

When a provider's practice is chiefly one of monitoring self-change, it may be advisable to have more frequent contacts for shorter periods of time—perhaps seeing the client for thirty minutes for twice as many sessions. An alternative possibility is to spread out the length of time between sessions. Instead of meeting once a week, consider once every other week to begin, and maybe taper to once every three weeks or so.

Self-change interventions are known to be effective. Published accounts of these interventions range from creative productivity to bulimia, anxiety, depression, health promotion, and a variety of other problems (Watson and Thorpe 1993).

Self-change programs are structured change programs or implementation plans for systematic change. In many respects, they are the treatment protocols that clients follow in the effort to direct their own change. Among the number of excellent publications on developing self-change programs is the widely read book by Watson and Thorpe (1993), now in its sixth edition and used extensively. Many psychology undergraduates got their first practice experience with this volume. It is a useful guide in developing self-change programs for managed care clients. There are other equally valuable references (e.g., Mahoney 1979), and many interventions that have homework assignments are suitable for integrating into a self-change intervention.

Self-change interventions are based on the premise that personal adjustment is primarily a matter of having the skills of adjustment, that is, the ability to respond to a task well in a variety of situations (Watson and Thorpe 1993). The model of developing self-change intervention is most appropriate for clients who present problems in coping or coping skills deficits. The change that is to occur is either an increase or a decrease of something—perhaps to increase the efficiency of social skills or to decrease self-defeating behavior. It is convenient to conceptualize the particular behavior to be increased according to whether it is cognitive, affective, or some particular action. (As we have throughout this book, we prefer to call the last category *action* instead of *behavior* because cognitive and affective activity are also behaviors. *Action* seems a good way to indicate something the client will do in a situation.)

The essential element of a self-change intervention is to change some cognition, affect, or action through self-knowledge, planning, information gathering, and then modifying the intervention in accordance with the feedback. Developing a self-change intervention requires deliberate steps; they are similar to those followed in developing a prospective utilization review.

Step 1: Goal Selection. At this initial stage you and the client identify a target behavior to change and the goal of that change. The GAS procedures are useful here. The target behavior may be changed by altering the events that set off the behavior, such as after-dinner coffee as a stimulus for a cigarette or driving past a pornographic video store on the way home from work for a person with a sexual addiction. You might alter the behavior by creating an antecedent that facilitates the desired behavior. The cigarette smoker may take a leisurely walk after dinner. Alternatively, the client's self-change intervention might remove antecedents that result in the undesired behaviors. For example, the sex addict might plot a different traffic course home from work to avoid the temptations of the flesh.

Alternatively, the change program might alter the behavior itself— perhaps developing new behaviors, such as time management in contrast to procrastination, while decreasing others, such as the amount of unproductive time spent procrastinating. Or a client who is depressed and lonely can acquire the interpersonal skills necessary for successful intimate relationships.

Behaviors can also be changed by intervening on the consequence that maintains the problem or facilitates change by using rewards and punishments to enhance the probability that the behavior will or will not occur again. The impact of a consequence is summarized in figure 9.1. The effect of a consequence is to increase or decrease the likelihood the behavior will occur again. This consequence may be controlled by presenting it or removing it. For example, a client may present a reward of a dinner at an expensive restaurant or remove something by making a contribution to a political party one holds in contempt. The impact of presenting or removing a consequence is to increase or decrease the likelihood of occurrence. These two factors (present-remove and increase-decrease) facilitate understanding how to use rewards and punishments and their likely impact.

Client behavior, regardless of whether it is a thought, feeling, or action, can be changed by intervening at any level of antecedent, behavior, or consequence.

Once the goal is established and the client has isolated the behavior to be changed, you must decide if the intervention is best at the level of the antecedent, the behavior, or the consequence. The most effective self-change interventions judiciously target all three avenues.

Figure 9.1   Nature and Effect of Consequences on Behavior

		Present	Remove
Impact on Likelihood of Performance	Increase	Positive reinforcement	Negative reinforcement
	Decrease	Positive Punishment	Negative Punishment

Step 2: Self-Observations. Once these decisions have been made, the client will need to observe the presenting problem and treatment goal systematically, demands similar to what is expected even if the client is not using a self-change intervention. These observations may be with anchored rating scales, goal assessment scaling, or any of a number of relevant rapid assessment instruments. If you are using a self-change intervention in conjunction with clinical therapy, it will be necessary to limit the number of observational systems used. You may consider using some measures for both the authorized clinical protocol and the self-change program.

The client could record the observations on a case summary form (see appendix I), which enables him or her to monitor any self-change concomitant with the clinical change. The client should be encouraged to report observations about antecedents, the behavior, and the consequences in the lined area of the form.

Step 3: Implementing the Self-Change Intervention. The self-change program is much like the treatment protocol. It is the strategy for intervening on the problem. This plan should have a variety of techniques that are useful in producing change, and the intervention should be at all possible levels of change. Additionally, when the client's goal is to eliminate an undesirable behavior, he or she should strive to replace it with something else. For example, a planned decrease in anxious feelings would be replaced with feelings of calm. Explosive behaviors would be replaced with appropriate expression of anger and other social skills. A variety of techniques for changing behavior are delineated in Watson and Thorpe (1993).

Step 4: Monitoring and Fine Tuning. The implementation should be monitored with the monitoring devices outlined in chapter 6. The monitoring becomes necessary for determining treatment effectiveness and for fine-tuning the intervention. The purpose of this step is to assess client progress and adjust the intervention in accordance with that information, much as a concurrent utilization review does. Together you and your client ask, "Is it working?" You are now serving the role of managed care reviewer to evaluate if the intervention was implemented correctly and to recommend any needed adjustments.

This evaluation should occur about halfway through the treatment.

If you are authorized for five sessions, you and your client should review progress during the third session. When self-directed interventions are used in conjunction with other components of clinical services, this evaluation may be delayed until about two-thirds completed, provided you monitor it regularly.

Information on self-change programs is also helpful in completing concurrent and retrospective utilization reviews. As with other clients, it is useful to have clients whose treatment is based on self-change interventions to complete a concurrent or retrospective review. You will find that these clients have a thorough understanding of how the intervention was implemented and how well it is working.

Much as you want your client to attend to the evidence of change found in your records and the managed care organization's records, so too you should pay attention to your client's record of change. Actively participate by examining the charting of the observations (e.g., scores on a rapid assessment instrument or goal attainment scale scores) and your client's written progress notes. Based on this information you and your client can adjust the self-change intervention. In essence, we are asking you to respond as a managed care reviewer would who is interested in ensuring quality.

Step 5: Establish a Maintenance Program. The final step in any change program, whether a treatment protocol or a self-directed intervention, is to establish mechanisms for maintaining the change. This may include ways to enhance compliance with newly developed and desired behaviors or some form of relapse prevention (Shelton and Levy 1981; Watson and Thorpe 1993). Many interventions may benefit from a planned "booster shot." Watson and Thorpe (1993) delineate a number of techniques for this purpose.

CONCLUSIONS

Client participation is associated with effective treatment outcomes and promotes the values of autonomy and self-determination. It fosters informed consent and the protection of clients' privacy rights. In essence, client participation generally seems to be a good thing.

We have delineated three ways to promote client participation in managed mental health care. This may be accomplished first by having clients actively involved in the managed care process, including completing utilization reviews. Participation was also considered in terms of the process of change. The very nature of managed mental health care is designed to maximize the client's active participation, including goal setting and monitoring change in the presenting problem and goal attainment. Two additional ways we have considered are through client homework assignment and self-change interventions. There are, of course, many other ways providers can encourage clients' involvement in their treatment. None of these ways should be considered separate from the treatment process. All the techniques to encourage participation should be integral to the treatment—purposive, goals directed, and designed to ensure quality of care.

Chapter 10

Conclusions

We have come a long way in our discussion of managed care—from the complicated issue of third party funding to some routine skills that will be useful in daily practice with managed care clients. Since managed care is developing so rapidly, in this chapter we briefly consider its future chiefly from the perspective of how it *should* develop. We will also show you where to look for the future of managed care.

STANDARDS FOR FUTURE DEVELOPMENT

Given the rapid change in managed care's short history, it is likely that this pace of development will continue into the next century. Change in the system will be driven from all directions: clients who are in need of services, clinicians who are frustrated, and third party payors who are questioning the effectiveness of this new fourth party.

The goals of cost containment and quality assurance will be accomplished to varying degrees by different managed care organizations. Varying degrees of success will be accompanied by failures, and this will be in terms of human suffering by needy clients and the cost of services. One way to see it: when managed care is not working, the costs are higher, and quality is lower. One must wonder if managed care is not similar to other advances in health care, not replacing but only supplementing other procedures (Office of Technological Assessment 1993). In this respect managed care may simply add to the costs rather than containing them.

This form of inquiry will not lead to the demise of managed care. It will, however, facilitate its development, which we think must be guided by sound and practical standards. We have considered three possible ones.

First, managed care must determine if it is truly cost-effective. This information will prove invaluable in evaluating the effectiveness of the system and for developing cost-effective practices. For example, some costly cost-containment practices, such as a second-opinion mandate, may be abandoned or used more judiciously, perhaps excluding this mandate for clinicians with proven track records. Others will be developed and will most likely be part of the electronic information highway.

Developments and advances in managed care must, however, first pass the threshold standard of saving money. If it does not, and cannot so develop, then the cost may be contained by containing managed care.

The second guideline to development is for the system to develop practices that are reasonable and responsive to cooperative clinicians and service providers. Practitioners' frustration and discontent is not without cause, and managed care must address these concerns head-on. These conflicts are issues of quality assurance. Failure to develop without formulating reasonable practices will eventually undermine the goal of ensuring quality of services. Practitioners who can get out of the system will. Those who remain will struggle to set aside their own sentiments when working with a client whose care is managed. This effort will be met with varying degrees of success and adverse impact on client care.

The development must be acknowledged as a reciprocal relationship between managed care and providers. The demand for reasonable cost-containment practices may be heard only if the clinician is cooperative with managed care's goals of cost containment and quality assurance. Professional organizations that on the one hand market utilization review services but then establish toll-free phone banks to collect horror stories about managed care are not inviting meaningful dialogue or development in the field.

Finally, we have argued that however managed care develops, provided it is cost-effective and a reasonable system, it must be pursued with the best interest of the potential client in mind. We say "potential" client deliberately in order to widen the scope of the duty to the person possibly in need of services. This notion includes those who are authorized for services as well as those who are seeking them. One is duty bound to a client. Similarly, there should be some duty to the best interest of the potential client.

It would be easy to contain costs by denying more and more persons seeking services—potential clients. But the public policy need is not simply to save money but to ensure access to a quality system. Thus, managed care must develop with a commitment and duty that is first to the potential client and then to cost containment.

FUTURE TRENDS

While it is difficult to predict the future, certain trends are apparent. We think three are likely: (1) a blurring between the private and public distinctions of managed care, (2) an increased restriction of what is covered while demand for diverse services increases, and (3) an ever expansive and pervasive system.

In the future, the distinctions between the public and private sector will decrease as more and more public recipients are covered by programs that encourage enrollment in private capitated managed care organizations. This policy will be greatly expanded in years to come. It will be most noticeable with Medicare and Medicaid recipients' enrolling in HMOs.

The blur between the two systems will also occur as private businesses begin aggressively to market managed care services to the public sector. In an era of fiscal deficit reduction, more and more programs will be reduced and offered through the private sector, which will claim it can be done cheaper and better. Federal and state policy markers are more likely to select "cheaper and better" services over program cuts.

The second trend that most would agree on is the increasing restrictions on what services will be covered by a third party. This, of course, will include more rigorous determination of preexisting conditions and exclusion of most interpersonal and social problems. This cost-savings practice will collide with the increasing prevalence of diverse cultures in both the private and public sectors with expectations for culturally competent services. In essence, conditions covered will be restricted, with the appropriateness of the needed services expanded. The practical outcome will be an increasing willingness of managed care to authorize culturally competent care under the notion of indigenous social support services. A shaman, after all, may be less costly than a psychiatrist.

Finally, the future of managed care is bound to be one of expansion. The future is clearly one of larger and larger managed care organizations, whether in the form of corporations or regional behavioral health

Table 10.1   Periodicals for Managed Care Development

Administration and Policy in Mental Health
American Journal of Health Promotion
American Journal of Psychiatry
American Journal of Public Health
American Psychologist
Business and Health
Employee Benefits Plan Review
Health Affairs
Health Care Financing Review
Health Policy
Health Policy Quarterly
Health Services Research
HMO Practice
Journal of the American Medical Association
Journal of Health Care Marketing
Journal of Health Economics
Journal of Policy Analysis and Management
Law and Contemporary Problems
Medical Benefits
Medical Care
New England Journal of Medicine
Prevention Medicine
Professional Psychology: Research and Practice
Psychiatric Hospitals
Psychiatric Services (formerly *Hospital and Community Psychiatry*)
Psychotherapy
Quality Management in Health Care
Quality Review Bulletin
Social Security Bulletin

care networks. Moreover, there will be ever increasing membership in managed care as more and more private and public payors encourage cost-containment practices.

These three trends suggest that it will be difficult to keep abreast of the future of managed care. This is especially so since managed mental health care includes so many different fields and disciplines: employment law, insurance, public policy, business administration and benefits management, public financing, law, and, of course, clinical practice by a variety of different professionals. Table 10.1 presents a list of important periodicals that frequently publish articles on the topic of managed mental health care.

The future trends in managed mental health care are hard to predict. Some are fairly obvious, like the ones we have mentioned. We think it is important for the development to be guided by standards of economic effectiveness, reasonable demands, and a commitment to the best interest of the potential client. Such standards, and others, are necessary if managed care is to contain costs while assuring quality.

Appendix A

Ecomap

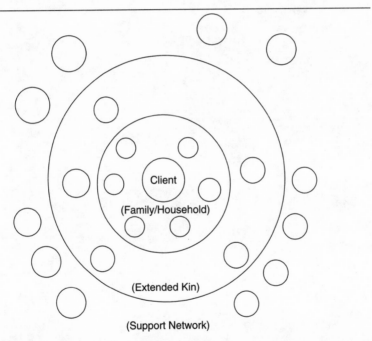

(Support Network)

Instructions: Have client identify all people and resources in support system fusing circles, then indicate relationship within those systems (using arrows, lines and dashes).

(———▶) Arrows are used to indicate the direction of the flow of energy or resources between systems.

◀——▶ Positive (reflects strong relationship)

◀---▶ Negatives (reflects a stressful or conflicted relationship)

Family/Household consists of all people/pets residing in the household.
Extended Kin consists of all relatives (extended/adopted) who may be involved in the client's life.
Support Network consists of all support systems that the client is connected with.

Appendix B

Prospective Utilization Review Form

REQUEST FOR AUTHORIZATION OF CLINICAL SERVICES

Instructions: Below are a number of questions regarding your client and the request to authorize services. Please complete each item with sufficient detail to enable the managed care organization to determine the need for services, the history of the problem and previous treatment, the treatment plan, and your qualifications. Information insufficient to evaluate thoroughly the request for services will delay authorization. Services that occur prior to authorization may not be authorized or reimbursed.

A. Identifying Information

1. Client name: _____

2. Client address: _____

3. Client phone number: _____

4. Client date of birth: _____/_____/19 _____
5. If client is a dependent, please identify parent or guardian:

   _____

6. Health care coverage/payment plan:_____

7. Source of referral: _____

8. Date of intake assessment: _____/_____/19 _____
9. Client presenting problems:

   (a) 1 _____

(b) 2 _____

(c) 3 _____

10. What was the date of onset of each presenting problem?

(a) Problem 1: _____ (b) Problem 2: _____ (c) Problem 3: _____

11. Please identify current symptoms observed for each problem for which you are requesting authorization of services:

(a) Problem 1: _____

_____.

(b) Problem 2: _____

_____.

(c) Problem 3: _____

_____.

12. What is the client's current functioning in each of the following areas?

(a) Psychological: _____

_____.

(b) Social: _____

_____.

(c) Occupational/educational: _____

_____.

13. How have you assessed the client's problems, symptoms, and functioning?

_____.

14. Please provide the following DSM diagnoses:

(a) Axis I: _____

(b) Axis II: _____

(c) Axis III: _____

(d) Axis IV: _____

Stressors: _____

(e) Axis V: (GAF)_____

B. History of Treatment
1. Was the client ever treated before for this or a similar problem?

    ____No ____Yes
2. If yes, what type of clinical services were provided?

    _____

3. Please summarize the outcome of previous treatment or clinical services.

    _____

4. Please indicate if medication was provided before, and include the type,

    dosage, and duration of the medication. _____

    _____.

C. Current Request for Clinical Services
Please provide information on the primary presenting problem for which you
are requesting treatment authorization. If additional problems exist and you
are requesting authorization for treatment, please complete this portion of the
form for each problem.
1. Summary statement of the presenting problem for which you are request-
    ing treatment:

    _____.

2. What is the short-term goal of treatment? That is, objectively define what
    you hope to achieve if treatment is authorized.

    _____

    _____

3. Please describe the treatment plan for reaching the short-term goal, in-
    cluding the specific steps you will follow in implementing it.

    _____

    _____

    _____.

4. Why is treatment necessary at this time? _____
_____.

5. What is the prognosis? _____.

6. How will you determine (i.e., assess/evaluate or monitor) the client's success in reaching this short-term goal?

_____

7. What is the long-term goal of treatment? That is, objectively define what you hope to achieve if treatment is authorized.

_____

_____

8. Please describe the treatment plan for reaching the long-term goal, including the specific steps you will follow in implementing it._____

_____

_____.

9. How will you determine (i.e., assess/evaluate or monitor) the client's success in reaching this long-term goal?

_____

10. How many sessions are you requesting? _____

11. How many minutes will each session last? _____

12. Will outside services be provided? ___Yes ___No

    (a) If yes, what services? _____

    _____.

    (b) Who will provide these services?_____

    _____.

    (c) When will these services begin and end? _____

    _____.

D. Provider Information

1. Name: _____

2. (a) Credentials: _____

   (b) License number: _____

3. Malpractice insurance carrier and policy number: _____

4. Provider address: _____

5. Phone number: _____

Semistructured Mental Status Exam

Instructions: Consider the content of each item in your intake interview. Indicate with an X in the space to the right of each question if the symptomatology was absent (a "no" response), "somewhat" evident, or clearly evident (a "yes a lot" response).

	No	*Yes Somewhat*	*Yes a Lot*
scores:	0	1	2

Presentation of Self

1. Was your client's hygiene, grooming, or clothing unclean or unkempt? ___ ___ ___

2. Was your client's clothing and jewelry noticeably atypical for his/her age and gender? ___ ___ ___

3. In comparison to most other people, was your client's posture and gait unusual? ___ ___ ___

4. Was there motor skill retardation or acceleration, or restlessness? ___ ___ ___

Behavioral

5. Did your client make peculiar facial expressions (e.g., grimace, fearful stare)? ___ ___ ___

6. Was speech atypical (e.g., loud, soft, whisper, slurred)? ___ ___ ___

	No	Yes Somewhat	Yes a Lot
scores:	0	1	2

7. Does your client report difficulty with interpersonal relationships at home or work?   ___ ___ ___

8. Was the client uncooperative, suspicious, or hostile?   ___ ___ ___

9. Does the client report problems meeting the demands of daily living (e.g., cooking, cleaning)?   ___ ___ ___

10. Does the client report repeated behaviors or intrusive thoughts?   ___ ___ ___

Cognition

11. Did the client show signs or report a history of hallucinations?   ___ ___ ___

12. Was there a reported history of delusions?   ___ ___ ___

13. Has the client ever had feelings of unreality or depersonalization?   ___ ___ ___

14. Was the client's attention span appropriate for his/her age and physical health status?   ___ ___ ___

15. Did the client show any problems in abstract thinking?   ___ ___ ___

16. Was he/she oriented to person, place, and time?   ___ ___ ___

17. Did he/she have problems with short- or long-term memory?   ___ ___ ___

18. Were thoughts of suicide reported?   ___ ___ ___

19. Has the client ever had ideas of reference or inference?   ___ ___ ___

20. Was thinking characterized by loss of association or circumstantiality?   ___ ___ ___

	No	Yes Somewhat	Yes a Lot
scores:	0	1	2

Affect

21. Did the client manifest appropriate affect for the circumstance and topic?   ___   ___   ___

22. Does the client report any worries or excessive concerns for his/her physical health status?   ___   ___   ___

23. Has the client reported unrealistic fears or experiences of panic?   ___   ___   ___

24. Was the client labile or report periods of lability?   ___   ___   ___

25. Did he/she show blunted or flat affect?   ___   ___   ___

Summary of clinical impression:

_____

_____

_____

_____

_____

Clinical Problem and Diagnostic Impression Checklist

Check each general diagnostic class and clinical problem that accurately reflects this client.

___ Substance-related problems _____

Diagnostic impression: _____.

___ Psychotic or schizophrenic disorder _____

Diagnostic impression: _____.

___ Problems and disorders of mood, excluding anxiety

Diagnostic impression: _____.

___ Anxiety disorders

Diagnostic impression: _____.

___ Psychophysical conditions

Diagnostic impression: _____.

___ Enduring problems of character and personality disorders

Diagnostic impression: _____.

___ Problems of conduct

Diagnostic impression: _____.

___ Problems with the community

Please specify: _____.

___ Family problems

Please specify: _____.

Measures for Clinical Practice

INSTRUMENTS FOR COUPLES
(Volume 1)

BEIER-STERNBERG DISCORD QUESTIONNAIRE	E. G. Beier and D. P. Sternberg
COMPETITIVENESS SCALE	M. R. Laner
DOMINANCE-ACCOMMODATION SCALE	C. N. Hoskins
DUAL EMPLOYED COPING SCALES	D. A. Skinner and H. I. McCubbin
DUAL-CAREER FAMILY SCALE	B. F. Pendleton, M. M. Poloma, and T. N. Garland
DYADIC ADJUSTMENT SCALE	G. B. Spanier
EQUITY/INEQUITY SCALE	J. Traupmann, R. Petersen, M. Utne, and E. Hatfield
HYPOTHETICAL, JEALOUSY-PRODUCING EVENTS SCALE	G. L. Hanson
INDEX OF MARITAL SATISFACTION	W. W. Hudson
KANSAS MARITAL CONFLICT SCALE	K. Eggeman, V. Moxley, and W. R. Schumm
KANSAS MARITAL GOALS ORIENTATION SCALE	K. Eggeman, V. Moxley, and W. R. Schumm
KANSAS MARITAL SATISFACTION SCALE	W. R. Schumm, L. A. Paff-Bergen, R. C. Hatch, F. C. Obiorah, J. M. Copeland, L. D. Meens, and M. A. Bugaighis
LIFE DISTRESS INVENTORY	E. J. Thomas, M. Yoshioka, and R. D. Ager

LOCKE-WALLACE MARITAL ADJUSTMENT TEST	H. J. Locke and K. M. Wallace
MARITAL ALTERNATIVES SCALE	J. R. Udry
MARITAL COMPARISON LEVEL INDEX	R. M. Sabatelli
MARITAL CONVENTIONALIZATION SCALE	V. H. Edmonds
MARITAL HAPPINESS SCALE	N. H. Azrin, B. T. Naster, and R. Jones
MARITAL INSTABILITY INDEX	J. N. Edwards, D. R. Johnson, and A. Booth
MILLER MARITAL LOCUS OF CONTROL SCALE	P. C. Miller, H. M. Lefcourt, and E. E. Ware
NON-PHYSICAL ABUSE OF PARTNER SCALE	J. W. Garner and W. W. Hudson
PARTNER ABUSE SCALE: NON-PHYSICAL	W. W. Hudson
PARTNER ABUSE SCALE: PHYSICAL	W. W. Hudson
PASSIONATE LOVE SCALE	E. Hatfield and S. Sprecher
PHYSICAL ABUSE OF PARTNER SCALE	J. W. Garner and W. W. Hudson
POSITIVE FEELINGS QUESTIONNAIRE	K. D. O'Leary, F. Fincham, and H. Turkewitz
PRIMARY COMMUNICATION INVENTORY	H. J. Locke, F. Sabaght, and M. M. Thomes
RELATIONSHIP ASSESSMENT SCALE	S. S. Hendrick
RELATIONSHIP EVENTS SCALE	C. E. King and A. Christensen
SEMANTIC DIFFERENTIAL OF SEX ROLES	R. J. Hafner
SPOUSE ENABLING INVENTORY	E. J. Thomas, M. Yoshioka, and R. D. Ager
SPOUSE SOBRIETY INFLUENCE INVENTORY	E. J. Thomas, M. Yoshioka, and R. D. Ager
SPOUSE TREATMENT MEDIATION INVENTORIES	R. D. Ager and E. J. Thomas

INSTRUMENTS FOR FAMILIES
(Volume 1)

ADOLESCENT-FAMILY INVENTORY OF LIFE EVENTS AND CHANGES	H. I. McCubbin, J. M. Patterson, E. Bauman, and L. H. Harris

FAMILY TIMES AND ROUTINES INDEX	H. I. McCubbin, M. A. McCubbin, and A. I. Thompson
FAMILY TRADITIONS SCALE	H. I. McCubbin and A. I. Thompson
FETAL HEALTH LOCUS OF CONTROL SCALE	S. M. Labs and S. K. Wurtele
INDEX OF BROTHER AND SISTER RELATIONS	W. W. Hudson, G. MacNeil, and J. Dierks
INDEX OF FAMILY RELATIONS	W. W. Hudson
INDEX OF PARENTAL ATTITUDES	W. W. Hudson
KANSAS FAMILY LIFE SATISFACTION SCALE	W. R. Schumm, A. P. Jurich, and S. R. Bollman
KANSAS PARENTAL SATISFACTION SCALE	W. R. Schumm and J. Hall
MEMORY AND BEHAVIOR PROBLEMS CHECKLIST	S. H. Zarit and J. M. Zarit
PARENT AFFECT TEST	M. N. Linehan
PARENT'S REPORT	E. Dibble and D. J. Cohen
PARENT-CHILD RELATIONSHIP SURVEY	M. A. Fine, J. R. Moreland, and A. Schwebel
PARENTAL AUTHORITY QUESTIONNAIRE	J. R. Buri
PARENTAL BONDING INSTRUMENT	G. Parker, H. Tupling, and L. B. Brown
PARENTAL LOCUS OF CONTROL SCALE	L. K. Campis, R. D. Lyman, and S. Prentice-Dunn
PARENTAL NURTURANCE SCALE	J. R. Buri, T. M. Misukanis, and R. A. Mueller
PERINATAL GRIEF SCALE	L. Potvin, J. Lasker, and T. Toediter
REALIZATIONS OF FILIAL RESPONSIBILITY	W. C. Seelbach
SELF-REPORT FAMILY INSTRUMENT	W. R. Beavers, R. B. Hampson, and Y. F. Hulgus

INSTRUMENTS FOR CHILDREN
(Volume 1)

ADOLESCENT COPING ORIENTATION FOR PROBLEM EXPERIENCES	J. M. Patterson and H. I. McCubbin
ASSERTIVENESS SCALE FOR ADOLESCENTS	D. Y. Lee, E. T. Hallberg, A. G. Slemon, and R. F. Haase

BEHAVIORAL SELF-CONCEPT SCALE
R. L. Williams and E. A. Workman

BEHAVIOR RATING INDEX FOR CHILDREN
A. R. Stiffman, J. G. Orme, D. A. Evans, R. A. Feldman, and P. A. Keeney

CHILDHOOD PERSONALITY SCALE
E. Dibble and D. J. Cohen

CHILD'S ATTITUDE TOWARD FATHER AND MOTHER SCALES
W. W. Hudson

CHILDREN'S ACTION TENDENCY SCALE
R. H. Deluty

CHILDREN'S BELIEFS ABOUT PARENTAL DIVORCE SCALE
L. A. Kurdek and B. Berg

CHILDREN'S COGNITIVE ASSESSMENT QUESTIONNAIRE
S. Zatz and L. Chassin

CHILDREN'S LONELINESS QUESTIONNAIRE
S. R. Asher

CHILDREN'S PERCEIVED SELF-CONTROL SCALE
L. L. Humphrey

COMMON BELIEF INVENTORY FOR STUDENTS
S. R. Hooper and C. C. Layne

COMPANION ANIMAL BONDING SCALE
R. H. Poresky, C. Hendrix, J. E. Mosier, M. L. Samuelson

COMPULSIVE EATING SCALE
D. M. Kagan and R. L. Squires

CONCERN OVER WEIGHT AND DIETING SCALE
D. M. Kagan and R. L. Squires

DEPRESSION SELF-RATING SCALE
P. Birleson

EYBERG CHILD BEHAVIOR INVENTORY
S. Eyberg

HARE SELF-ESTEEM SCALE
B. R. Hare

HOMEWORK PROBLEM CHECKLIST
K. M. Anesko, B. Scholock, R. Ramirez, and F. M. Levine

HOPELESSNESS SCALE FOR CHILDREN
A. E. Kazdin

HOSPITAL FEARS RATING SCALE
B. G. Melamed and M. A. Lumley

IMPULSIVITY SCALE
P. P. Hirschfield, B. Sutton-Smith, and B. G. Rosenberg

INDEX OF PEER RELATIONS
W. W. Hudson

INVENTORY OF PARENT AND PEER ATTACHMENT
G. C. Armsden and M. T. Greenberg

MOOD THERMOMETERS	B. W. Tuckman
MULTI-ATTITUDE SUICIDE TENDENCY SCALE	I. Orbach, I. Milstein, D. Har-Even, A. Apter, S. Tiano, and A. Elizur
NOWICKI-STRICKLAND LOCUS OF CONTROL SCALE	S. Nowicki, Jr. and B. R. Strickland
PEER AND SELF-RATING SCALE	R. A. Glow and P. H. Glow
PERSISTENCE SCALE FOR CHILDREN	D. Lufi and A. Cohen
PERSONAL ATTRIBUTE INVENTORY FOR CHILDREN AND NONSEXIST PERSONAL ATTRIBUTE INVENTORY	T. S. Parish
ROSENBERG SELF-ESTEEM SCALE	M. Rosenberg
SELF-CONCEPT SCALE FOR CHILDREN	L. P. Lipsitt
SELF-CONTROL RATING SCALE	P. C. Kendall and L. E. Wilcox
YOUNG CHILDREN'S SOCIAL DESIRABILITY SCALE	L. H. Ford and B. M. Rubin

INSTRUMENTS FOR ADULTS
(Volume 2)

ACHIEVEMENT ANXIETY TEST	R. Alpert and R. N. Haber
ACTIVITY-FEELING SCALE II	J. Reeve
ADULT HEALTH CONCERNS QUESTIONNAIRE	R. L. Spoth and D. M. Dush
ADULT SELF-EXPRESSION TEST	M. L. Gay, J. G. Hollandsworth, Jr., and J. P. Galassi
AFFECT BALANCE SCALE	N. Bradburn and E. Noll
AGGRESSION INVENTORY	B. A. Gladue
AGGRESSION QUESTIONNAIRE	A. H. Buss and M. Perry
AGORAPHOBIC COGNITIONS QUESTIONNAIRE	D. L. Chambless, G. C. Caputo, P. Bright, and R. Gallagher
ALCOHOL BELIEFS SCALE	G. J. Connors and S. A. Maisto
ARGUMENTATIVENESS SCALE	D. A. Infante and A. S. Rancer
ASCRIPTION OF RESPONSIBILITY QUESTIONNAIRE	A. R. Hakstian and P. Suedfeld
ASSERTION INVENTORY	E. Gambrill and C. Richey

CLIENT SATISFACTION QUESTIONNAIRE	C. C. Attkisson
CLINICAL ANXIETY SCALE	B. A. Thyer
COGNITIVE COPING STRATEGY INVENTORY	R. W. Butler, F. L. Damarin, C. Beaulieu, A. Schwebel, and B. E. Thorn
COGNITIVE PROCESSES SURVEY	R. F. Martinetti
COGNITIVE SLIPPAGE SCALE	T. C. Miers and M. L. Raulin
COGNITIVE-SOMATIC ANXIETY QUESTIONNAIRE	G. E. Schwartz, R L. Davidson, and D. J. Goleman
COGNITIVE TRIAD INVENTORY	E. E. Beckham, W. R. Leber, J. T. Watkins, J. L. Boyer, and J. B. Cook
COMBAT EXPOSURE SCALE	T. M. Keane, J. A. Fairbank, J. M. Caddel, R. T. Zimmering, K. L. Taylor, and C. A. Mora
COMPULSIVENESS INVENTORY	D. M. Kagan and R. L. Squires
CONCERN ABOUT DEATH-DYING AND COPING CHECKLISTS	P. S. Fry
COSTELLO-COMREY DEPRESSION AND ANXIETY SCALES	C. G. Costello and A. L. Comrey
DATING AND ASSERTION QUESTIONNAIRE	R. W. Levenson and J. M Gottman
DEATH DEPRESSION SCALE	D. I. Templer, M. LaVoie, H. Chalgujian, and S. Thomas-Dobson
DENTAL ANXIETY SCALE	N. Corah, E. N. Gale, and S. J. Illig
DENTAL FEAR SURVEY	R. A. Kleinknecht, R. K. Klepac, L. D. Alexander, and D. A. Bernstein
DIETARY INVENTORY OF EATING TEMPTATIONS	D. G. Schlundt and R. T. Zimering
DIETING BELIEFS SCALE	S. Stotland and D. C. Zuroff
DISSOCIATIVE EXPERIENCES SCALE	E. M. Bernstein and F. W. Putman
DYSFUNCTIONAL ATTITUDE SCALE	A. Weissman
EATING ATTITUDES TEST	D. M. Garner and P. E. Garfinkel

EATING QUESTIONNAIRE—REVISED	D. A. Williamson, C. J. Davis, A. J. Goreczny, S. J. McKenzie, and P. Watkins
EATING SELF-EFFICACY SCALE	S. M. Glynn and A. J. Ruderman
EGO IDENTITY SCALE	A. L. Tan, R. J. Kendis, J. Fine, and J. Porac
EMOTIONAL ASSESSMENT SCALE	C. R. Carlson, F. L. Collins, J. F. Stewart, J. Porzelius, J. A. Nitz, and C. O. Lind
EMOTIONAL/SOCIAL LONELINESS INVENTORY	H. Vincenzi and F. Grabosky
EVALUATION OF OTHERS QUESTIONNAIRE	J. P. Shapiro
FEAR OF AIDS SCALE	R. A. Bouton, P. E. Gallagher, P. A. Garlinghouse, T. Leal, L. D. Rosenstein, and R. K. Young
FEAR OF INTIMACY SCALE	C. J. Descutner and M. Thelen
FEAR OF NEGATIVE EVALUATION	D. Watson and R. Friend
FEAR QUESTIONNAIRE	I. M. Mark and A. M Mathews
FEAR SURVEY SCHEDULE-II	J. H. Geer
FREQUENCY OF SELF-REINFORCEMENT QUESTIONNAIRE	E. M. Heiby
FRIENDLINESS—UNFRIENDLINESS SCALE (SACRAL)	J. M. Reisman
FROST MULTIDIMENSIONAL PERFECTIONISM SCALE	R. O. Frost, P. Martin, C. Lahart, and R. Rosenblate
GENERALIZED CONTENTMENT SCALE	W. W. Hudson
GENERALIZED EXPECTANCY FOR SUCCESS SCALE	B. Fibel and W. D. Hale
GERIATRIC DEPRESSION SCALE	T. L. Brink, J. A. Yesavage, O. Lum, P. Heersema, V. Huang, T. L. Rose, M. Adey, and V. D. Leirer
GOLDFARB FEAR OF FAT SCALE	L. A. Goldfarb
HARDINESS SCALE	P. T. Bartone, R. J. Ursano, K. M. Wright, and L. H. Ingraham

HENDRICK SEXUAL ATTITUDE SCALE	S. Hendrick and C. Hendrick
HOMOPHOBIA SCALE	R. A. Bouton, P. E. Gallagher, P. A. Garlinghouse, T. Leal, L. D. Rosenstein, and R. K. Young
HUNGER-SATIETY SCALES	P. E. Garfinkel
HYPERCOMPETITIVE ATTITUDE SCALE	R. M. Ryckman, M. Hammer, L. M. Kaczor, and J. A. Gold
HYPOCHONDRIASIS SCALE FOR INSTITUTIONAL GERIATRIC PATIENTS	T. L. Brink, J. Bryant, J. Belanger, D. Capri, S. Jasculca, C. Janakes, and C. Oliveira
ILLNESS ATTITUDE SCALE	R. Kellner
ILLNESS BEHAVIOR INVENTORY	I. D. Turkat and L. S. Pettegrew
ILLNESS BEHAVIOR QUESTIONNAIRE	I. Pilowsky and N. D. Spence
IMPACT OF EVENT SCALE	M. J. Horowitz
INDEX OF ALCOHOL INVOLVEMENT	G. MacNeil
INDEX OF ATTITUDES TOWARD HOMOSEXUALS	W. W. Hudson and W. Ricketts
INDEX OF CLINICAL STRESS	N. Abell
INDEX OF SELF-ESTEEM	W. W. Hudson
INDEX OF SEXUAL SATISFACTION	W. W. Hudson
INTERACTION AND AUDIENCE ANXIOUSNESS SCALES	M. R. Leary
INTERNAL CONTROL INDEX	P. Dutteiler
INTERNAL VERSUS EXTERNAL CONTROL OF WEIGHT SCALE	L. L. Tobias and M. L. MacDonald
INTERPERSONAL DEPENDENCY INVENTORY	R. M. A. Hirschfield, G. L. Klerman, H. G. Gough, J. Barrett, S. J. Korchin, and P. Chodoff
INTIMACY SCALE	A. J. Walker and L. Thompson
INVENTORY TO DIAGNOSE DEPRESSION	M. Zimmerman, W. Coryell, C. Corenthal, and S. Wilson
IRRATIONAL VALUES SCALE	A. P. MacDonald
IRRITABILITY/APATHY SCALE	A. Burns, S. Folstein, J. Brandt, and M. Folstein

JOB INTERVIEW SELF-STATEMENT SCHEDULE	R. G. Heimberg, K. E. Keller, and, T. Peca-Baker
LIFE EVENTS QUESTIONNAIRE	T. S. Brugha
LIFE SATISFACTION INDEX–Z	B. Neugarten, R. J. Havighurst, and S. S. Tobin
LIKING PEOPLE SCALE	E. E. Filsinger
LONELINESS RATING SCALE	J. J. Scalise, E. J. Ginter, and L. H. Gerstein
LOVE ATTITUDES SCALE	C. Hendrick and S. S. Hendrick
MAGICAL IDEATION SCALE	M. Eckblad and L. J. Chapman
MATHEMATICS ANXIETY RATING SCALE—REVISED	B. S. Plake and C. S. Parker
MAUDSLEY OBESSIONAL-COMPULSIVE INVENTORY	R. J. Hodgson and S. Rachman
MCGILL PAIN QUESTIONNAIRE	R. Melzack
MCMULLIN ADDICTION THOUGHT SCALE	R. F. McMullin
MEDICAL OUTCOME SCALE	A. L. Stewart, R. D. Hays, and J. Ware, Jr.
MENSTRUAL SYMPTOM QUESTIONNAIRE	M. Chesney
MICHIGAN ALCOHOLISM SCREENING TEST	M. K. Selzer
MILLER SOCIAL INTIMACY SCALE	R. S. Miller and H. M. Lefcourt
MISSISSIPPI SCALE	T. Keenne, J. M. Caddell, and K. L. Taylor
MOBILITY INVENTORY FOR AGORAPHOBIA	D. L. Chambless, G. Caputo, S. E. Jasin, E. Gracely, and C. Williams
MOOD RELATED PLEASANT EVENTS SCHEDULE	D. J. MacPhillamy and P. M. Lewinsohn
MOOD SURVEY	B. Underwood and W. J. Froming
MULTIDIMENSIONAL BODY-SELF RELATIONS QUESTIONNAIRE	T. F. Cash
MULTIDIMENSIONAL DESIRE FOR CONTROL SCALES	L. A. Anderson
MULTIDIMENSIONAL HEALTH LOCUS OF CONTROL SCALES	K. A. Wallston, B. S. Wallston, and R. DeVellis
MULTIDIMENSIONAL LOCUS OF CONTROL SCALES FOR PSYCHIATRIC PATIENTS	H. Levenson

MULTIDIMENSIONAL SCALE OF PERCEIVED SOCIAL SUPPORT — G. D. Zimet, N. W. Dahlem, S. G. Zimet, and G. K. Farley

MULTI-DIMENSIONAL SUPPORT SCALE — H. R. Winefield, A. H. Winefield, and M. Tiggemann

NEGATIVE ATTITUDES TOWARD MASTURBATION INVENTORY — P. R. Abramson and D. L. Mosher

NETWORK ORIENTATION SCALE — A. Vaux, P. Burda, and D. Stewart

NONCONTINGENT OUTCOME INSTRUMENT — J. P. Shapiro

OBSESSIVE-COMPULSIVE SCALE — G. D. Gibb, J. R. Bailey, R. H. Best, and T. T. Lambirth

PANIC ATTACK COGNITIONS QUESTIONNAIRE — G. A. Clum, S. Broyles, J. Borden, and P. L. Watkins

PANIC ATTACK SYMPTOMS QUESTIONNAIRE — G. A. Clum, S. Broyles, J. Borden and P. L. Watkins

PATIENT REACTIONS ASSESSMENT — J. P. Galassi, R. Schanberg, and W. B. Ware

PERCEIVED GUILT INDEX—STATE AND PERCIEVED GUILT INDEX—TRAIT — J. R. Otterbacher and D. C. Munz

PERCEIVED SOCIAL SUPPORT—FRIEND SCALE AND PERCEIVED SOCIAL SUPPORT—FAMILY SCALE — M. E. Procidano and K. Heller

PERSONAL ASSERTION ANALYSIS — B. L. Hedlund and C. U. Lindquist

PERSONAL STYLE INVENTORY — C. J. Robins and A. G. Luten

PHYSICAL SELF-EFFICACY SCALE — R. M. Ryckman, M. A. Robbins, B. Thonton, and P. Cantrell

PROBLEM SOLVING INVENTORY — P. P. Heppner

PROCRASTINATION ASSESSMENT SCALE—STUDENTS — L. J. Solomon and E. D. Rothblum

PROCRASTINATION SCALE — B. W. Tuckman

PROVISION OF SOCIAL RELATIONS — R. J. Turner, B. G. Frankel, and D. M. Levin

PURSUING-DISTANCING SCALE — D. M. Bernstein, J. Santelli, K. Alter-Reid, and V. Androsiglio

QUESTIONNAIRE OF EXPERIENCES OF DISSOCIATION — K. C. Riley

RAPE AFTERMATH SYMPTOM TEST — D. G. Kilpatrick

RATHUS ASSERTIVENESS SCHEDULE	S. A. Rathus
RATIONAL BEHAVIOR INVENTORY	C. T. Shorkey and V. C. Whiteman
RAULIN INTENSE AMBIVALENCE SCALE	M. L. Raulin
REACTION INVENTORY INTERFERENCE	D. R. Evans and S. S. Kazarian
REASONS FOR LIVING INVENTORY	M. M. Linehan
REID-GUNDLACH SOCIAL SERVICE SATISFACTION SCALE	P. N. Reid and J. P. Gundlach
RESTRAINT SCALE	C. P. Herman
REVISED KINSHIP SCALE	K. G. Bailey and G. R. Nava
REVISED MARTIN-LARSEN APPROVAL MOTIVATION	H. J. Martin
REVISED UCLA LONELINESS SCALE	D. Russell, L. Peplau, and C. Cutrona
ROLE PERCEPTION SCALE	M. S. Richardson and J. L. Alpert
SATISFACTION WITH LIFE SCALE	E. Diener, R. A. Emmons, R. J. Larsen, and S. Griffin
SCALE FOR THE ASSESSMENT OF NEGATIVE SYMPTOMS	N. C. Andreasen
SCALE FOR THE ASSESSMENT OF POSITIVE SYMPTOMS	N. C. Andreasen
SELF-ATTITUDE INVENTORY	M. Lorr and R. A. Wunderlich
SELF-CONSCIOUSNESS SCALE	M. F. Scheier
SELF-CONTROL QUESTIONNAIRE	L. P. Rehm
SELF-CONTROL SCHEDULE	M. Rosenbaum
SELF-EFFICACY SCALE	M. Sherer, J. E. Maddux, B. Mercadante, S. Prentice-Dunn, B. Jacobs, and R. W. Rogers
SELF-ESTEEM RATING SCALE	W. R. Nugent and J. W. Thomas
SELF-RATING ANXIETY SCALE	W. W. K. Zung
SELF-RATING DEPRESSION SCALE	W. W. K. Zung
SELF-RIGHTEOUSNESS SCALE	T. Falbo
SELFISM SCALE	E. J. Phares and N. Erskine
SEMANTIC DIFFERENTIAL FEELING AND MOOD SCALES	M. Lorr and R. A. Wunderlich
SENSATION SCALE	S. A. Maisto, V. J. Adesso, and R. Lauerman

SENSE OF SYMBOLIC IMMORTALITY SCALE	J. L. Drolet
SEPARATION-INDIVIDUATION PROCESS INVENTORY	R. M. Christenson and W. P. Wilson
SESSION EVALUATION QUESTIONNAIRE	W. B. Stiles
SEVERITY OF SYMPTOMS SCALE	B. Vitiello, S. Spreat, and D. Behar
SEXUAL AROUSABILITY INVENTORY AND SEXUAL AROUSABILITY INVENTORY—EXPANDED	E. F. Hoon and D. L. Chambless
SEXUAL ASSAULT SYMPTOM SCALE	L. O. Ruch, J. W. Gartell, S. R. Amedeo, and B. J. Coyne
SEXUAL ATTITUDE SCALE	W. W. Hudson, G. I. Murphy, and P. S. Nurius
SEXUAL BEHAVIOR INVENTORY— FEMALE	P. M. Bentler
SEXUAL BEHAVIOR INVENTORY— MALE	P. M. Bentler
SIMPLE RATHUS ASSERTIVENESS SCHEDULE	I. A. McCormick
SMOKING SELF-EFFICACY QUESTIONNAIRE	G. Colletti and J. A. Supnick
SOCIAL ADJUSTMENT SCALE—SELF REPORT	M. M. Weissman and E. S. Paykel
SOCIAL ANXIETY THOUGHTS QUESTIONNAIRE	L. M. Hartman
SOCIAL AVOIDANCE AND DISTRESS SCALE	D. Watson and R. Friend
SOCIAL FEAR SCALE	M. L. Raulin and J. L. Wee
SOCIAL INTERACTION SELF- STATEMENT TEST	C. R. Glass, T. V. Merluzzi, J. L. Biever, and K. H. Larsen
SOCIAL PROBLEM-SOLVING INVENTORY	T. J. D'Zurilla and A. M. Nezu
SOCIAL RHYTHM METRIC	T. Monk, J. F. Flaherty, E. Frank, and D. J. Kupfer
SOCIAL SUPPORT APPRAISALS SCALE	A. Vaux, J. Philips, L. Holley, B. Thompson, D. Williams, and D. Stewart
SOCIAL SUPPORT BEHAVIORS SCALE	A. Vaux, S. Riedel, and D. Stewart
SOCIOPOLITICAL CONTROL SCALE	M. A. Zimmerman and J. H. Zahniser

SOMATIC, COGNITIVE, BEHAVIORAL ANXIETY INVENTORY	P. M. Lehrer and R. L. Woolfolk
SPLITTING SCALE	M. J. Gerson
STATE-TRAIT ANGER SCALE	C. Spielberger and P. London
STRESS-AROUSAL CHECKLIST	C. Mackay and T. Cox
STRESSFUL SITUATIONS QUESTIONNAIRE	W. F. Hodges and J. P. Felling
STUDENT JENKINS ACTIVITY SURVEY	P. R. Yarnold and F. B. Bryant
SURVEY OF HETEROSEXUAL INTERACTION	C. T. Twentyman and R. M. McFall
SYMPTOM QUESTIONNAIRE	R. Kellner
SYMPTOMS CHECKLIST	P. T. Bartone, R. J. Ursano, K. M. Wright, and L. H. Ingraham
TCU DEPRESSION AND DECISION-MAKING SCALES	G. W. Joe, L. Knezek, D. Watson, and D. D. Simpson
TEMPLER DEATH ANXIETY SCALE	D. I. Templer
TEST OF NEGATIVE SOCIAL EXCHANGE	L. S. Ruehlman and P. Karoly
THREAT APPRAISAL SCALE	K. E. Hart
TIME URGENCY AND PERPETUAL ACTIVATION SCALE	L. Wright, S. McCurdy, and G. Rogoll
TRUST IN PHYSICIAN SCALE	L. A. Anderson and R. F. Dedrick
VALUES CONFLICT RESOLUTION ASSESSMENT	R. T. Kinnier
VERBAL AGGRESSIVENESS SCALE	D. A. Infante and C. J. Wigley, III
WAY OF LIFE SCALE	L. Wright, K. von Bussmann, A. Friedman, M. Khoury, F. Owens, and W. Paris
WEST HAVEN–YALE MULTI-DIMENSIONAL PAIN INVENTORY	R. D. Kerns, D. C. Turk, and T. E. Rudy
WORKING ALLIANCE INVENTORY	A. O. Horvath
YOUNG ADULT FAMILY INVENTORY OF LIFE EVENTS AND CHANGES	H. I. McCubbin, J. M. Patterson, and J. R. Grochowski
YOUNG ADULT SOCIAL SUPPORT INVENTORY	H. I. McCubbin, J. M. Patterson, and J. R. Grochowski

INSTRUMENTS CROSS-INDEXED BY PROBLEM AREA

(Instruments in **boldface** are in Volume 1 and those in standard type are in Volume 2.)

PROBLEM AREA	INSTRUMENT
Abuse (also see Rape)	**Non-Physical Abuse of Partner Scale** **Partner Abuse Scale: Physical** **Partner Abuse Scale: Non-Physical** **Physical Abuse of Partner Scale**
Addiction and Alcoholism (See Substance Abuse)	
Anger and Hostility	Aggression Inventory Aggression Questionnaire Argumentativeness Scale Bakker Assertiveness-Aggressiveness Inventory **Conflict Tactics Scales** State-Trait Anger Scale Symptom Questionnaire
Anxiety and Fear (also see Phobia and Mood)	Achievement Anxiety Test **Children's Cognitive Assessment Questionnaire** Clinical Anxiety Scale Cognitive-Somatic Anxiety Questionnaire Combat Exposure Scale Concern About Death-Dying and Coping Checklist Costello-Comrey Anxiety Scale Dental Anxiety Scale Dental Fear Survey Fear of Intimacy Scale Fear of Negative Evaluation Scale **Hospital Fears Rating Scale**

Interaction and Audience
  Anxiousness Scales
Mathematics Anxiety Rating Scale—
  Revised
Self-Consciousness Scale
Self-Rating Anxiety Scale
Social Anxiety Thoughts
  Questionnaire
Social Avoidance and Distress Scale

Social Fear Scale
Social Interaction Self-Statement
  Test
Somatic, Cognitive, Behavioral
  Anxiety Inventory
Stressful Situations Questionnaire

Symptom Questionnaire
Threat Appraisal Scale

Assertiveness   Assertion Inventory
  (also see Anxiety and   Assertion Self-Statement Test—
  Interpersonal Behavior)   Revised
                                               Assertive Job-Hunting Survey
                                               **Assertiveness Scale for
                                                 Adolescents**
                                               Assertiveness Self-Report Inventory

                                               Assertiveness Self-Statement Test

                                               Bakker Assertiveness-Aggressiveness
                                                 Inventory
                                               Children's Action Tendency Scale

                                               Conflict Tactics Scale
                                               Personal Assertion Analysis
                                               Rathus Assertiveness Schedule
                                               Simple Rathus Assertiveness
                                                 Schedule

Beliefs (Rational and Irrational)   Ascription of Responsibility
                                                 Questionnaire
                                               Authoritarianism Scale

Beliefs Associated with Childhood
  Sexual Abuse
Cognitive Triad Inventory
Common Belief Inventory for
  Students
Evaluation of Others Questionnaire

Family Beliefs Inventory
Hardiness Scale
Irrational Values Scale
Rational Behavior Inventory
Self-Righteousness Scale
Separation-Individuation Process
  Inventory

Children's Behaviors/Problems

Behavior Rating Index for
  Children
Childhood Personality Scale
Children's Beliefs about Parental
  Divorce Scale
Companion Animal Bonding Scale

Eyberg Child Behavior Inventory

Homework Problem Checklist
Peer and Self-Rating Scale
Persistence Scale for Children
Self-Control Rating Scale

Couple Relationship
(See Marital/Couple Relationship)

Death Concerns

Concern About Death-Dying and
  Coping Checklists
Death Depression Scale
Sense of Symbolic Immortality
  Scale
Templar Death Anxiety Scale

Depression and Grief
(also see Mood, Suicide)

Automatic Thoughts Questionnaire

Brief Depression Rating Scale
Brief Screen for Depression
Center for Epidemiologic Studies—
  Depressed Mood Scale

Chinese Depressive Symptom Scale

Costello-Comrey Depression Scale

Depression Self-Rating Scale
Dysfunctional Attitude Scale
Evaluation of Others Questionnaire

Frequency of Self-Reinforcement
    Questionnaire
Generalized Contentment Scale
Hopelessness Scale for Children

Inventory to Diagnose Depression

Mood Related Pleasant Events
    Schedule
Perinatal Grief Scale
Personal Style Inventory
Self-Control Questionnaire
Self-Rating Depression Scale
Social Rhythm Metric
Symptoms Questionnaire

Eating Problems

Bulimia Test—Revised
Compulsive Eating Scale
**Concern over Weight and Dieting
    Scale**
Dietary Inventory of Eating
    Temptations
Dieting Beliefs Scale
Eating Attitudes
Eating Questionnaire—Revised
Eating Self-Efficacy Scale
Goldfarb Fear of Fat Scale
Hunger-Satiety Scales
Internal Versus External Control of
    Weight Scale
Restraint Scale

Family Functioning
(also see Parent-Child
Relationships)

Environmental Assessment Index

**Family Adaptability and Cohesion
    Evaluation Scale**
Family Assessment Device
Family Awareness Scale

Family Celebrations Index
Family Crisis Oriented Personal
    Evaluation Scales
Family Functioning Scale
Family Inventory of Resources for
    Management
Family-of-Origin Scale
Family Responsibility Index
Family Sense of Coherence Scale

Family Times and Routines Index

Family Traditions Scale
Index of Brother and Sister
    Relations
Index of Family Relations
Kansas Family Life Satisfaction
    Scale
Self-Report Family Instrument

Separation-Individuation Process
    Inventory

Geriatric
(also see listings under
problem areas)

Attitude Toward the Provision of
    Long-Term Care
Caregiver Strain Index
Caregiver's Burden Scale
Concern About Death-Dying and
    Coping Checklists
Geriatric Depression Scale
Irritability/Apathy Scale
Memory and Behavior Problems
    Checklist
Realizations of Filial
    Responsibility

Guilt
(also see Anxiety, Beliefs)

Perceived Guilt Index—State and
    Perceived Guilt Index—Trait

Health Issues

Adult Health Concerns
    Questionnaire
Cognitive Coping Strategy
    Inventory
Coping Health Inventory for
    Parents

Hospital Fears Rating Scale
Hypochondriasis Scale for
  Institutional Geriatric Patients
Illness Attitude Scale
Illness Behavior Inventory
Illness Behavior Questionnaire
McGill Pain Questionnaire
Medical Outcome Scale
Menstrual Symptom Questionnaire

Multidimensional Body-Self
  Relations Questionnaire
Multidimensional Health Locus of
  Control Scales
Patient Reactions Assessment
Symptom Questionnaire
Time Urgency and Perpetual
  Activation
Trust in Physician Scale
West Haven–Yale Multidimensional
  Pain Inventory

Identity   Ego Identity Scale
                                         Separation-Individuation Process
                                           Inventory

Interpersonal Behavior   Argumentativeness Scale
  (also see related issues)   Authority Behavior Inventory
                                         Barnett Liking of Children Scale
                                         Boredom Proneness
                                         Conflict Tactics Scale
                                         Dating and Assertion Questionnaire

                                         Friendliness-Unfriendliness Scale
                                           (SACRAL)
                                         Hypercompetitive Attitude Scale
                                         Index of Peer Relations
                                         Index of Attitudes Toward
                                           Homosexuals
                                         Interpersonal Dependency Inventory

                                         Job Interview Self-Statement
                                           Schedule
                                         Liking People Scale

Miller Social Intimacy Scale
Pursuing-Distancing Scale
Separation-Individuation Process
    Inventory
Revised Martin-Larsen Approval
    Motivation
Test of Negative Social Exchange

Verbal Aggressiveness Scale
**Young Children's Social
    Desirability Scale**

Locus of Control

Ascription of Responsibility
    Questionnaire
Belief In Personal Control Scale
Family Empowerment Scale
**Fetal Health Locus of Control
    Scale**
Generalized Expectancy for Success
    Scale
Hardiness Index
Internal Control Index
Internal Versus External Control of
    Weight Scale
**Miller Marital Locus of Control
    Scale**
Multidimensional Desire for Control
    Scales
Multidimensional Health Locus of
    Control Scales
Multidimensional Locus of Control
    Scales for Psychiatric Patients
Noncontingent Outcome Instrument

**Nowicki-Strickland Locus of
    Control Scale**
Parental Locus of Control Scale

Sociopolitical Control Scale
Way of Life Scale

Loneliness
(also see Interpersonal Behaviors)

**Adolescent-Family Inventory of
    Life Events and Changes**
**Children's Loneliness
    Questionnaire**

Emotional/Social Loneliness
  Inventory
Loneliness Rating Scale
Revised UCLA Loneliness Scale

Love

Intimacy Scale
Love Attitudes Scale
Parental Nurturance Scale
Passionate Love Scale
Revised Kinship Scale

Marital/Couple Relationship
  (also see Sexuality)

**Beier-Sternberg Discord
  Questionnaire
Competitiveness Scale
Dominance-Accommodation Scale**

**Dual-Career Family Scale
Dual Employed Coping Scales
Dyadic Adjustment Scale
Equity/Inequity Scale
Hypothetical, Jealousy-Producing
  Events Scale
Index of Marital Satisfaction
Kansas Marital Conflict Scale
Kansas Marital Goals Orientation
  Scale
Kansas Marital Satisfaction Scale**

**Life Distress Inventory
Locke-Wallace Marital Adjustment
  Test
Marital Alternatives Scale
Marital Comparison Level Index**

Marital Conventionalization Scale

**Marital Happiness Scale
Marital Instability Index
Positive Feelings Questionnaire**

**Primary Communication
  Inventory
Relationship Assessment Scale
Relationship Events Scale**

| | Semantic Differential for Sex Roles |
| | Spouse Treatment Mediation Inventories |

Mood	Mood Survey
(also see Depression)	**Mood Thermometer**
	Semantic Differential Mood Scale

| Narcissism | Selfism Scale |

Obsessive-Compulsive	Compulsiveness Inventory
	Maudsley Obsessional-Compulsive Inventory
	Obsessive-Compulsive Scale
	Reaction Inventory Interference
	Severity of Symptoms Scale

Parent-Child Relationship	**Adult-Adolescent Parenting**
(also see Family Functioning)	**Inventory**
	Child's Attitude Toward Father
	and Mother Scale
	Conflict Tactics Scales
	Family Empowerment Scale
	Inventory of Parent and Child
	Attachment
	Inventory of Parent and Peer
	Attachment
	Kansas Parental Satisfaction Scale
	Parent Affect Test
	Parent's Report
	Parent-Child Relationship Survey
	Parental Authority Questionnaire
	Parental Bonding Instrument
	Parental Nurturance Scale

| Perfectionism | Frost Multidimensional Perfectionism Scale |

| Phobias | Agoraphobic Cognitions |
| (see also Anxiety) | Questionnaire |

Body Sensation Questionnaire
Fear of AIDS Scale
Fear Questionnaire
Fear Survey Schedule-II
Homophobia Scale
Hospital Fears Rating Scale
Mobility Inventory for Agoraphobia

Panic Attack Symptoms
   Questionnaire
Panic Attack Cognitions
   Questionnaire

Problem-Solving

Problem-Solving Inventory
Social Problem-Solving Inventory

Values Conflict Resolution
   Assessment

Procrastination

Procrastination Assessment Scale—
   Students
Procrastination Scale

Psychopathology (General) and
   Psychiatric Symptoms

Activity-Feeling Scale II
Auditory Hallucinations
   Questionnaire
Body Image Avoidance
   Questionnaire
Dissociative Experiences Scale
Emotional Assessment Scale
Hardiness Scale
Questionnaire of Experiences of
   Dissociation
Raulin Intense Ambivalence Scale

Scale for the Assessment of Negative
   Symptoms
Scale for the Assessment of Positive
   Symptoms
Separation-Individuation Process
   Inventory
Student Jenkins Activity Survey
Symptom Questionnaire
Symptoms Checklist

Rape	Rape Aftermath Symptom Test
	Sexual Assault Symptom Scale
Satisfaction with Life	Life Satisfaction Index–Z
(also see Depression)	Satisfaction with Life Scale
Schizotypical Symptoms	Cognitive Slippage Scale
	Magical Ideation Scale
	Raulin Intense Ambivalence Scale
	Splitting Scale
Self-Concept and Esteem	Affect Balance Scale
	Behavioral Self-Concept Scale
	Ego Identity Scale
	Hare Self-Esteem Scale
	Index of Self-Esteem
	Personal Attribute Inventory for Children and Nonsexist Personal Attitude Inventory
	Self-Concept Scale for Children
	Self-Esteem Rating Scale
	Semantic Differential of Sex Roles
Self-Control	**Children's Perceived Self-Control Scale**
(also see Locus of Control)	**Impulsivity Scale**
	Peer and Self-Rating Scale
Self-Efficacy	Physical Self-Efficacy Scale
	Self-Efficacy Scale
	Smoking Self-Efficacy Questionnaire
Sexuality	Hendrick Sexual Attitude Scale
	Index of Sexual Satisfaction
	Negative Attitudes Toward Masturbation Inventory
	Sexual Attitude Scale
	Sexual Arousability Inventory
	Sexual Arousability Inventory— Expanded

Sexual Behavior Inventory—Female

Sexual Behavior Inventory—Male

Survey of Heterosexual Interaction

Smoking

Smoking Consequences
  Questionnaire
Smoking Self-Efficacy
  Questionnaire

Social Functioning
  (also see Interpersonal Behavior)

Social Adjustment Scale—Self-
  Report
Mood Related Pleasant Events
  Schedule

Social Support

Multi-Dimensional Support Scale

Multidimensional Scale of Perceived
  Social Support
Network Orientation Scale
Perceived Social Support-Family
  Scale
Perceived Social Support—Friend
  Scale
Provision of Social Relations
Social Support Appraisals Scale
Social Support Behaviors Scale
Young Adult Social Support
  Inventory

Stress

**Adolescent Coping Orientation for
  Problem Experiences**
**Adolescent-Family Inventory of
  Life Events and Changes**
Family Hardiness Index
**Family Inventory of Life Events
  and Changes**
Hardiness Scale
Impact of Event Scale
Index of Clinical Stress
Life Events Questionnaire
Self-Control Schedule

Stress-Arousal Checklist
**Young Adult Family Inventory of
Life Events and Changes**

Suicide   **Hopelessness Scale for Children**
  (also see Depression,
  Satisfaction with Life)   **Multi-Attitude Suicide Tendency
                                              Scale**
                                           Reasons for Living Inventory

Substance Abuse   Alcohol Beliefs Scale
                                           Assertion Questionnaire in Drug
                                              Use
                                           **Beck Codependence Assessment
                                              Scale**
                                           Co-dependency Inventory
                                           Index of Alcohol Involvement
                                           McMullin Addiction Thought Scale

                                           Michigan Alcoholism Screening
                                              Test
                                           Sensation Scale
                                           Spouse Enabling Inventory
                                           **Spouse Sobriety Influence
                                              Inventory**
                                           TCU Depression and Decision-
                                              Making Scales

Treatment Satisfaction   Client Satisfaction Questionnaire

                                           Reid-Gundlach Social Service
                                              Satisfaction Scale
                                           Session Evaluation Questionnaire

                                           Working Alliance Inventory

Source: Fischer, J. and Corcoran, V. (1994). *Measures for Clinical Practices.* NY: The Free Press.

Goal Setting Work Sheets

CLIENT GOAL ATTAINMENT SCALING WORK SHEET

This form is designed to establish the goal of clinical services and how we will be able to determine whether we have met that goal. Please complete this form in advance of your scheduled intake.

What behavior (either the way you think, feel, or act) do you expect at the end of clinical services?

_____

_____

Describe how that behavior would look to you or someone else if he or she observed it.

_____

_____

How would you describe that behavior if the outcome of clinical services was *somewhat better* than you expect?

_____

_____

How would you describe that behavior if the outcome of clinical services was *a lot better* than expected?

_____

_____

How would you describe that behavior if the outcome of clinical services was *somewhat worse* than expected?

_____

_____

How would you describe that behavior if the outcome of clinical services was *a lot worse* than expected?

_____

_____

_____

Client-Clinician Goal Attainment Work Sheet

Client Problems   **Priority Rating**

1._____

_____   _____

2._____

_____   _____

3._____

_____   _____

4._____

_____   _____

Treatment Goals

1. _____

_____

2. _____

_____

3. _____

_____

4. _____

_____

Objective Statements

1._____ will do _____
    (who)   (what)
_____ by _____ .
    (and to what extent)   (when)

2._____ will do _____
    (who)   (what)
_____ by _____ .
    (and to what extent)   (when)

3._____ will do _____
    (who)   (what)
_____ by _____ .
    (and to what extent)   (when)

4._____ will do _____
    (who)   (what)
_____ by _____ .
    (and to what extent)   (when)

Appendix F

Concurrent Utilization Review Form

REQUEST FOR AUTHORIZATION OF CONTINUATION OF SERVICES

Instructions: Below are a number of questions regarding your client and the request to authorize additional services. Please complete each item with sufficient detail to enable the managed care organization to determine the need for additional services. Information insufficient to evaluate thoroughly the request for services will delay authorization. Services that occur prior to authorization may not be authorized or reimbursed.

A. Identifying Information

1. Client name: _____

2. Client address: _____

3. Client phone number: _____

4. Client date of birth: _____ / _____ /19_____
5. If client is a dependent, please identify parent or guardian:

_____

6. Health care coverage/payment plan:_____

7. Source of referral: _____

8. Date of intake assessment: _____ / _____ /19_____
9. Client presenting problems:

    (a) 1 _____

    (b) 2 _____

(c) 3 _____

10. What was the date of onset of each presenting problem?

    (a) Problem 1: _____ (b) Problem 2: _____ (c) Problem 3: _____

11. Please identify current symptoms observed for each problem for which you are requesting authorization of services:

    (a) Problem 1: _____

    _____.

    (b) Problem 2: _____

    _____.

    (c) Problem 3: _____

    _____.

12. Contrast the client's current functioning in each of the following areas with his/her functioning at intake:

    (a) Psychological: _____

    _____.

    (b) Social: _____

    _____.

    (c) Occupational/educational: _____

    _____.

13. How did you assess the client's problems, symptoms, and functioning?

    _____

    _____.

14. Please provide the following DSM diagnoses:

    (a) Axis I: _____

    (b) Axis II: _____

    (c) Axis III: _____

    (d) Axis IV: _____

Stressors: _____

(e) Axis V: (GAF) _____

B. History of Treatment

1. Was the client ever treated before for this or a similar problem?

   ____No ____Yes

2. If yes, what type of clinical services were provided?

   _____

3. Please summarize the outcome of previous treatment or clinical services.

   _____

4. Please indicate if medication was provided before, and include the type,

   dosage, and duration of the medication. _____

   _____ .

C. Current Request for Continuation of Services

Please provide information on the primary presenting problem for which you
are requesting a continuation of clinical services. If additional problems exist
and you are requesting a continuation of authorization for treatment, please
complete this portion of the form for each problem.

1. Summary statement of the presenting problem for which you are requesting a continuation of treatment:

   _____ .

2. What was the short-term goal of treatment? That is, objectively define
   what you hope to achieve if further treatment is authorized.

   _____

   _____

3. Please describe the additional treatment plan you will use to reach the short-
   term goal, including the specific steps you will follow in implementing it.

   _____

   _____

   _____

   _____ .

4. How did you determine (i.e., assess/evaluate or monitor) the client's success so far in reaching this short-term goal?

_____

_____.

5. What was the long-term goal of treatment? That is, objectively define what you hope to achieve if further treatment is authorized.

_____

_____

6. Please describe the additional treatment plan you will use to reach the long-term goal, including the specific steps you will follow in implementing it.

_____

_____

_____.

7. How did you determine (i.e., assess/evaluate or monitor) the client's success so far in reaching this long-term goal?

_____

8. What progress is still required to warrant continuation of services?

_____.

9. What is the prognosis? _____.

10. How many addiditonal sessions are you requesting? _____

11. How many minutes will each session last?   _____

12. Were outside services provided? ___Yes ___No

    (a) If yes, what services?   _____

    _____.

    (b) Who provided these services?_____

    _____.

    (c) When did these services begin and end?_____

    _____.

13. Will more outside services be provided? ___Yes ___No

(a) If yes, what services? _____

_____.

(b) Who will provide these services?_____

_____.

(c) When will these services begin and end? _____

_____.

D. Provider Information

1. Name: _____

2. (a) Credentials: _____

(b) License number: _____

3. Malpractice insurance carrier and policy number: _____

4. Provider address:_____

5. Phone number: _____

Retrospective
Utilization Review Form

REQUEST FOR PAYMENT OF CLINICAL SERVICES

Instructions: Below are a number of questions regarding your client and the request to authorize payment for services. Please complete each item with sufficient detail to enable the managed care organization to determine the quality of those services provided. Information insufficient to evaluate thoroughly the request for services will delay authorization.

A. Identifying Information

1. Client name: _____

2. Client address: _____

3. Client phone number: _____

4. Client date of birth: _____/_____/19_____

5. If client is a dependent, please identify parent or guardian:

_____

6. Health care coverage/payment plan:_____

7. Source of referral: _____

8. Date of intake assessment:: _____/_____/19_____

9. Client presenting problems during the course of treatment:

(a) 1 _____

291

(b) 2 _____

(4) 3 _____

10. What was the date of onset of each presenting problem?

    (a) Problem 1: _____ (b) Problem 2: _____ (c) Problem 3: _____

11. Please identify the symptoms observed for each problem for which you are requesting authorization of payment for services:

    (a) Problem 1: _____

    _____.

    (b) Problem 2: _____

    _____.

    (c) Problem 3: _____

    _____.

12. Contrast the client's current functioning in each of the following areas with his/her functioning at intake:

    (a) Psychological: _____

    _____.

    (b) Social: _____

    _____.

    (c) Occupational/educational: _____

    _____.

13. How did you assess the client's problems, symptoms, and functioning?

    _____

    _____.

14. Please provide the following DSM diagnoses:

    (a) Axis I: _____

    (b) Axis II: _____

    (c) Axis III: _____

(d) Axis IV: _____

   Stressors: _____

(e) Axis V: (GAF)_____

B. History of Treatment

1. (a) Was the client ever treated before for this or a similar problem?

   ____No ____Yes

   (b) If yes, what type of clinical services were provided?

   _____

2. Please summarize the outcome of previous treatment or clinical services.

   _____.

3. Please indicate if medication was provided before, and include the type,

   dosage, and duration of the medication. _____

   _____.

C. Type of Treatment Provided

Please provide information on the primary presenting problem for which you are requesting authorization of payment for services. If additional problems were the focus of treatment and you are requesting payment, please complete this portion of the form for each problem.

1. Summary statement of the presenting problem for which you provided clinical services:

   _____.

2. What was the short-term goal of treatment? That is, objectively define what you had intended to achieve in treatment.

   _____

   _____

3. Please describe the treatment plan you used to reach the short-term goal, including the specific steps you followed.

   _____

   _____

   _____.

4. How did you determine (i.e., assess/evaluate or monitor) the client's success in reaching this short-term goal?

_____

5. What was the long-term goal of treatment? That is, objectively define what you had intended to achieve in treatment.

_____

_____

6. Please describe the treatment plan you used to reach the long-term goal, including the specific steps you followed.

_____

_____

_____.

7. How did you determine (i.e., assess/evaluate or monitor) the client's success in reaching this long-term goal?

_____

8. Why was treatment necessary?

_____.

9. What was the prognosis? _____.

10. For how many sessions are you requesting payment? _____

11. How many minutes did each session last? _____

12. Were outside services provided? ___Yes ___No

    (a) If yes, what services? _____

    _____.

    (b) Who provided these services? _____

    _____.

    (c) When did these services begin and end? _____

    _____.

D. Provider Information

1. Name: _____

2. (a) Credentials: _____

   (b) License number: _____

3. Malpractice insurance carrier and policy number: _____

4. Provider address: _____

5. Phone number: _____

Appendix H

Anchored Rating Scale Work Sheet

Step 1. In the space below write a description of what is to be rated (frequency, duration, or intensity or thinking, feeling, or action).

_____

_____

_____

Step 2. Consider the person who will be doing the rating and his or her ability to distinguish different attributes of what will be rated (listed in step 1). Select a range of scores (e.g., 1–4, 1–5, 1–7, 1–9, or 1–10), and arrange them on a continuum from 1 to the highest score.

1	*highest*

Step 3. In the boxes under the lowest rating, describe this extreme attribute of what is to be rated. In the box under the highest score, describe the other extreme attribute. Be certain these descriptions are in clear, concise, and observable terms.

Step 4. Draw boxes under at least one point toward the middle of the continuum and describe the attribute for this level of what is to be rated.

Appendix I

Case Summary Form

Case Summary Sheet

Client Name: _____ GAF: _____

Problem: _____

Goals/Objective: _____

Tx Protocol: _____

Measurement of Problem: _____

Measurement of Goal: _____

SCORES

NOTES:

P.U.R. Summary:	C.U.R. Summary:	R.U.R. Summary:

Appendix J

Biopsychosocial Cultural Assessment Checklist

Biopsychosocial Cultural Assessment Checklist for DSM-IV Use

Instructions: The following checklist is designed to guide the evaluator in making an assessment and diagnosis that is culturally sensitive to the ethnic background of the client/patient.

Questions	Comments/Narrative	DSMIV Notes
A. Establish Cultural Identity: ___ Ethnicity ___ Preferred language ___ Clan/Tribe/Faith ___ Country of origin? ___ Family/Community ___ How long in U.S.? Identity		

B. Cultural Explanation of (Physical) Illness/Symptoms:
 	
___ Use of folk words to explain illness
     (refer to DSM Glossary)
___ Meaning and explanation of client symptoms
     compared to reference group
___ Context of "illness" (location, frequency, occasion)
___ Types of help sought (traditional healers, folk medicine)
		Axis III - Medical

C. Cultural Factors Related to Psychosocial Environment and Level of Functioning: • Psychosocial Environment: What are the perceived stressors? ___ Support ___ Legal/Criminal ___ Educational ___ Violence/Trauma ___ Occupational ___ Access to health care system ___ Housing ___ Racism/discrimination ___ Economics ___ Other___ ___ Spiritual		Axis IV - Psychosocial Environmental
• Level of Functioning (wellness or unwellness): ___ degree of acculturation/biculturalism or assimilation ___ level of family/community stability		Axis V - Functioning

D. Cultural Elements of Provider-Client Relationship:

___ Gender issues   ___ Any other issues to influence
___ Age issues   how symptoms would be
___ Social status   expressed or how diagnosis/
___ Race/Ethnicity   treatment would be effected?
___ Language
___ Credibility within ethnic community

E. Overall Cultural Assessment (Diagnosis and Care):

___ How can cultural considerations influence diagnosis
      and care?
___ What is potential for compliance to health care plan?
___ Has family and/or significant community members (elders)
      been consulted?

F. DSM-IV Considerations:

• Axis I Clinical Syndrome

    ___ Appropriate?
    ___ V - Codes?

• Axis II Personality Disorders, Mental Retardation, and/or

    Defense Mechanisms

    ___ Appropriate?
    ___ V - Codes?

(Alternative) Recommendations:

Axis I: _____

Axis II: _____

Axis III _____

Axis IV: _____

Axis V: _____

303

GLOSSARY

The terms here reflect common definitions that you will encounter in managed care settings. The definitions may vary in different settings and should be used as a general guideline.

access   The ability of potential clients to seek and participate in available and appropriate services.

administrative-services-only (ASO)   A management system or service for the administration of self-funded health care plans.

adverse selection   A situation in which healthier individuals change to a less costly insurance plan, leaving the old plan with less healthy individuals who use more services. Due to adverse selection, the cost in the old plan constantly increases as the number of low-service users leaving the plan rises. Also refers to the disproportionate enrollment of insurance risks who are poorer or more prone to suffer more loss or make more claims than the average risk. That is, people at risk of poor health are more likely to seek insurance.

alternative delivery systems   Health care delivery modes that directly provide or finance the delivery of services with the goal of improving efficiency and/or containing cost.

ancillary services   Services provided in conjunction with physicians and hospitals (e.g., lab tests and radiology). Ancillary services include home health care (e.g., home nursing, home infusion or IV therapy), long-term nursing care, hospice care, and prosthetics and orthotics.

appropriateness   The degree of positive fit between a person's specific health care needs and available services. This is a term used to evaluate planned treatment protocols. Appropriateness of services may be determined by such factors

305

as level of service needs and severity of illness; treatment options; cultural match of clinician, organization, and client; motivation; and informed consent.

at risk   The state of being subject to some uncertain event's occurring that connotes loss or difficulty. In the financial sense, this refers to an individual, organization, or insurance company's assuming the chance of loss through running the risk of having to provide or pay for more services than are paid for through premiums or per capita payments—that is, at risk of losing money.

automated treatment planning   Software programs for clinicians that enable them to develop treatment plans using information that reflects current research-based standards of care. The forerunner of automated treatment planning that will occur in the future.

behavioral health/medicine   Applying psychological principles and procedures to the treatment of medical disorders.

capitation   A payment system in which the risk is absorbed by the provider, and funds are provided on a prospective basis per person (e.g., $1,500 per client per year).

capitation funding   A method of at-risk contracting between a payor and provider that involves preset funding for the number of persons covered by the benefit plan. Payment of a provider or organization for services to a given population, based on a fixed amount per person for a stated period of time rather than on the cost of actual services rendered (fee for service). The plan provides all covered services with additional costs to the enrollee. Health maintenance organizations typically use a capitation payment plan.

carve-out   A system in which a health maintenance organization and a group of providers, usually an individual practice association, make all mental health referrals to a specific group practice rather than to independent practitioners. The group practice is often under a capitation or other contract.

case mix   The diagnosis-specific makeup of a health program's workload. Case mix directly influences the length of stay, intensity, cost, and scope of services provided by a health or mental health program.

case-rate funding   A method of at-risk contracting between a payor and provider that involves prospective and preset funding. The amount of funding is assigned on the basis of the number and type of enrolled persons who present for services.

closed-panel PPO   A preferred provider organization (PPO) variation. For the patient to be allowed to use services, he or she must utilize services only by clinicians who are members of the panel. Also called *closed-panel provider* or *exclusive provider organization*.

community mental health organization (CMHO)   A term used to denote the changing face of community mental health centers (CMHC). These organizations operate with many of the same principles of the CMHC for public mental health care. Additionally, CMHOs incorporate principles of marketing, access, availability of care, efficiency, productivity, and capitated financing systems.

community rating   A method of calculating premiums according to the expected benefit utilization of the population as a whole rather than the utilization of specific groups.

comorbidity   The concurrence of two or more diseases in the same patient. Also called *complications*.

concurrent review   An assessment of the treatment necessity or appropriateness of services currently being rendered.

consultation   Obtaining additional information or a second opinion regarding a patient's health care. The primary provider continues to maintain responsibility for the client's care.

consumer   A person who receives and/or purchases services. Consumers may also advocate for service quality and appropriateness.

controlled-cost model   A health care delivery system with specific provisions to control cost.

copayment   A cost-sharing arrangement in which an insured person pays either a flat charge per visit (copay) or a percentage of the total cost (coinsurance).

cost containment   Mechanisms or procedures to control health care costs.

cost sharing   Financing arrangements such as deductibles, copayments, and coinsurance that shift some of the cost of services to the covered person.

delivery system   An organized array of service providers coordinated to deliver a set of services.

demand risk   The risk that enrollees will demand a different level of service from that projected in estimating costs for capitated programs.

diagnosis-related group (DRG)   A patient classification system used in the prospective reimbursement system of the federal Medicare program for hospital care. For each diagnosis, a specific amount of money will be paid to the hospital or organization regardless of the actual services provided or number of days of care. Payments are based on a person's primary and secondary diagnoses, demographics, and complicating factors. There are very few DRGs in mental health, with the largest category being "pscyhosis."

direct contracting   Employers, individually or in coalitions, contract directly with physicians or a medical facility for services. This is a form of self-insurance and is done without an insurance company intermediary in order to control cost.

direct payment model   A model in which the patient pays the provider directly for the services received. (Contrast this with the third-party payment model, in which some third party assumes responsibility for all or partial payment.) Also known as *fee for service.*

direct recognition laws   Laws that require insurance carriers to pay psychologists or social workers for services rendered. Patients have the freedom to choose a psychologist, social worker, or physician to provide services.

employee assistance program (EAP)   An in-house plan in which limited assessment, counseling, and referral services are made available to employees. Historically, EAPs were oriented toward the treatment of employees with alcohol problems. Today, EAPs are expanding to provide a broader range of services to help employees, their families, and the employer resolve personal and workplace problems through behavioral interventions.

enrollee   An individual eligible for services from a health plan, as either a subscriber or a dependent.

exclusive provider organization (EPO)   A type of managed care plan. EPOs are similar to preferred provider organizations but allow members to choose providers from a much smaller panel. The smaller panel is supposed to allow the insurance company to maintain high standards among its providers and to negotiate rates more aggressively.

fee-for-service (FFS) model   A model in which a separate fee is generated for each service provided.

gatekeeper   A person who screens patients and makes referrals to other providers. The gatekeeper, who is often a primary care physician or other professional (e.g., case manager), serves as the patient's first contact in a managed care system and controls access to other providers in the system. The gatekeeper will authorize access to the rest of the health care system, including specialty services, inpatient hospital services, and ancillary services.

group practice   Two or more professionals working together to provide a broader array of services than either could provide alone.

Health Care Financing Administration (HCFA)   The federal agency that administers Medicare and oversees the states' administration of Medicaid.

health maintenance organization (HMO)   A type of managed care plan; a prepaid health care delivery system in which patients receive all covered medical services without additional costs. In the HMO, provider payment is independent of utilization. HMOs are true managed care entities. Providers working for HMOs are usually employees of the HMO, and patients may have no choice as to which provider-physician they see at any particular office visit or hospitalization. Capitated payments are more common in HMOs, because they are federally regulated to accept such risks and to administer services. HMOs offer an organized system for providing health care within a specific geographic area, provide a set of basic and supplemental health maintenance and treatment services, and provide care to an enrolled group of people.

indemnity insurance The traditional form of medical insurance, which reimburses a patient for covered expenses after the services are rendered but only to the limits of the policy.

independent practice association (IPA) A type of health maintenance organization (HMO) in which practitioners retain their private practice but agree to provide a certain amount of service to HMO enrollees for a set fee.

integrated delivery system A combination of two or more traditionally separate components of the medical system, such as physician, hospital, ancillary services, risk contracting, and administration.

managed care Any health care delivery system in which various strategies are employed to optimize the value of provided services by controlling their cost and utilization, promoting their quality, and measuring performance to ensure cost-effectiveness. A managed care system actively manages both the medical and financial aspects of a patient's care.

medical model Refers to the disease model of illness or a model that asserts that a physician must be in charge of all patient health care.

medical necessity The determination that a specific health care service is medically appropriate, necessary to meet the person's health needs, consistent with the person's diagnosis, the most cost-effective option, and consistent with clinical standards of care.

morbidity The incidence and severity of situations requiring treatment (e.g., illness and accidents) within a specific group of persons.

morbidity risk The risk that service needs among a group of enrollees will differ from an expected amount. This does not translate directly into utilization risk but can affect it.

outcome measures Statistical barometers of the effectiveness of treatment for a particular disease or condition, including morbidity, mortality, cost, and patient satisfaction.

outcomes research Formal studies designed to measure the effectiveness of a given service or benefit package.

partially self-funded   A self-funded plan that relies on reinsurance or stop-loss insurance as protection against unexpected catastrophic losses.

payor   An entity that pays for medical services, usually an insurance company, Medicare, or Medicaid.

peer review   A form of professional services retrospective review in which one or more professionals are asked to make an expert judgment about a professional service. In order to effect a judgment, peer review may be based on a variety of data, including documents. Compliance with professional standards of care is based on judgment as to the congruence between a practice and a standard.

point of service (POS)   A type of managed care plan. POS plans allow members to vary their choice of providers and coverage from visit to visit. The terms for reimbursement depend on the options chosen. For instance, a plan may provide PPO coverage as long as a network physician is seen but will reimburse at standard indemnity insurance rates for services provided by other doctors. The choices are made prior to each encounter. A POS plan may also include basic HMO features with indemnity coverage for out-of-network services.

preferred provider organization (PPO)   A type of managed care plan. A health care benefit program designed to control benefit costs by giving members incentives to use health care providers who are designated as "preferred." Such an arrangement also provides substantial coverage for services from other health care providers. PPOs are created by insurance companies to contract with a limited number of clinicians. To ensure some level of quality, the providers must meet certain criteria, or credentials. The physicians agree to discount their customary fees in exchange for the chance to participate in caring for a large number of patients. Patients usually pay a small fee, or copayment, for each office visit. Most plans cover services outside the network only in the event of an emergency.

prepaid model   A health care system in which payment is received prior to and independent of any services rendered. A capitated model. Contrast with the fee-for-service model.

primary care   Refers to first-contact care that is longitudinal, comprehensive, and coordinated. *First contact* indicates that the provider is the point at which individuals seek entry into the health care system. *Longitudinality* means that the caregiver is the principal provider of care to the patient over time and implies an ongoing relationship between patient and provider. HMOs serve this purpose as organizations. *Comprehensiveness* means that the primary care facilities must be able to arrange for all types of health care services, even those not provided efficiently within the facility. Services would include preventive care, acute care, referral and consultative services, psychosocial services, and family planning. *Coordination* means that the provider is capable of integrating all the care that patients receive. This includes using various means to promote such coordination (e.g., physical proximity of providers and effective communication systems).

primary care physician Usually a family doctor, general internist, or pediatrician, and in some managed care plans, obstetricians and gynecologists.

professional services review Utilization review through some procedure involving a professional judgment.

prospective payment system (PPS) A system used to establish in advance the rate at which a service will be reimbursed. Diagnosis-related groups are an example of a PPS.

protocols Acceptable treatment plans in the event of certain diagnoses.

provider Physician, therapist, social worker, psychologist, dentist, hospital, laboratory, pharmacy, or other entity that provides medical services or supplies to the general public.

purchaser The buyer of health care services and benefits, either directly or for a third party, including individuals, employers, and governments.

quality assurance A professional services review in which an expert opinion is rendered as to the degree to which a given practice approximates an ideal.

quality of care The ability of a provider to meet the real or perceived needs of his or her patients; the degree to which health care services for individuals and populations increase the likelihood of the desired outcomes and are consistent with current professional knowledge.

race A composite measure of social, psychological, biological, and genetic influences on a person's life.

referral To turn over responsibility and control of a patient's health care to another provider.

risk Generally, any chance of loss. In insurance, designates the individual or property insured by an insurance policy against loss from some peril or hazard. Also used to denote the probability that the loss will occur.

risk sharing An arrangement between the program administrator and provider whereby the provider shares any funds remaining at the end of the period that have not been expended for services. They also share in shortages occasioned when spending for program services exceeds the available budget.

salaried practice A practice in which the employees of a private practice or institution receive a salary for their services.

self-funded   A health care plan funded by the employees that assumes the risks for all losses.

skimming   The practice in health programs paid on a prepayment or capitation basis and in health insurance of seeking to enroll only the healthiest people as a way of controlling program costs. Also known as *cherry picking*. Also, the practice of some providers of offering only those services that are favorably reimbursed by insurers (also called *creaming*).

subscriber   Often used synonymously with the terms *member* or *beneficiary*. In the strictest sense, *subscriber* means only the individual (family head or employee) who has elected to contract for, participate in, or subscribe to an insurance plan or HMO.

supervision   An educational process in which one individual with more knowledge, skills, and expertise (supervisor) teaches these skills to another individual (supervisee). Manditory supervision is a quality assurance practice of managed care organizations.

third-party payor   Insurance companies, government agencies, or other entities that provide monies to patients for the treatment of physical and mental illnesses.

urgent care center   Neighborhood medical clinic that is equipped and staffed to deal with most nonemergency problems.

utilization   The rate at which medical services are provided; patterns or rates of use of a single service or type of service (e.g., hospital care, physician visits, prescription drugs). Measurement of utilization of all clinical services. This is usually done in terms of dollar expenditures. For example, use is expressed in rates per unit of population at risk for a given period (e.g., number of hospital admissions per 1,000 persons over age sixty-five per year or number of visits to a physician per person per year for family planning services).

utilization management   Anticipating and setting standards for clinical services and monitoring the actual level of services achieved.

utilization review   The process of using predefined criteria to evaluate the necessity and appropriateness of allocated services and resources to ensure that a facility's services are necessary, cost-efficient, and effectively utilized. Also determines the medical necessity, efficiency, and appropriateness of the level of services provided, in advance, as the services are provided, or after the fact. Utilization review may be done by a committee, professional standards review organization, peer review group, public agency, or private company.

vendor   A provider, institution, agency, organization, or individual practitioner who signs an agreement with the payor to provide health or medical services or equipment.

References

Adler, S. (1990). Mental health benefit revisited. *Business Insurance*. February 27–28.

Allred v. State (1976) 554 P.2d 411.

Alpert, S. (1993). Smart cards, smarter policy: Medical records, privacy and health care reform. *Hastings Center Report, 23*, 13–23.

American Psychiatric Association (1994a). *Diagnostic and statistical manual* (4th ed.). Washington, DC: Author.

American Psychiatric Association (1994b). Practice guidelines for the treatment of patients with bipolar disorders. *American Journal of Psychiatry, 151*, Supp.

American Psychiatric Association (1993a). *Practice guidelines for eating disorders*. Washington, DC: Author.

American Psychiatric Association (1993b). *Practice guidelines for major depressive disorders*. Washington, DC: Author.

American Psychiatric Association (1992). *Utilization management: A handbook for psychiatrists*. Washington, DC: Author.

American Psychiatric Association (1987a). Guidelines on confidentiality. *American Journal of Psychiatry, 144*, 1522–1526.

American Psychiatric Association (1987b). *Economic fact book for psychiatry* (2d ed.). Washington, DC: Author.

Anclote Manor Foundation v. Wilkinson (1972), 263 So. 2d 256.

Anderson, D. F., and Berlant, J. L. (1993). Managed mental health and substance abuse services. In P. R. Kongstvedt (ed.), *The managed health care handbook*. Gaithersburg, MD: Aspen.

Anderson, S. C. (1989). Goal-setting in social work practice. In B. R. Compton and B. Galaway (eds.), *Social work process*. Belmont, CA: Wadsworth.

Andrews, G., and Harvey, R. (1981). Does psychotherapy benefit the neurotic patient: A reanalysis of Smith, Glass and Miller data. *Archives of General Psychiatry, 38*, 1203–1208.

Appel, K. E., and Bartemeier, L. H. (1961). *Action for mental health: Findings of the Joint Commission on Mental Illness and Health*. New York: Basic Books.

Applebaum, P. S. (1993). Legal liability and managed care. *American Psychologist, 48*, 251–257.

Applebaum, P. S. (1992). Practice guidelines in psychiatry and their implications for malpractice. Hospital and Community Psychiatry, 43, 341–342.

Austad, M. F., and Hoyt, C. S. (1992). The managed care movement and the future of psychotherapy. Psychotherapy, 29, 109–118.

Austin, M. J., Knopp, J., and Smith, P. L. (1986). Delivering human services. New York: Longman.

Bachofer, H. J. (1988). Prospective pricing psychiatric services. In D. J. Scherl, J. T. English, and S. S. Sharfstein (eds.), Prospective payment and psychiatric care (pp. 9–39). Washington, DC: American Psychiatric Press.

Bachrach, L. (1989). The legacy of model programs. Hospital and Community Psychiatry, 40, 234–235.

Baldwin, J. A., and Bell, Y. R. (1985). The African self-consciousness scale: An Afrocentric personality questionnaire. Western Journal of Black Studies, 9(2), 65–68.

Barlow, D. H. (ed.) (1993). Clinical handbook of psychological disorders. New York: Guilford.

Barlow, D. H., Hayes, S. C., and Nelson, R. O. (1984). The scientist practitioner: Research and accountability in clinical and educational settings. NY: Pergamon Press.

Becker, R. E., Heimberg, R. G., and Bellack, A. S. (1987). Social skills training for depression. Elmsford, NY: Pergamon.

Berg, I. K. & Jaya, A. (1993). Different and same: Family therapy with Asian-American families. Journal of Marital and Family Therapy, 19(1), 31–38.

Berman, J. S., Miller, C. R., and Massman, P. J. (1985). Cognitive therapy versus systematic desensitization: Is one treatment superior? Psychological Bulletin, 97, 451–461.

Bernstein, C. (1994). Is managed care good for mental health clients? No. In S. Kirk and S. Einbinder (eds.), Controversial Issues in Mental Health. Needham Heights, MA: Allyn & Bacon.

Berry, J. (1980). Acculturation as variations of adaptation. In A. M. Padilla (ed.), Acculturation: Theory, Models, and Some New Findings (pp. 9–23). Boulder, CO: Westview.

Bickman, L., Guthie, P. R., Foster, E. M., Lambert, E. W., Summerfelt, W. T., Breda, C. S., and Heflinger, C. A. (1995). Evaluating managed mental health services: The Fort Bragg experiment. New York: Plenum.

Biglan, A. & Campbell, D. R. (1981). Depression. In J. L. Shelton & R. L. Levy (eds.), Behavioral Assignment and Treatment Compliance: A Handbook of Clinical Strategies, (111–146). Champaign, IL: Research Press.

Bloom B. L. (1992). Planned Short-term Psychotherapy: A Clinical Handbook. Needham Heights, MA: Allyn & Bacon.

Bloom, M. (1975). The paradox of helping: Introduction to the philosophy of scientific practice. New York: Wiley.

Bloom, M. (ed.) (1993). Single-system designs in the social services for the 1990's. Binghamton, NY: Haworth Press.

Bloom, M., Fischer, J., and Orme, J. G. (1995). Evaluating practice: Guidelines for the accountable professional (2d ed.). Needham, MA: Allyn and Bacon.

Blythe, B. J. (1983). An examination of practice evaluation among social workers. Unpublished doctoral dissertation, University of Washington.

Bornstein, D. B. (1990). Managed care: A means of rationing psychiatric treatment. Hospital and Community Psychiatry, 41, 1095–1098.

Boyer, J. F., and Sobel, L. (1993). CHAMPUS and the Department of Defense managed care programs. In P. R. Kongstvedt (ed.), *The Managed health care handbook* (pp. 382–391). Gaithersburg, MD: Aspen.

Briar, S. (1973). The age of accountability. *Social Work, 18,* 14.

Brown, S. (1982, May). *Native generations, diagnosis, and placement on the conflicts/resolution chart.* Paper presented at the annual meeting of the School of Addiction Studies, Center for Alcohol and Addiction Studies, University of Alaska, Anchorage.

Bruvold, W. H. (1993). A meta-analysis of adolescent smoking prevention programs. *American Journal of Public Health, 83,* 872–880.

Butler, J. P. (1992). Of kindred minds: The ties that bind. In M. A. Orlandi (ed.), *Cultural competence for evaluators: A guide for alcohol and other drug abuse prevention practitioners working with ethnic/racial communities* (pp. 23–54). Rockville, MD: U.S. Department of Health and Human Services-Office of Substance Abuse Prevention.

Ceullar, I., Harris, I. C., and Jasso, R. (1980). An acculturation scale for Mexican American normal clinical populations. *Hispanic Journal of Behavioral Science, 2,* 199–217.

Chadwick, B. A. & Strauss, J. H. (1975). The assimilation of American Indians into urban society: The Seattle case. *Human Organizations, 34,* 359–369.

Cienfuegos, A. J., and Monelli, C. (1983). The testimony of political repression as a therapeutic instrument. *American Journal of Orthopsychiatry, 53,* 43–51.

Clum, G. A., Clum, G. A., and Surls, R. (1993). A meta-analysis of treatment for panic disorders. *Journal of Consulting and Clinical Psychology, 61,* 317–326.

Compton, B. R. & Galaway, B. (eds.) (1989). *Social Work Processes.* Belmont, CA: Wadsworth.

Corcoran, K. (1994). Is managed care good for mental health clients? Yes. In Stuart A. Kirk and Susan Einbinder (eds.), *Controversial issues in mental health* (pp. 240–245). New York: Allyn and Bacon.

Corcoran, K. (1993). Practice evaluation: Problems and promises of single-system design in clinical practice. *Journal of Social Service Research, 18,* 147–159.

Corcoran, K. (1992a). Doing family therapy with an acting-out adolescent: Applying the empirical clinical practice model. In C. W. LeCroy (ed.), *Case studies in social work practice* (pp. 262–267). Belmont, CA: Wadsworth Press.

Corcoran, K. (1992b). *Structuring change: Effective practice for common client problems.* Chicago: Lyceum.

Corcoran, K. (1985). Clinical practice with non-behavioral methods: Strategies for evaluation. *Clinical Social Work Journal, 3,* 78–86.

Corcoran, K., and Gingerich, W. (1994). Practice evaluation in the context of managed care: Case recording methods for quality assurance review. *Research on Social Work Practice, 4,* 326–337.

Corcoran, K., and Gingerich, W. (1992). Practice evaluation: Setting goals, measuring and assessing change. In *Structuring change: Effective practice for common client problems* (pp. 26–45). Chicago: Lyceum Books.

Corcoran, K., and Keeper, C. (1992). Psychodynamic treatment of persons with borderline personality. In *Structuring change: Effective practice for common client problems* (pp. 255–271). Chicago: Lyceum Books.

Corcoran, K., and Videka-Sherman, L. (1992). Some things we know about effective practice. In *Structuring change: Effective practice for common client problems* (pp. 13–25). Chicago: Lyceum Books.

Corcoran, K., and Winslade, W. J. (1994). Eavesdropping on the 50-minute hour: Confidentiality and managed mental health care. *Behavioral Sciences and the Law, 12*, 351–365.

Corin, E. (1994). The social and cultural matrix of health and disease. In R. E. Evans, M. L. Barer, and T. R. Marmor (eds.), *Why are some people healthy and others not? The determinants of health of populations* (pp. 93–132). Hawthorne, NY: Aldine de Gruyter.

Cox, B. J., Swinson, R. P., Morrison, B., and Lee, P. S. (1993). Clomipramine, fluoxetine, and behavior therapy in the treatment of obsessive-compulsive disorder: A meta analysis. *Journal of Behavioral Therapy and Experimental Psychiatry, 24*, 149–153.

Craighead, L. W., Craighead, W. E., Kazdin, A. E., and Mahoney, M. J. (1994). *Cognitive and behavioral interventions: An empirical approach to mental health problems.* Needham Heights, MA: Allyn & Bacon.

Cross, T. (1987). *Cross-cultural skills in Indian child welfare—A guide for the non-Indian.* Portland, OR: Northwest Indian Child Welfare Institute.

Cutler, D. (1992). A historical overview of community mental health centers in the United States. In S. Cooper and T. Lantner (eds.), *Innovations in community mental health* (pp. 1–22). Miami, FL: Professional Resource Press.

Dana, R. H. (1993). *Multicultural assessment perspectives for professional psychology.* Needham Heights, MA: Allyn & Bacon.

Davis, J. M., Wang, Z., and Janicak, P. G. (1993). A quantitative analysis of clinical drug trials for the treatment of affective disorders. *Psychopharmacology Bulletin, 29*, 175–181.

Delgado, M. (1988). Groups in Puerto Rican spiritism: Implications for clinicians. In C. Jacobs & D. D. Bowles (eds.), *Ethnicity and race: Critical concepts in social work* (pp. 34–37). Silver Spring, MD: National Association of Social Workers.

Derogatis, L., and Melisaratos, N. (1983). The brief symptom inventory: An introductory report. *Psychological Medicine, 13*, 595–605.

Dickey, B., and Azeni, H. (1992). Impact of managed care on mental health services. *Health Affairs, 11*, 197–204.

Dilulio, J. J. (1991). *No escape: The future of American corrections.* New York: Basic Books.

Dobson, D. J. G., McDougal, G., Busheikin, J., and Aldous, J. (1995). Effects of social skills training and social milieu treatment on symptoms of schizophrenia. *Psychiatric Services, 46*(4), 376–380.

Dorwart, R. A. (1990) Managed mental health care: Myths and realities in the 1990s. *Hospital and Community Psychiatry, 41*, 1087–1091.

Doverspite, W. F. (1990). Multiaxial Diagnostic Inventory: Adult clinical scales and personality scales. *Innovations in Clinical Practice, 9*, 241–263.

Durham, M. L. (1994). Healthcare's greatest challenge: Providing services for people with severe mental illness in managed care. *Behavioral Sciences and the Law, 12*, 331–349.

DuVal, M. K. (1988). Changing reimbursement patterns and the realities of health care finance. In D. J. Scherl, J. T. English, and S. S. Sharfstein (eds.), *Prospective Payment and Psychiatric Care* (pp. 1–8). Washington, DC: American Psychiatric Press.

Eddy, D. M. (1990). Designing a practice policy: Standards, guidelines, options. *Journal of the American Medical Association, 263*, 3077, 3081, 3084.

Edinburgh, G., and Cottler, J. (1990). Implications of managed care for social work in psychiatric hospitals. *Hospital and Community Psychiatry, 41*, 1063–1064.

Eisenberg, J. M. et al. (1989). Substituting diagnostic services: New tests only partially replace older ones. *Journal of the American Medical Association, 262*, 1196–1200.

Engels, G. I., Garnefski, N., and Diekstra, R. F. (1993). Efficacy of rational-emotive therapy: A quantitative analysis. *Journal of Consulting and Clinical Psychology, 61*, 1083–1090.

English, J. T., Sharfstein, S. S., Scherl, D. J. Astrachan, and Muszynski (1986). Diagnosis-related groups and general hospital psychiatry. *American Journal of Psychiatry, 143*, 135.

Eppley, K. R., Abrams, A. I., and Shore, J. (1989). Differential effects of relaxation techniques on trait anxiety: A meta analysis. *Journal of Clinical Psychology, 45*, 957–974.

Eysenck, H. (1952). The effects of psychotherapy: An evaluation. *Journal of Consulting Psychology, 16*, 319–324.

Fauman, M. A. (1992). Quality assurance monitoring in psychiatry. In M. R. Mattson (ed.), *Manual of psychiatric quality assurance* (pp. 57–68). Washington, DC: American Psychiatric Press.

Feleppa, R. (1986). Emics, etics, and social objectivity. *Current Anthropology, 27*, 243–255.

Field, M. J., and Gray, B. H. (1989). Should we regulate "utilization management"? *Health Affairs, 8*, 103–112.

Fischer, J. (1990). Problems and issues in meta-analysis. In L. Videka-Sherman and W. J. Reid (eds.), *Advances in clinical social work research.* Silver Spring, MD: National Association of Social Workers.

Fischer, J. (1978). *Effective casework practice: An eclectic approach.* NY: McGraw-Hill.

Fischer, J. (1976). *The effectiveness of social casework.* Springfield, IL: Thomas.

Fischer, J. (1973). Is casework effective? A review. *Social Work, 18*, 5–20.

Fischer, J., and Corcoran, K. (1994a). *Measures for Clinical Practice: A sourcebook. Vol. 1: Adults.* New York: The Free Press.

Fischer, J., and Corcoran, K. (1994b). *Measures for clinical practice: A sourcebook. Vol. 2: Couples, children and families.* New York: The Free Press.

Fischer, S. G. (1980). The use of time limits in brief psychotherapy: A comparison of six-session, twelve-session, and unlimited treatment with families. *Family Process, 19*, 377–392.

Fleming, C. M. (1992). American Indians and Alaska Natives: Changing societies past and present. In M.A. Orlandi (ed.), *Cultural competence for evaluators: A guide for alcohol and other drug abuse prevention practitioners working with ethnic/racial communities* (pp. 147–172). Rockville, MD: U.S. Department of Health and Human Services-Office of Substance Abuse Prevention.

Forer, L. G. (1994). *A rage to punish: The unintended consequences of mandatory sentencing.* New York: Norton.

Friesen, B. J., and Poertner, J. (eds.) (1995). *Building on family strength.* Baltimore, MD: Brooks.

Fuchs, V. R. (1993). No pain, no gain: Perspectives on cost containment. *Journal of American Medical Association, 269*, 631–633.

Fuller, M. G. (1994). A new day: Strategies for managing psychiatric and substance abuse benefits. *Health Care Management Review, 19*, 20–24.

Furrow, B. R., Johnson, S. H., Jost, T. S., and Schwartz, R. L. (1991). *Health law: Cases, materials and problems.* St. Paul, MN: West Publishing.

Gabbard, G. O. (1995). *Treatments of psychiatric disorders.* Washington, DC: American Psychiatric Press.

Gabbard, G. O. (1994). Inpatient services: The clinician's view. In R. K. Schreter, S. S. Sharfstein, and C. A. Schreter (eds.), *Allies and adversaries: The impact of managed care on mental health services.* Washington, DC: American Psychiatric Press.

Gabbard, G. O. (1992). The big chill: The transition from residency to managed care nightmare. *Academic Psychiatry, 16,* 119–126.

Garcia, M., and Lega, L. I. (1979). Development of a Cuban ethnic identity questionnaire. *Hispanic Journal of Behavioral Sciences, 1,* 247–261.

Garfield, S. L., and Bergin, A. E. (eds.) (1986). *Handbook of psychotherapy and behavior change.* New York: Wiley.

Garnick, D. W., Hendricks, A. M., Dulski, J. D., Thorpe, K. E., and Hogen, C. H. (1994). Characteristics of private-sector managed care for mental health and substance abuse treatment. *Hospital and Community Psychiatry, 45,* 1201–1205.

Gary, L. (1987). Religion and mental health in an urban Black community. *Urban Research Review, 7*(2), 5–7.

Gelso, C. J. & Hazel-Johnson, D. (1983). *Exploration in time-limited counseling and psychotherapy.* New York: Teachers College Press.

Giles, T. R. (1993). *Managed mental health care: A guide for practitioners, employers, and hospital administrators.* Needham Heights, MA: Allyn & Bacon.

Giles, T. R. (ed.) (1993). *Handbook of effective psychotherapy.* New York: Plenum.

Giles, T. R. (1991). Managed mental health care and effective psychotherapy: A step in the right direction? *Journal of Behavior Therapy and Experimental Psychiatry, 22,* 83–86.

Gingerich, W. J. (1990). Rethinking single case-evaluation. In L. Videka-Sherman and W. J. Reid (eds.), *Advances in clinical social work research.* Silver Spring, MD: NASW.

Gingerich, W. J. (1984). Generalizing single-case evaluation from classroom to practice. *Journal of Education for Social Work 20,* 74–82.

Goodman, M., Brown, J. and Deitz, P. (1992). *Managing managed care: A mental health practitioners' survival guide.* Washington, DC: American Psychiatric Press.

Gostin, L. O., Turek-Brezina, J., Powers, M., Kozloff, R., Faden, R., and Steinauer, D. D. (1993). Privacy and security of personal information in a new health care system. *Journal of American Medical Association, 270,* 2487–2493.

Grace, C. A. (1992). Practical considerations for program professionals and evaluators working with African-American communities. In Orlandis (pp. 55–74).

Graham, M. D. (1995). Managed care: The American Academy of Child and Adolescent Psychiatry's managed care strategy. *Psychiatric Services, 46,* 659–660.

Griswold v. Connecticut (1965). 381 U.S. 479.

Grumet, G. W. (1989). Health care rationing through inconvenience. *New England Journal of Medicine, 231,* 607–611.

Hakstian, A. R., and McLean, P. D. (1989). Brief screen for depression. *Psychological Assessment, 1,* 139–141.

Hall, R. C. W. (1994a). Social and legal implications of managed care in psychiatry. *Psychosomatic, 35,* 150–158.

Hall, R. C. W. (1994b). Legal precedents affecting managed care: The physician's responsibility to patients. *Psychosomatic, 35,* 105–117.

Hamilton, J. M. (1992). Introduction to the American Psychiatric Association's involvement in quality assurance and utilization review. In M. R. Mattson (ed.), *Manual of psychiatric quality assurance* (pp. 7–9). Washington, DC: American Psychiatric Press.

Hanrahan, P., and Reid, W. J. (1984). Choosing effective interventions. *Social Services Review, 58,* 244–258.

Hargreaves, W. A. (1992). A capitation model for providing mental health service in California. *Hospital and Community Psychiatry, 43,* 275–277.

Harris, J. S. (1994). *Strategic health management: A guide for employees, employers, and policy makers.* San Francisco: Jossey-Bass.

Hartman, D. P., Gottman, J. M. Jones, R. R., Williams, G. Kazdin, A. E., and Vaught, R. (1981). Interrupted timed series analysis and its application to behavioral data. *Journal of Applied Behavior Analysis, 13,* 543–560.

Havinghurst, C. C. (1991). Practice guidelines as legal standards governing physician liability. *Law and Contemporary Problems, 54,* 87–117.

Hazelrigg, M. D., Cooper, H. M., and Bordin, J. (1987). Evaluating the effectiveness of family therapies: An integrative review and analysis. *Psychological Bulletin, 101,* 428–442.

Health Insurance Association of America (1992). *Source book of health insurance data.* Washington, DC: Author.

Heineman-Piper, M. D. (1981). The obsolete scientific imperative in social work research. *Social Service Review, 55,* 371–397.

Helms, J. E. (1986). Expanding racial identity theory to cover the counseling process. *Journal of Counseling Psychology, 33,* 62–64.

Herrick, R. R. (1993). Medicaid and managed care. In P. R. Kongstvedt (ed.), *The managed health care handbook* (pp. 373–381). Gaithersburg, MD: Aspen.

Hersen, M., and Barlow, D. H. (1986). *Single case experimental designs.* New York: Pergamon Press.

Hillman, A. L., Welch, W. P., and Pauly, M. V. (1992). Contractual agreements between HMOs and primary care physicians: Three-tiered HMOs and risk pools. *Medical Care, 30,* 136–148.

Ho, M. K. (1987). *Family therapy and ethnic minorities.* Newbury Park, CA: Sage.

Hoffman, T., Dana, R. H., and Bolton, B. (1985). Measured acculturation and MMPI-168 performance of Native American adults. *Journal of Cross-Cultural Psychology, 16,* 243–256.

Hogarty, G. E. (1989). Meta-analysis of the effects of practice with the chronically mentally ill: A critique and reappraisal of the literature. *Social Work, 34,* 363–373.

Hood, L., and Sharfstein, S. S. (1992). Managed care for patients who are treatment resistant. *Hospital and Community Psychiatry, 43,* 774–775.

Horak v. Biris (1985). 130 Ill. App. 3d 140.

Horne v. Patton (1973). 287 So. 2d 824.

Howard, G. S. (1980). Response-shift bias: A problem in evaluating interventions with pre/post self reports. *Evaluation Review, 4,* 93–106.

Hudson, W. W. (1992). *MPSI technical manual.* Tempe, AZ: WALMYR Publishing.

Hudson, W. W. (1982). *The clinical measurement package: A field manual.* Chicago: Dorsey.

Hughes v. Blue Cross of Northern California (1988). 245 Cal. Rptr. 273.

Hustig, H. H., and Hafner, R. J. (1990). Persistent auditory hallucinations and their relationship to delusions and mood. *Journal of Nervous and Mental Disease, 178,* 264–267.

Jackson, G. (1986) Conceptualizing Afrocentric and Eurocentric mental health training. In H.P. Lefley & P.B. Pedersen (eds.), *Cross-cultural training for mental health professionals* (pp. 131–149). Springfield, IL: Thomas Publishing.

Jackson, J. A. (1987). Clinical social work and peer review: A professional leap ahead. *Social Work, 32,* 213–220.

Jayaratne, S. (1978). Analytic procedures for single-subject designs. *Social Work Research and Abstracts, 14,* 30–40.

Jayaratne, S., and Levy, R. L. (1979). *Empirical clinical practice.* New York: Columbia University Press.

Jecker, N. S., Carress, J. A., and Pearlman, R. A. (1995). Care for patients in cross-cultural settings. *Hastings Center Report, 25,* 6–14.

Jellinek, M. S., and Nurcombe, B. (1993). Two wrongs don't make a right: Managed care, mental health, and the marketplace. *Journal of the American Medical Association, 270,* 1737–1739.

Jordon, C., and Franklin, C. (1995). *Clinical assessment for social workers: Quantitative and qualitative methods.* Chicago: Lyceum Books.

Kagle, J. D. (1982). Using single-subject measures in practice decisions: Systematic documentation or distortion? *Arete, 7,* 1–9.

Kane, R. L., Bartlett, J., and Potthoff S. (1995). Best practices: Building an empirically based outcomes information system for managed mental health care. *Psychiatric Services, 46,* 459–461.

Kaplan, H.I., Sadock, B.J., and Grebb, J.A. (1994). *Synopsis of psychiatry: Behavioral sciences of clinical psychiatry* (7th ed.). Baltimore, MD: Williams & Wilkins.

Katz, S. E. and Trainor, R. E. (1988). Impact of cost containment strategies on state mental health delivery system. In D. J. Scherl, J. T. English, and S. S. Sharfstein (eds.), *Prospective payment and psychiatric care* (pp. 55–65). Washington, DC: American Psychiatric Press.

Kellner, R. (1987). A symptom questionnaire. *Journal of Clinical Psychiatry, 48,* 268–274.

Kendall, P. C., and Braswell, L. (1993). *Cognitive-behavioral therapy for impulsive children.* New York: Guilford.

Kennedy, J. F. (1963). Message from the President of the United States relative to mental illness and mental retardation. 88th Cong. 1st sess., House of Representatives, Doc. No. 58, February 5, 1963.

Kim, S., McLeod, J.H., and Shantzis, C. (1992). Cultural competence for evaluators working with Asian-American communities: Some practical considerations. In M.A. Orlandi (ed.), *Cultural competence for evaluators: A guide for alcohol and other drug abuse prevention practitioners working with ethnic/racial communities* (pp. 203–260). Rockville, MD: U.S. Department of Health and Human Services-Office of Substance Abuse Prevention.

Kinzie, J. D., and Manson, S. M. (1987). The use of cross-cultural rating scales in cross-cultural psychiatry. *Hospital and Community Psychiatry, 38*(2), 190–196.

Kiresuk, T. S., and Sherman, R. E. (1968). Goal attainment scaling: A general method for evaluating comprehensive community mental health programs. *Community Mental Health Journal, 4,* 443–453.

Kiresuk, T. S., Smith, A., and Cardillo, J. E. (eds.) (1994). *Goal attainment scaling: Applications, theory and measurement.* Hillsdale, NJ: Erlbaum.

Kirk, S. A., and Kutchins, H. (1992). *The Selling of DSM: The rhetoric of science in psychiatry.* New York: Aldine.

Kirmayer, L. J. (1994). Is the concept of mental disorder culturally relative? In S.A. Kirk and S.D. Einbinder (eds.), *Controversial Issues in Mental Health* (pp. 1–20). Needham Heights, MA: Allyn and Bacon.

Kiser, L. J., Heston, J. D., Milsap, P. A., and Pruitt, D. B. (1991). Treatment protocols in child and adolescent day treatment. *Hospital and Community Psychiatry, 42*, 597–600.

Klerman, G. L., Olfson, M., Leon, A. C., and Weissman, M. M. (1992). Measuring the need for mental health care. *Health Affairs, 11*, 23–33.

Kongstvedt, P. R. (ed.) (1993). *The managed health care handbook.* Gaithersburg, MD: Aspen.

Kratochwill, T. R. (ed.) (1978). *Single-system research: Strategies for evaluating change.* New York: Academic Press.

Kuhl, V. (1994). The managed care revolution: Implications for humanistic psychotherapy. *Journal of Humanistic Psychology, 34*, 62–81.

Kutchins, H. (1991). The fiduciary relationship: The legal basis for social workers' responsibility to clients. *Social Work, 36*, 106–113.

Lacey v. Bressler (1987). 358 S.E.2d 560.

Larson, A. (1992). *Worker's compensation law: Cases, materials and text.* New York: Matthew Bender.

Larson, D. L., Attkisson, C. C., Hargreaves, W. A., and Nguyen, T. D. (1979). Assessment of client/patient satisfaction: Development of a general scale. *Evaluation and Planning, 2*, 197–207.

Lazarus, J. A., and Sharfstein, S. S. (1994). Changes in the economics and ethics of health and mental health care. *Review of Psychiatry, 13*, 389–413.

LeClere, F. B., Jensen, L., and Biddlecom, A. E. (1994). Health care utilization, family context, and adaptation among immigrants to the United States. *Journal of Health and Social Behavior, 35*, 370–384.

LeCroy, C. W. (1994). *Handbook of child and adolescent treatment manuals.* New York: Lexington Books.

Lehman, A., Rachuba, L.T., and Postrado, L.T. (1995). Demographic influences on quality of life among persons with chronic mental illnesses. *Evaluation and Program Planning, 18*(2), 155–164.

Levy, R. L. (1981). On the nature of the clinical-research gap: The problems with some solutions. *Behavioral Assessment, 3*, 235–242.

Levy, R. L., and Shelton, J. L. (1990). Tasks of brief therapy. In R. A. Wells and V. J. Giannetti (eds.), *Handbook of the Brief Psychotherapies* (pp. 145–163). New York: Plenum.

Lin, N. (1989). Measuring depression symptomatology in Chinese. *Journal of Nervous and Mental Disorders, 177*, 121–131.

Linehan, M. M., and Kehrer, C. A. (1993). Borderline personality disorder. In D. H. Barlow (ed.), *Clinical handbook of psychological disorders* (pp. 396–441). New York: Guilford.

Lipsey, M. W., and Wilson, D. B. (1993). The efficacy of psychological, educational, and behavioral treatment: Confirmation from meta-analysis. *American Psychologists, 48*, 1181–1209.

Littrell, J. (1995). Clinical practice guidelines for depression in primary care: What social workers need to know. *Research on Social Work Practice, 5*, 131–151.

Loewenberg, F. M., and Dolgoff, R. (1992). *Ethical decisions for social work practice* (4th ed.). Itasca, IL: Peacock.

Luft, L. L., Sampson, L. M., and Newman, D. (1976). Effects of peer review on outpatient psychotherapy: Therapist and patient follow-up survey. *American Journal of Psychiatry, 133*, 891–895.

MacDonald v. Clinger (1982), 446 N.Y.S.2d 801.

MacKenzie, K. R. (1995a). *Introduction to time-limited group psychotherapy.* Washington, DC: American Psychiatric Press.

MacKenzie, K. R. (1995b). *Effective use of group therapy in managed care.* Washington, DC: American Psychiatric Press.

MacLeod, G. K. (1993). An overview of managed health care. In P. R. Pongstvedt (ed.), *The managed care handbook* (2d.ed.) (pp. 3–11). Gaithersburg, MD: Aspen Press.

Mahoney, M. J. (1979). *Self-change: Strategies for solving personal problems.* New York: Norton.

Marin, G., Sabogal, F., Van Oss Marin, B., Otero-Sabogol, R., and Perez-Stable, E. J. (1987). Development of a short acculturation scale for Hispanics. *Hispanic Journal of Behavioral Science, 9*, 183–205.

Marin, G., and Van Oss Marin, B. (1991). *Research with Hispanic populations.* Newbury Park, CA: Sage.

Markowitz, J. C. (1994). Psychotherapy of dysthymia. *American Journal of Psychiatry, 151*, 1114–1121.

Markowitz, J. C., and Klerman, G. L. (1993). *Manual for interpersonal psychotherapy of dysthymia.* New York: Cornell University Medical College, Department of Psychiatry.

Marmar v. Health Care Plan of New Jersey (1995). *National Law Journal.*

Masuda, M., Matsumoto, G. H., and Meredith, G. M. (1970). Ethnic identity in three generations of Japanese Americans. *Journal of Social Psychology, 81*, 199–207.

Mattaini, M. A. (1993). *More than a thousand words: Graphics for clinical practice.* Silver Spring, MD: National Association of Social Workers.

Mattson, M. R. C. (1992). *Manual of psychiatric quality assurance.* Washington, DC: American Psychiatric Press.

Mazza v. Huffaker (1983). 300 S.E.2d 833.

McCall-Perez, F. (1993). What employers want in managed care programs. *Hospital and Community Psychiatry, 44*, 682–683.

McCullough, J. P. (1992). *The manual for therapists treating the chronic depressions and using the cognitive-behavioral analysis system of psychotherapy.* Richmond, VA: Virginia Commonwealth University, Department of Psychiatry.

McGovern, M. P., Lyons, J. S., and Pomp, H. (1990). Capitation payment systems and public mental health care: Implication for psychotherapy with the seriously mentally ill. *American Journal of Orthopsychiatry, 60*, 298–304.

Menendez v. Superior Court (1991), 228 Cal. App. 3d 1320.

Menendez v. Superior Court, No. S017206.

Milliones, J. (1980). Construction of a black consciousness measure: Psychotherapeutic implications. *Psychotherapy: Theory, Research, and Practice, 17*, 175–182.

Millon, T. (1985a). The MCMI provides a good assessment of DSM-III disorder: The MCMI-II will prove even better. *Journal of Personality Assessment, 49*, 379–391.

Millon, T. (1985b). *Millon clinical multiaxial inventory* (2d ed.). Minneapolis, MN: National Computer Systems.

Mizrahi, T. (1993). Managed care and managed competition: A primer for social work. *Health and Social Work, 18*, 86–91.

Mollica, R., Caspi-Yavin, Y., Bollini, P., Truong, T., Tor, S., and Lavelle, J. (1992). The

Harvard trauma questionnaire: Validating a cross-cultural instrument for measuring torture, trauma, and post traumatic stress disorder in Indochinese refugees. *Journal of Nervous and Mental Disease, 180*(2), 111–116.

Mollica, R. F., Wyshak, G., de Marneffe, D., Khuan, F., and Lavelle, J. (1987). Indochinese versions of the Hopkins Symptom Checklist—25: A screening instrument for the psychiatric care of refugees. *American Journal of Psychiatry, 144*(4), 497–500.

Mollica, R. F., Wyshak, G., de Marneffe, D., Tu, B., Yang, T., Khuon, F., Coelho, R., and Lavelle, J. (1994). *Hopkins Symptom Checklist—25: Indochinese version: Manual.* Boston: Harvard School of Public Health–Harvard Program in Refugee Trauma.

Morreim, E. H. (1995). The ethics of incentives in managed care. *Trends in Health Care, Law and Ethics, 10,* 56–62.

Morreim, E. H. (1991). Economic disclosure and economic advocacy: New duties in the medical standard of care. *Journal of Legal Medicine, 12,* 275–329.

Motwani, J., Hodge, J., and Crampton, S. (1995). Managing diversity in the health care industry: A conceptual model and an empirical investigation. *Health Care Supervisor, 13,* 16–23.

Murphy, J. M., and Helzer, J. E. (1990). Epidemiology of adult schizophrenia. *Psychiatry, 1,* 1–19.

Mutschler, E. (1984). Evaluating practice: A study of research utilization by practitioners. *Social Work, 29,* 332–337.

Namerow, M. J. & Gibson, R. W. (1988). Prospective payment for private psychiatric specialty hospitals: The National Association of Private Psychiatric Hospitals' prospective payment study. In D. J. Scherl, J. T. English, & S. S. Sharfstein (eds.), *Prospective payment and psychiatric care* (pp. 41–53). Washington, DC: American Psychiatric Press.

NASW (1993). *National Association of Social Workers policy statements: Managed care.* Silver Spring, MD: Author.

Nelsen, J. C. (1993). Testing practice wisdom: Another use of single-system research. *Journal of Social Service Research, 18,* 65–82.

Nelsen, J. C. (1981). Issues in single-subject research for non-behaviorists. *Social Work Research and Abstracts, 17,* 31–37.

Nickens, H. W. (1995). The role of race/ethnicity and social class in minority health status. *Health Services Research, 30,* 151–162.

Norcross, J. C. (1986). *Handbook of eclectic psychotherapy.* New York: Brunner/Mazel.

Nuehing, E. M., and Pascone, A. B. (1986). Single-subject evaluation: A tool for quality assurance. *Social Work, 31,* 359–365.

Nunnally, J., and Bernstein, I. H. (1994). *Psychometric Theory.* New York: McGraw-Hill.

Obeyesekere, G. (1985). Depression, Buddhism, and the work of culture in Sri Lanka. In A. M. Kleinmanit and B. Good (eds.), *Culture and depression* (pp. 134–152.). Berkeley: University of California Press.

O'Hara, T. (1995). Problem severity among outpatient mental health clients: Development and validation of the South Shore Problem Inventory. *Research on Social Work Practice, 5,* 107–119.

Olfson, M., and Pincus, H. A. (1994a). Outpatient psychotherapy in the United States, II: Patterns of utilization. *American Journal of Psychiatry, 151,* 1289–1294.

Olfson, M., and Pincus, H. A. (1994b). Outpatient psychotherapy in the United States, I: Volume, costs, and user characteristics. *American Journal of Psychiatry, 151,* 1281–1288.

Olmedo, E. L., Martinez, J. L., and Martinez, S. R. (1978). Measure of acculturation for Chicano adolescents. *Psychological Reports, 42,* 159–170.

Orlandi, M. A. (1992). Defining cultural competence: An organizing framework. In M. A. Orlandi (ed.), *Cultural competence for evaluators: A guide for alcohol and other drug abuse prevention practitioners working with ethnic/racial communities* (pp. 293–299). Rockville, MD: U.S. Department of Health and Human Services-Office of Substance Abuse Prevention.

Osman, S., and Shueman, S. A. (1988). A guide to the peer review process for clinicians. *Social Work, 33,* 345–348.

Padilla, A. M. and de Salgado, V. N. (1992). Hispanics: What the culturally informed evaluator needs to know. In M. A. Orlandi (ed.), *Cultural competence for evaluators: A guide for alcohol and other drug abuse prevention practitioners working with ethnic/racial communities* (pp. 117–146). Rockville, MD: U.S. Department of Health and Human Services-Office of Substance Abuse Prevention.

Parmet, W. (1981). Public health protection and the privacy of medical records. *Harvard Civil Rights–Civil Liberties Law Review, 16,* 265–304.

Parsi K. P., Winslade, W. J., and Corcoran, K. (1995). Does confidentiality have a future? The computer-based patient record and managed mental health care. *Trends in Health Care, Law and Ethics, 10,* 78–82.

Patterson, D. Y. (1990). Managed care: An approach to rational psychiatric treatment. *Hospital and Community Psychiatry, 41,* 1092–1094.

Patterson, D. Y., and Sharfstein, S. S. (1992). The future of mental health care. In J. L. Feldman and R. J. Fitzpatrick (eds.), *Managed mental health care: Administration and clinical issues* (pp. 335–343). Washington, DC: American Psychiatric Press.

Paulson, R. I. (1996). Swimming with the sharks or walking in the Garden of Eden: Two versions of managed care. In P. R. Raffoil and A. C. NcNeece (eds.), *The future of social work.* Needham Heights, MA: Allyn & Bacon.

People v. Clark (1990). 268 Cal. Rptr. 399.

People v. O'Gorman (1977). 398 N.Y.S.2d 336.

People v. Wharton (1991). 953 Cal. 3d 522.

Pickett, S. A., Lyons, J. S., Polonus, T., Seymour, T., and Miller, S. (1995). Factors predicting patients' satisfaction with managed mental health care. *Psychiatric Services,* 46(7), 722–723.

Pieper-Heineman, M. (1987). Comments on "Scientific imperatives in social work research: Pluralism is not skepticism." *Social Services Review, 61,* 368–370.

Pinkston, E. M., Levitt, J. L., Green, G. R., Linsk, N. L., and Rzepnicki, T. L. (1982). *Effective social work practice: Advanced techniques for behavioral intervention with individuals, families, and institutional staff.* San Francisco: Jossey-Bass.

Pomales, J., Claiborn, C., and LaFromboise, T. (1986). Effects of Black students' racial identity on perceptions of white counselors varying in cultural sensitivity. *Journal of Counseling Psychology 33,* 57–61.

Poynter, W. L. (1994). *The preferred provider's handbook: Building a successful private practice in the managed care marketplace.* New York: Brunner/Mazel.

Poythress, N. G., and Miller, R. B. (1991). The treatment of forensic patients: Major issues. In S. A. Shah and B. D. Sales (eds.), *Law and mental health: Major developments and research needs.* No. (ADM) 91-1875. Rockville, MD: U.S. Department of Health and Human Services.

Price, S. B., & Greenwood, S. K. (1988). Using treatment plans for quality assurance monitoring in a residential center. *Quality Review Bulletin, 14,* 266–274.

Prosser, W. L., Wade, J. W., and Schwartz, V. E. (1988). *Torts: Cases and materials* (8th ed.). Mineola, NY: Foundation Press.

Public Health Service (1991). *Healthy people 2000: National health promotion and disease prevention objectives.* DHHS Pub. No. 91-50212. Washington, DC: U.S. Government Printing Office.

Quinlivan R., Hough, R., Crowell, A., Beach, C., Hofstetter, R., and Kenworthy, K. (1995). Service utilization and costs of care for severely mentally ill clients in an intensive care management program. *Psychiatric Services, 46*(4), 365–371.

Rabinowitz, J., and Lufkoff, I. (1995). Clinical decision making of short- versus long-term treatment. *Research on Social Work Practice, 5,* 62–79.

Ramirez, M. (1991). *Psychotherapy and counseling with minorities: A cognitive approach to individual and cultural differences.* New York: Pergamon Press.

Ray, C., and Oss, M. (1993). Community mental health and managed care. *New Directions for Mental Health Services, 59,* 89–98.

Reid, W. J. (1994). The empirical practice movement. *Social Services Review, 37,* 165–184.

Reid, W. J. (1992). *Task strategies: An empirical approach to social work.* New York: Columbia University Press.

Reid, W. J. (1975). A test of the task-centered approach. *Social Work, 22,* 3–9. ·

Reid, W. J., and Hanrahan, P. (1982). Recent evaluations of social work: Grounds for optimism. *Social Work, 27,* 328–340.

Reid, W. J., and Shyne, A. W. (1969). *Brief and extended casework.* New York: Columbia University Press.

Reiger, D. R., and Burke, J. D. (1989). Epidemiology. In H. J. Kaplan and B. J. Sadack (eds.), *Comprehensive textbook of psychiatry* (vol. 1, 5th ed.). Baltimore, MD: Williams & Wilkins.

Reisner, R., and Slobogin, C. (1990). *Law and the mental health system: Civil and criminal aspects.* St. Paul, MN: West.

Ridgewood Finance Institute (1995). Survey report. *Psychotherapy Finances, 21.*

Ridgewood Finance Institute (1991). Survey report. *Psychotherapy Finances, 17.*

Robinson, M. O. (1989). Relationship between HMOs and mental health providers. *Social Casework, 70,* 195–200.

Rodriques, A. R. (1984) Peer review program set trends in claims processing. *Business and Health, 1,* 22.

Rodwin, M. C. (1995). Conflicts in managed care. *New England Journal of Medicine, 332,* 604–607.

Roe v. Doe (1977). 400 N.Y.S.2d 668.

Roe v. Wade (1973). 410 U.S. 113.

Rogers, W. H., Wells, K. B., Meredith, L. S., Sturm, R., and Burman, A. (1993). Outcomes of adult outpatients with depression under prepaid and fee-for-services financing. *Archives of General Psychiatry, 50,* 517–525.

Rogler, L. H. (1993). Culturally sensitizing psychiatric diagnosis: A framework for research. *Journal of Nervous and Mental Disease, 181,* 401–408.

Rubin, H. R., Cardek, B., Rogers, W. H., Kosinski, M. McHorney, C. A., and Ware, J. E. (1993). Patient's ratings of outpatients visits in different practice settings: Results from the Medical Outcomes Study. *Journal of the American Medical Association, 270,* 835–840.

Rukdeschel, R., and Farris, B. (1981). Science: Critical faith or dogmatic ritual? *Social Casework, 63,* 272–275.

Sabin, J. E. (1994). Care about patients and caring about money: The American Psychiatric Association Code of Ethics meets managed care. *Behavioral Sciences and the Law, 12,* 317–330.

Sands, R. (1991). *Clinical social work practice in community mental health.* New York: Merrill.

Sargent, S. L. (1992). Contracting and managed care payment options. In J. L. Feldman and R. J. Fitzpatrick (eds.), *Managed mental health care: Administration and clinical issues* (pp. 53–67). Washington, DC: American Psychiatric Press.

Schreter, R. K. (1993). Ten trends in managed care and their impact on the biopsychosocial model. *Hospital and Community Psychiatry, 44*(4), 325–327.

Scogin, F., and McElreath, L. (1994). Efficacy of psychosocial treatments for geriatric depression: A quantitative review. *Journal of Consulting and Clinical Psychology, 62,* 69–73.

Sederer, L. I. (1992). Judicial and legislative responses to cost containment. *American Journal of Psychiatry, 149,* 1157–1161.

Sederer, L. I., Eisen, S. V., Dill, D., Grob, M. C., Gougeon, M. L., and Mirin, S. M. (1992). Case-based reimbursement for psychiatric hospital care. *Hospital and Community Psychiatry, 43,* 1120–1126.

Seltzer, D. A. (1988). Limitations on HMO services and the emerging redefinition of chronic mental illness. *Hospital and Community Psychiatry, 39,* 137–139.

Selzer, M. L. (1971). The Michigan Alcoholism Screening Test: The quest for a new diagnostic instrument. *American Journal of Psychiatry, 127,* 89–94.

Shadish, W. R., Montgomery, L. M., Wilson, P., and Wilson, M. R. (1993). Effects of family and marital psychotherapies: A meta-analysis. *Journal of Consulting and Clinical Psychology, 61,* 992–1002.

Shapiro, B. A., and Shapiro, D. (1982). Meta-analysis of comparative therapy outcome studies: A replication and refinement. *Psychological Bulletin, 92,* 581–604.

Sharfstein, S. S., Dunn, L., and Kent, J. (1988). The clinical consequences of payment limitations: The experience of a private psychiatric hospital. *Psychiatric Hospital, 19,* 63–66.

Shelton, J. L., and Levy, R. L. (1981). *Behavioral assignments and treatment compliance: A handbook of clinical strategies.* Champaign, IL: Research Press.

Shore, J. H. (1989). Community psychiatry. In H. I. Kaplan and B. J. Sadack (eds.), *Comprehensive textbook of psychiatry* (Vol. 2, 5th Ed.). (pp. 2063–2067). Baltimore, MD: Williams & Wilkins.

Shulman, K. A., Rubenstein, L. E., Chelsey, F. and Eisenberg, J. M. (1995). The roles of race and socioeconomic factors in health services research. *Health Services Research, 30*(1), 179–195.

Sifneos, P. E. (1992). *Short-term anxiety provoking psychotherapy: A treatment manual.* New York: Basic Books.

Simmons v. United States of America (1986) 805 F.2d 1363.

Simon, G., Ormel, J., VonKorff, M., and Barlow, W. (1995). Health care costs associated with depressive and anxiety disorders in primary care. *American Journal of Psychiatry, 152*(3), 352–357.

Simons, R. L., and Aigner, S. M. (1985). *Practice Principles: A Problem-Solving Approach to Social Work.* New York: Macmillan.

Singleton v. Wulff (1976). 428 U.S. 106.

Siverman, W. H., Comerford, R., and Stoker, T. (1988). Patient care monitoring review at a psychiatric hospital for adolescents. *Quality Review Bulletin, 14,* 307–310.

Skinner, K. (1980) Vietnamese in America: Diversity in adaptation. *California Sociologist, 3*(2), 103–124.

Smith, M. L., and Glass, G. V. (1977). Meta-analysis of psychotherapy outcome studies. *American Psychologist, 32* 752–760.

Smith, M. L., Glass, G. V., and Miller, T. I. (1980). *The benefits of psychotherapy.* Baltimore, MD: Johns Hopkins University Press.

Smith, S. R., and Meyer, R. G. (1987) *Law, behavior and mental health.* New York: New York University Press.

Solomon, P., and Draine, J. (1995). One-year outcomes of a randomized trial of consumer case management. *Evaluation and Program Planning, 18,* 117–127.

Spector, R. E. (1991). *Cultural diversity in health and illness.* (3rd ed.) Norwalk, CT: Appleton and Lange.

Staines, V. S. (1993). Potential impact of managed care on national health spending. *Health Affairs, 12,* 248–257.

Starr, P. (1982). *The social transformation of American medicine.* New York: Basic Books.

State v. Miller (1985), 709 P.2d 225

Stern, S. (1993). Managed care, brief treatment, and treatment integrity. *Psychotherapy, 30,* 162–175.

Steward, A. L., Hays, R. D., and Ware, J. E. (1988). The MOS short form general health survey. *Medical Care, 26,* 724–735.

Strom, K. (1992). Reimbursement demands and treatment decisions: A growing dilemma for social workers. *Social Work, 37,* 398–403.

Sue, S., and Zane, N. (1987). The role of culture and cultural techniques in psychotherapy. *American Psychologist, 42,* 37–45.

Sundberg, N. D., Hadiyono, J. P., Latkin, C. A., and Padilla, J. (1995). Cross-cultural prevention program transfer: Questions regarding developing countries. *Journal of Primary Prevention, 15,* 361–375.

Tajfel, H., and Turner, J. (1979). An integrative theory of intergroup conflict. In W. G. Austin and Worchel (eds.), *The social psychology of intergroup relations* (pp. 33–47). Belmont, CA: Brooks/Cole.

Tan, H. (1967). Intercultural study of counseling expectancies. *Journal of Counseling Psychology, 14,* 122–130.

Tarasoff v. Regents of the University of California (1974). 18 Cal. Rptr. 129.

Thelan, M. H., Farmer, J., Wonderlich, S., and Smith, M. (1991). A revision of the bulimia test: The BULIT-R. *Psychological Assessment, 3,* 119–124.

Thomas, E. J. (1978). Research and service in single-case experimentation: Conflicts and choices. *Social Work Research and Abstracts, 14,* 20–31.

Thomlison, R. J. (1984). Something works: Evidence from practice effectiveness studies. *Social Work, 29,* 51–57.

Thompson, J. W., Burns, B. J., Goldman, H. H., and Smith, J. (1992). Initial level of care and clinical status in a managed mental health care program. *Hospital and Community Psychiatry, 43,* 599–607.

Thorne, J. I. (1992). The Oregon Plan approach to comprehensive and rational health care. In M. A. Strosberg, J. M. Wiener, R. Baker, and I. A. Fien (eds.), *Rationing America's medical care: The Oregon plan and beyond* (pp. 24–34). Washington, DC: Brookings.

Thyer, B. A. (1987). *Treating anxiety disorders.* Newbury Park, CA: Sage.

Tischler, G. L. (1990a). Utilization management and the quality of care. *Hospital and Community Psychiatry, 41,* 1099–1102.

Tischler, G. L. (1990b). Utilization management of mental health services by private third parties. *American Journal of Psychiatry, 147,* 967–973.

Toner, R., and Pear, R. (1995). Medicare: Birthday brouhaha. *The Oregonian,* July 28, p. A22, 1995.

Triandis, H. C., Marin, G., Betancourt, H., Lisansky, J., and Chang, B. (1982). *Dimensions of familism among Hispanic and mainstream Navy recruits.* Chicago: University of Illinois.

Trimble, J. E. (1988). Stereotypical images, American Indians, and prejudice. In P. A. Katz & D. A. Taylor (Eds.), *Eliminating racism: Profiles in controversy* (pp. 181–202). New York: Plenum.

Tyson, K. (1995). *New foundations for scientific social and behavioral research: The heuristic paradigm.* Needham Heights, MA: Allyn & Bacon.

Tyson, K. (1992). A new approach to relevant and scientific research for practitioners: The heuristic paradigm. *Social Work, 37,* 541–556.

U.S. Congress. Office of Technology Assessment (1994). *Identifying health technologies that work: Search for evidence.* OTA-608. Washington, DC: U.S. Government Printing Office.

Van Den Berg, N. (1992). Feminist treatment for people with depression. In K. Corcoran (ed.), *Structuring change: Effective interventions for common client problems.* Chicago: Lyceum.

Vandiver, V., Jordan, C., Keopraseuth, K., and Yu, M. (1995). Family empowerment and service satisfaction: An exploratory study of Laotian families who care for a mentally ill family member. *Psychiatric Rehabilitation, 19*(1), 47–54.

Vandiver, V. L., and Kirk, S. A. (1992). Case management for persons with schizophrenia. In K. Corcoran (ed.), *Structuring change: Effective practice for common client problems.* Chicago: Lyceum.

van Gelder, D. W. (1992). Surviving in an era of managed care: Lessons from Colorado. *Hospital and Community Psychiatry, 43,* 1145–1147.

Van-Si, C. (1992). *Understanding Southeast Asian cultures.* Bend, OR: Maverick Publications.

Videka-Sherman, L. (1990). A user's perspective on meta-analysis. In L. Videka-Sherman and W. J. Reid (eds.), *Advances in clinical social work research.* Silver Spring, MD: NASW Publications.

Videka-Sherman, L. (1988). Meta-analysis of research in social work practice in mental health. *Social Work, 33,* 325–338.

Videka-Sherman, L. (1985). *Harriet M. Bartlett Practice Effectiveness Project.* Silver Spring, MD: NASW Publications.

Wagner, M. (1991). Managing diversity. *Modern Healthcare, 21*(39), 24–29.

Wakefield, J. C. (1994). Is the concept of mental disorder culturally relative? No. In S. A. Kirk and S. D. Einbinder (eds.), *Controversial issues in mental health.* Needham Heights, MA: Allyn and Bacon.

Watson, D. L., and Thorpe, R. G. (1993). *Self-directed behavior: Self modification for personal adjustment.* Belmont, CA: Wadsworth.

Weiner, B. A., and Wettstein, R. M. (1993). *Legal issues in mental health care.* New York: Plenum.

Welch, G. (1983). Will graduates use single-subject designs to evaluate their casework practice? *Journal of Education for Social Work, 19,* 42–47.

Wells, K., Burnam, M., and Rogers, W. (1992). Course of depression for adult outpatients: Results from the Medical Outcomes Study. *Archives General Psychiatry, 49,* 788–794.

Wells, R. A. (1994). *Planned short-term treatment.* New York: The Free Press.

Wells, R. A., and Giannetti, V. I. (1990). *Handbook of the brief psychotherapies.* New York: Plenum.

Westermeyer, J. (1991). Problems with managed psychiatric care without a psychiatrist manager. *Health and Community Psychiatry, 42,* 1221–1224.

Whalen v. Roe (1977), 410 U.S. 113.

White-Means, S. I. (1995). Conceptualizing race in economic models of medical utilization: A case study of community-based elders and the emergency room. *Health Services Research, 30*(1), 207–223.

Wickline v. California (1986), 228 Cal. Reptr. 661.

Wiener, J. M. (1992). Rationing in America: Overt and covert. In M. A. Strosberg, J. M. Wiener, R. Baker, and I. A. Fern (eds.), *Rationing America's medical care: The Oregon plan and beyond.* Washington, DC: Brookings.

Williamson, D. A., Davis, C. J., Goreczny, A. J., McKenzie, S. J., and Witkins, P. (1989). The Eating Questionnaire—Revised: A symptom checklist for bulimia. *Innovations in Clinical Practice, 8,* 321–326.

Wilson, G. F. (1992). Defining and measuring quality. In M. R. Mattson (ed.), *Manual of psychiatric quality assurance* (pp. 19–21). Washington, DC: American Psychiatric Press.

Wilson v. Blue Cross of Southern California (1990), 271 Cal. Rptr. 876.

Winegar, N. (1992). *The clinician's guide to managed mental health care.* Binghamton, NY: Hayworth Press.

Winslade, W. J. (1982). Confidentiality and medical records. *Journal of Legal Medicine, 3,* 497–425.

Winslade, W. J., and Ross, J. W. (1986). *Choosing life or death: A guide for patients, families, and professionals.* New York: The Free Press.

Winslade, W. J., and Ross, J. W. (1985). Privacy, confidentiality, and autonomy in psychotherapy. *Nebraska Law Review, 64,* 578–636.

Witkins, S. (1991). Empirical clinical practice: A critical analysis. *Social Work, 36,* 158–163.

Wolf, S. M. (1994). Health care reform and the future of physician ethics. *Hastings Center Report, 24,* 28–41.

Wood, K. (1978). Casework effectiveness: A new look at the research evidence. *Social Work, 23,* 437–459.

Woolsey, S. L. (1993). Managed care and mental health: The silencing of a profession. *International Journal of Eating Disorders, 14,* 387–401.

Wylie, M. S. (1994). Endangered species. *Family Networker, 18,* 20–33.

Yen, S. (1992). Cultural competence for evaluators working with Asian/Pacific Island-

American Communities: Some common themes and important implications. In M. A. Orlandi (ed.), *Cultural competence for evaluators: A guide for alcohol and other drug abuse prevention practitioners working with ethnic/racial communities* (pp. 261–292). Rockville, MD: U.S. Department of Health and Human Services-Office of Substance Abuse Prevention.

Young, J. E., Beck, A. T., and Weinberger, A. (1993). Depression. In D. H. Barlow (ed.), *Clinical handbook of psychological disorders* (240–277). New York: Guilford.

Zarabozo, C., and LeMasurier, J. D. (1993). Medicare and managed care. In P. R. Kongstvedt (ed.), *The managed health care handbook* (pp. 321–344). Gaithersburg, MD: Aspen.

Zarin, D. H., Pincus, H. A., and McIntyre, J. S. (1993). Practice guidelines. *American Journal of Psychiatry, 150,* 175–177.

Zimmerman, M., Coryell, W., Corenthal, L., and Wilson, S. (1986). A self-report scale to diagnosis major depressive disorder. *Archives of General Psychiatry, 43,* 1076–1081.

Zuckerman, R. L. (1989). Iatrogenic factors in "managed" psychotherapy. *American Journal of Psychotherapy, 43,* 118–131.

Index

Batista, Fulgencio, 173
Behavioral assignments. See Homework as-
    signments
Behavioral health/medicine, 306
Beneficence, 191–92, 193, 202, 215
Bilateral contracts, 227
Bio Psychosocial Cultural Assesment
    Checklist, 155
    form for, 301–3
Bipolar affective disorder, 48, 63, 91, 105
Block grants, 21
Blue Cross, 8–10, 14
Blue Shield, 9–10, 14
Body humors, 166
Borderline personality disorder, 18, 93
Bracero program, 172
Brennan, William, 196
Buddhists, 165, 166, 167
Bulimia, 128–29

California Physician Services, 9
Cambodians, 164, 165
Capitated managed care, 2–5, 6, 43–59,
    61–62
    basis of rates in, 45
    cost containment and, 4–5, 33–34,
        47–48
    evaluation in, 55–57
    limitations and benefits of, 58–59
    in private sector, 44, 46–48
    in public sector, 44, 46, 48–57
    spending caps in, 44, 46, 49, 58
    types of services in, 50–52
Capitation, defined, 306
Capitation funding, defined, 306
Carve-out, 306
Case management. See Clinical case
    management
Case mix, 306
Case-rate funding, 306
Case summary sheet, 137–39, 299–300
Castro, Fidel, 172–73
Catholics, 153, 165, 171
Channeling, 5, 26
Chicanos. See Mexican Americans
Children, measurement tools for, 256–58
Chinese Americans, 164, 165, 166–67, 169,
    170
Chinese Depressive Symptom Scale
    (CDSS), 169, 170
CIGNA, 36
Civilian Health and Medical Program of
    Uniformed Services (CHAMPUS),
    18, 21
Civil service, 18

Class. See Socioeconomic status
Client autonomy, 193
Client participation, 219–33
    in change process, 224–32
    in concurrent utilization reviews, 222–23
    in follow-up assessments, 223–24
    informed consent and confidentiality
        and, 221–22
    in preauthorization, 220–21
    in retrospective utilization reviews, 223
Client Satisfaction Survey, 56–57
Client satisfaction surveys, 55–57, 224
Clincal control, 27–31
Clinical case management, 7, 35, 50–51, 59
    benefits of, 51
    recommendations for, 54–55
Clinical samples, comparison with, 76–77
Clinician autonomy, 27–31
Clinton, Bill, 8
Clomipramine, 96
Closed-panel preferred provider organiza-
    tions (PPO), 306
Cognitive-behavioral approach, 103
Collectivism (allocentrism), 173–74, 175
Communitarianism, 191–92
Community, sense of, 182
Community mental health organizations
    (CMHO), 46
    defined, 307
    essential services provided by, 20–21
    intervention/prevention services in, 52
    target population for, 48
    utilization reviews and, 55
Community rating, 9
    defined, 307
Comorbidity, 307
Concurrent review, 307
Concurrent utilization reviews, 22, 83–84,
    102, 109–31. See also Practice evalua-
        tion model
    abandonment issue and, 206
    benefits of, 115–16
    in capitated managed care, 48–49, 55
    case summary sheet and, 139
    client participation in, 222–23
    confidentiality and, 198–99
    cost-effectiveness of, 35, 37–38
    defined, 5–6
    form for, 285–89
    methods for evidencing change in,
        123–25
    procedures in, 116–23
    retrospective utilization reviews com-
        pared with, 115–16
    by telephone, 214